German Villages in Crisis

STUDIES IN GERMAN HISTORIES

Editors: Thomas A. Brady, Jr., University of California, Berkeley
and Roger Chickering, Georgetown University

Studies in German Histories aims to present original works and translations on the histories of the German-speaking and closely related peoples of Central Europe between the Middle Ages and the present. The series brings forward new and neglected perspectives on important subjects and issues in the histories of these peoples.

German Villages in Crisis

Rural Life in Hesse-Kassel and the Thirty Years' War, 1580–1720

John Theibault

HUMANITIES PRESS
NEW JERSEY

First published in 1995
by Humanities Press International, Inc.
165 First Avenue, Atlantic Highlands, New Jersey 07716

© John Theibault, 1995

Library of Congress Cataloging-in-Publication Data
Theibault, John, 1957–
    German villages in crisis : rural life in Hesse-Kassel and the
Thirty Years' War, 1580–1720 / John Theibault.
        p.   cm.—(Studies in German histories)
    Originally presented as the author's thesis (Ph.D.).
    Includes bibliographical references and index.
    ISBN 0-391-03839-7
    1. Villages—Germany—Hesse-Kassel (Electorate)—History—17th
century. 2. Thirty Years' War, 1618–1648—Social aspects—Germany—Hesse-Kassel (Electorate) 3. Hesse-Kassel (Electorate)—Social
life and customs. 4. Germany—History—1517–1648. 5. Hesse-Kassel
(Electorate)—Rural conditions. 6. Hesse-Kassel (Electorate)—
Economic conditions. 7. Germany—Politics and government—
1517–1648. I. Title. II. Series.
DD801.H57T47 1994
943'.412041—dc20   93-28755
                                        CIP

A catalog record for this book is available from the British Library

Printed in the United States of America

Contents

List of Illustrations

Maps

Graphs

List of Tables

MAP 1

HESSE KASSEL CIRCA 1580

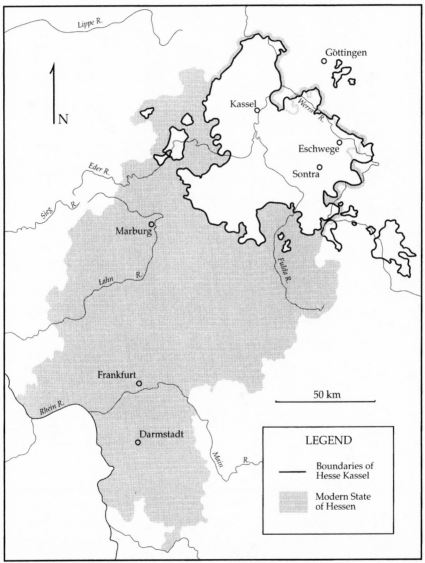

50 km

LEGEND

——— Boundaries of
Hesse Kassel

Modern State
of Hessen

Sources: Heinemeyer, Walter. *Das Werden Hessens*, Marburg: N.G. Elwert Verlag, 1986.
U.S. Central Intelligence Agency. *West Germany*. 1:1,620,000. Washington D.C.: CIA , 1972.

D.Moon 1993

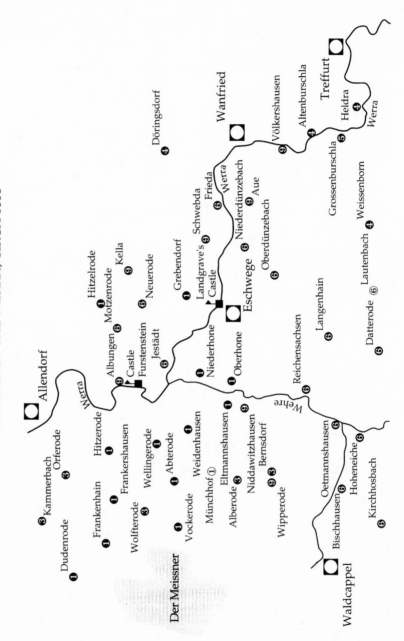

MAP 2
VILLAGES OF THE WERRA, CIRCA 1600

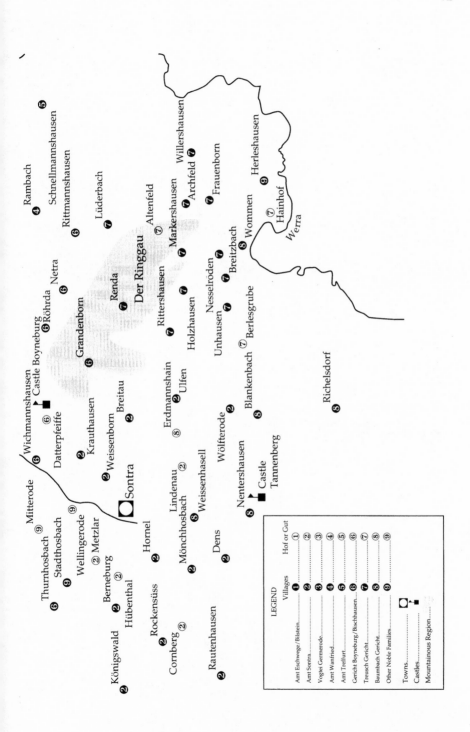

Rambach

Schnellmannshausen

Rittmannshausen

Lüderbach

Willershausen

Archfeld

Frauenborn

Markershausen

Herleshausen

Wommen

Altenfeld

Breitzbach

Netra

Hainhof

Der Ringgau

Werra

Renda

Röhrda

Castle Boyneburg

Grandenborn

Rittershausen

Holzhausen

Nesselroden

Unhausen

Blankenbach

Berlesgrube

Wichmannshausen

Mitterode

Datterpfeiffe

Krauthausen

Breitau

Weissenborn

Erdmannshain

Ulfen

Richelsdorf

Thurnhosbach

Stadthosbach

Wellingerode

Metzlar

Berneburg

Hübenthal

Sontra

Lindenau

Mönchhosbach

Weissenhasell

Wölfterode

Nentershausen

Castle Tannenberg

Königswald

Rockensüss

Cornberg

Hornel

Dens

Rautenhausen

LEGEND

Villages		Hof or Gut	
Amt Eschwege/Bilstein........	❶	①	
Amt Sontra......................	❷	②	
Vogtei Germerode.............	❸	③	
Amt Wanfried..................	❹	④	
Amt Treffurt...................	❺	⑤	
Gericht Boyneburg/Bischhausen.	❻	⑥	
Treusch Gericht................	❼	⑦	
Baumbach Gericht.............	❽	⑧	
Other Noble Families..........	❾	⑨	

Towns.................

Castles................

Mountainous Region.......

Acknowledgments

Like many first books, this one started as a Ph.D. thesis. In the years of researching and writing the thesis, and researching and revising the book, I naturally incurred many debts and saw the contours of my study change. I am particularly happy to acknowledge the collegiality of Mack Walker, Tom Brady, and Lisa Rosner, each of whom read more than one draft of the entire manuscript as it followed its course to the version you see here; they provided innumerable valuable suggestions. Other people made important contributions at various moments in the creation of the manuscript, including Heide Wunder, Walter Heinemeyer, Christina Vanja, Hans Medick, David Peal, Peter Taylor, Orest Ranum, Vernon Lidtke, Roger Chickering, John Nicols, Michael Wolfe, and Jim McNaughton. My research in Marburg and the Werra region was facilitated by the excellent advice of Dr. Gerhard Menk and the rest of the staff of the Staatsarchiv Marburg and by Heike Petersen, Georg and Liselotte Spenner, Werner Simon, Fritz Delius, Karl Kollmann, Herbert Fritsche, and Ilse Gromes in the Werra region. Robert Greenebaum and David Moon devoted meticulous attention to the preparation of the maps. Portions of Chapters 1 and 5 appeared in slightly different forms in the *Journal of Modern History* and the *Journal of Social History*. I would like to thank the University of Chicago Press and the *Journal of Social History* for permission to use them here. The research was supported by two grants from the German Academic Exchange Service (DAAD), and the writing was supported by a summer grant from the office of Research and Sponsored Programs at the University of Oregon. I am grateful to them all. None should be held responsible for any errors or omissions in the book. I dedicate the book to my parents, John and Mary Ann Theibault, and to the memory of my sister, Bonnie Jo Blevens.

Introduction

ARGUMENT

This is a study of villages in seventeenth-century Germany and how they experienced that century's most wrenching crisis, the Thirty Years' War. Both themes—the nature of the village and the impact of the war—are emphasized in the book because each is necessary to explain the other. During the past twenty years, the social history of the rural world of early modern Germany has been studied with renewed vigor.[1] French, English, and American methods of social history have begun to reshape early modern German history through the study of such topics as the Peasants' War, the genesis of rural industry in the eighteenth century, and the roots of popular mentalities under the German rubric *Alltagsgeschichte*. The Thirty Years' War, however, occupies an awkward position in the social history of early modern Germany and figured marginally, if at all, in the revival of interest in social history. The relative neglect of this war in recent social histories stands in stark contrast to the preoccupation with it before 1945, when the social consequences of the war was one of the most fiercely debated topics in historical research. This book aims to revive interest in the war by linking it to the concerns that have animated recent works on European social history.

War and crisis have often been linked in the historical imagination, and the Thirty Years' War has long epitomized the terrors that warfare can wreak in the countryside. Contemporary accounts, such as H. J. C. von Grimmelshausen's novel *Simplicius Simplicissimus*, Jacques Callot's etchings "The Miseries and Calamities of War," and a host of less accomplished chronicles, created a vivid impression of the devastation caused by the war.[2] All manner of purported ills of the Holy Roman Empire in the late seventeenth and eighteenth centuries have been attributed to the debilitating effects of the war. Beginning with Gustav Freytag's powerful depiction of death and misery in *Pictures from the German Past*, based on archival material from Saxony and Thuringia, historians have debated whether the war was a catastrophe for the countryside or merely a temporary derailment of everyday life with few lasting consequences.[3] Some argued that Freytag exaggerated the extent of destruction in the region he studied; others argued that he painted too rosy a picture of the situation before the war, which led him to see the war as a more dramatic interruption of rural life than was justified. The debate crystallized around two positions, identified by T. K. Rabb as the "disastrous war" and "earlier decline" schools of interpretation.[4] Freytag's view of a disastrous war found favor with many generations of German educators and can be called the popular view. When Hessian villagers were

1

asked in the 1960s to rank seven crises between the Black Death and defeat in the Second World War in terms of their impact on the German countryside, they selected the Thirty Years' War by a wide margin as the greatest historical calamity to befall their villages.[5]

But while villagers continued to view the war as a local as well as national catastrophe, historians became more concerned with emphasizing the war as part of the big picture of historical transformation. The social history of the Thirty Years' War was relegated to a burgeoning number of literature reviews and grand interpretive frameworks that drew on the same prewar pool of local studies. In 1940, Günther Franz made the first important contribution by compiling the various local studies into a general overview of the demographic effects of the war, which, in a slightly updated version, remains the standard work on the subject.[6] His conclusions corroborated Freytag's position to some extent, since he showed that much of central Germany lost more than 40 percent of its population during the war. His most important contribution, however, was to demonstrate that different regions had very different experiences of the war. Some regions lost more than half their population, while others were unaffected. Franz did no primary research, and his "method" consisted of accepting the demographic work of others with relatively little criticism. Perhaps because of Franz's lack of methodological reflection, the broad frameworks that were produced after 1945 tended to get stuck in an increasingly arid discussion of the limitations of other broad frameworks.

S. H. Steinberg's effort to reject Franz's figures as inflated and contrary to "common sense," without giving evidence of any primary or secondary research of his own, was the most extreme example of the turn away from local context.[7] Some historians included the war in the framework of the general crisis of the seventeenth century, though there was uncertainty whether the war should be conceived as a symptom or a cause of the crisis.[8] Still, the most characteristic broad frameworks continued to be "disastrous war" and "earlier decline," now integrated into the long-term trajectory of European economic development in the works of Friedrich Lütge and Wilhelm Abel.[9] Abel used macroeconomic indicators to argue that the German economy was already in crisis by 1608. Lütge, however, rejected such a pessimistic assessment of the German economy on the eve of the war. He portrayed an economy responding creatively to population pressures by shifting its center of gravity to new forms of production. Once again, the lack of detailed local studies made it difficult to resolve the debate; but even if local studies had been available, the way the debate was framed continued to limit the social historical importance of the war to a determination of how bad it was.

In an attempt to break through the limitations of the "disastrous war" and "earlier decline" dichotomy of the Abel-Lütge debate, Heiner Haan proposed that the war be treated as one of the results of the social trends of the sixteenth-century—that is, that it be treated as a social phenomenon. Haan began from a position similar to Lütge's, with the argument that Germany was prospering on the eve of the war. But instead of using that argument to bemoan the destructive effects of the war, he argued that prosperity caused the social instability that led to the war: The classes that were not well poised to take advantage of prosperity attempted to fend off those groups that profited.[10] The primary beneficiaries of the prosperity were the territorial princes, who gained new resources to exercise their power.

Haan's argument is suggestive, but it draws on very few local studies within the empire to buttress his claims of widespread prosperity or to show how traditional elites responded to that prosperity. Most conspicuous for its absence from Haan's presentation was Christopher Friedrichs's study of Nördlingen, which had appeared two years earlier.[11] Friedrichs's study was the first to link the methods of quantitative social history at the local level to the problem of the impact of the Thirty Years' War. His conclusions about the prosperity of Nördlingen on the eve of the war were mixed. When adjusted for inflation, the wealth of the city as a whole began to decline after 1615 and faced a sharp downturn with the *Kipper und Wipper* inflation of 1622.[12] But within the city, the relations of different trades changed in response to economic circumstances, so that some people were able to profit while others faced crisis. Friedrichs did not limit his interpretation of the war to the question of prewar prosperity. An important contribution of his work was to treat the Thirty Years' War as the midpoint of a larger transformation rather than as the beginning or end of a process. He did not minimize the war's consequences for Nördlingen but argued that its effects must be seen in conjunction with a series of incursions during the wars of Louis XIV that caused the city's retreat into insignificance in the eighteenth century.

Recently, Bernd Roeck followed up Friedrichs's arguments for Nördlingen with an even more detailed presentation of the city of Augsburg, one of the largest and most important urban centers of the era.[13] He reemphasized the complicated relationship between prosperity and decline in the late sixteenth and early seventeenth centuries and complained about the inadequate base of research that could address Haan's claim. He stated that "whether one can, in fact, create a picture of prosperity from the fragments of the economic trends that previous research has provided, depends on how one defines 'prosperity,' but even more on what sector of economic life one looks at."[14] He disputed those historians who believed that Augsburg was prospering on the eve of the war by claiming that there was an increasing polarity between rich and poor in the city rather than an expansion of a middle stratum. He thereby confirmed the image presented by Friedrichs, but with even greater detail and more careful differentiation of the experiences of various trades.

Roeck's work is exemplary both for the wealth of detailed information he presented and for the framework in which he placed that information. Indeed, his aspirations in the book are almost as important as his conclusions, because they can serve as the impetus for research in other regions. He argued for an integrated history that can deal simultaneously with structures and events. He therefore presented many different sectors of economic life and showed their connections to political and cultural life. By making those connections, he was able to chart the impact of the war over a wider range of issues than Friedrichs was able to do. Unfortunately, in one respect his work did not go as far as Friedrichs's. His presentation ended in 1648, too early to examine the long-range impact of the changes he charted.

Important as the works of Friedrichs and Roeck are, there are obvious limits to what one can learn about the range of responses to the Thirty Years' War from studies that focus on the urban world. The experience of the rural world is excluded entirely from Roeck's analysis, except for some references to the streams of people seeking protection within the walls when troops threatened. No one has undertaken research on a scale even approaching Roeck's for any rural region during the war. There are, however, two recent works that open some of the same questions and, together, frame the chronological contours of this work: Thomas Robisheaux's work on the small territory of Hohenlohe and Rudolf Schlögl's work on Upper Bavaria.[15] Robisheaux's book begins with the era of the Peasants' War and traces the development of rural society through the Thirty Years' War. His treatment of the war takes up the final eighth of the book, and although it is filled with suggestive ideas, it does not provide the careful exposition of influences that Roeck's does. Schlögl does not try to follow the trajectory of development prior to the war. He begins his story with a snapshot view on the eve of the war and traces the war's long-term impact into the late seventeenth century. A feature that both Robisheaux's and Schlögl's works share with Roeck's is that they pay close attention to the interrelationships of local social structure and administrative interests.

Robisheaux interprets the rural world as the site of increasing tensions between those villagers who had access to the most productive and consolidated properties and those who could hold on to only small properties, which were unable to support an expanding population. These social tensions found expression in a desperate search for some alternative system of order. This provided the impetus for social discipline, which succeeded in buying time for an unstable system at the end of the sixteenth century. The war is important to this story because it destroyed the tenuous order that had been created and forced readjustment throughout rural society. But at the same time, the war was produced by the social tensions that pervaded society as a whole. Robisheaux argues that "the unresolved tensions led, almost inexorably, to a wrenching crisis. . . . With this argument in mind, the Thirty Years' War looms as both more and less important than is commonly portrayed. The war becomes more important because it was part of a crisis of the whole society. . . . But the war alone could not have caused a crisis as deep and profound as this. One must keep in mind that its origins lay in other conditions as well."[16]

Robisheaux concludes his work with a discussion of the remarkable social and political stability that came about after the war. Schlögl's discussion of Bavarian conditions gives a more differentiated picture of the postwar recovery process. His analysis echoes Roeck's observation that whether one can identify stability depends on how one defines stability and what sector of society one looks at. Schlögl points out with some justification that the precise mechanisms of reorganization and regeneration in the rural world have been neglected in favor of simple summaries of the extent of damage. His close analysis of peasant productivity and state fiscal practices helps him show how many factors figured in the process of recovery.

The works of Roeck, Robisheaux, and Schlögl all provide inspiration and arguments for the present work. They attempt to connect the social history of early modern Germany to the social history of the Thirty Years' War. They show that it is impossible to describe the social impact of a crisis only in terms of the numbers of deaths and houses destroyed. Like other recent works, they argue that all social crises are to some extent socially constructed.[17] The contours of any crisis are inevitably shaped by a complex set of relationships revolving around work, wealth, gender, access to power, and acceptance of risk. We must be aware of the extent to which social and cultural patterns were able to assimilate the pressures brought to bear by the war and the extent to which the war prompted people to change their social and cultural patterns. If we are to address both issues, we cannot treat the war as either the end or the beginning of a social trend, as Robisheaux, Roeck, and Schlögl have done. It must be dealt with as part of a continuing process of adaptation and adjustment within early modern rural society.

Such an investigation must rely on a local study. David Sabean recently argued that the best way to study early modern social history as a process is by means of "socially specific, exacting accounts of power, resistance, and constraints in loci."[18] Sabean's argument forces us to confront the problem of what constitutes "location." For the vast majority of the population, that location was the village. To understand power and resistance, one must understand what the village was and how it served to locate actions. The idea of the village helps us fix location. This book presents several different views of the village, because the village appeared different, depending on how one looked at it. The village was a political, social, and cultural construct that must be understood in terms of all the groups that constructed it. It focused other relations and therefore is the point from which other analyses (of peasant society or popular culture) can proceed.

Conversely, any understanding of the social order of the village and the rural world in the seventeenth century must confront the crises that were an integral part of that order. To that extent, the story of German villages in the Thirty Years' War is part of a larger story about the ways in which the rural world participated in and was influenced by larger historical forces. Although we emphasize the local in the village, we must be aware that villages are not isolated and that interconnectedness is an essential feature of location. This book, like the works of Robisheaux and Schlögl, addresses problems of the relationship of state power to local rural social, economic, and political organization. The Thirty Years' War itself provides the most dramatic illustration of the interconnections of structure and event. The events of the war serve as both a window onto the internal dynamic of the village and a link to early modern society as a whole that was a source of change in that dynamic. They provide insight into the connections between local structuring and larger historical processes.

This book is constructed in three parts in order to balance the explication of the context of the village and the specific moment of the impact of the war. Each part gives a definition of the village from a specific point of view. The first part is concerned with the village as a totality or corporate body. Chapter 1 presents that corporate body as viewed by those who wished to control the village as it related to outsiders, most notably the landgrave of Hesse, his central and local officials, agents of the church, townspeople, and the territorial nobility. It sees the village primarily as an aspect of administration, but it also shows how an administrative definition shaped the way in which villagers were integrated into larger structures. Chapter 2 reverses the angle of vision to show how the village was also perceived as a corporate body by those who lived in it. It provides an insiders' definition of the village by exploring how space within the village was allocated and how conformity to corporate norms could be enforced. It argues that the corporate character of this internal definition benefited some inhabitants and worked against others. Both chapters take into account the fact that there were numerous ways of seeing the village as a corporate body, and these ways of seeing could reinforce or undermine one another, depending on many complex influences.

The second part of the book looks behind the purported atom of the village to show that the interior dimension was as subject to the pull of competing interests as were relations between inhabitants of the village and outsiders. Both chapters of Part II use terms or pose questions that are familiar in modern social historical analysis as they search for the contemporary terms for those same social relations. Chapter 3 treats the village as composed of variations on units of production and consumption or kin affiliations, either households or lineages. These units modified how individuals expressed their interest in the give-and-take of the village as a whole. They gave definition to work, gender, and age. Chapter 4 presents the variations in the village differently by placing both households and individuals in other networks—of wealth, status, voluntary association, or violence—which also modified their contributions to the village as a whole.

The first two parts of the book are structural analyses. They give a snapshot view of the prewar situation, though they admittedly draw on evidence from during and occasionally after the war. However, they do not portray the prewar world as static. They identify currents of change, such as the religious reorganization of the region under Landgrave Moritz, as part of the structuring of the village. The third part of the book, by contrast, treats change over time as the central feature of analysis. It shows the institutions of the village in constant flux due to the impact of the war. Chapter 5 introduces the war as a factor from outside the village that forces a reconceptualization of the relationship between the village and the outside world, with repercussions for the internal dynamic of the village as well. It focuses on the nonmaterial impact of the frequent incursion of troops and sets the stage for Chapter 6, which explores the more traditional question of the material impact of the war. In that chapter, mortality and economic disruption are not treated as a general trend in society but are situated in the specific circumstances of the affected villages, so that one can see how the material and institutional frameworks of the village were connected. Chapter 7 brings the strands of material and institutional together during the postwar period in order to chart the long-term effects of the war. It investigates the phase of recovery after the war and the new relationships that emerged, not merely to see what the war had wrought but also to view the internal composition of the village by examining how it responded to new circumstances.

This order of presentation is somewhat different from that of many social histories based on small regions. It has become commonplace to begin with the material base of society—the agricultural economy—and then to build the institutions that cover that economy on top of the base. I consider the structure of the rural economy and the conditions of expropriation of peasant products, but only after I have considered how the political organization of the territory located rural society. The argument that one must begin with either the elite or the peasantry because of the alleged priority of one over the other in historical development is moot by the sixteenth century, since the two had become deeply intertwined. The interactions of material base and cultural order are exceedingly complex, and I can offer no simple solution to the debate whether attitudes shape circumstances or circumstances shape attitudes. It seems to me that each influences the other through a continuous process of action and response, but such a dialectical framework often does not lead to clear exposition. The advantage of beginning with an essentially political perspective is that it provides the most explicit definition of the village as a unit.[19] My aim is to see the village as holding both material givens and cultural assumptions in a constant tension. Circumstances and attitudes—material and cultural—should not be reified, because they change from moment to moment. It is precisely this fluidity that is best studied in the local context. But fluidity does not mean that anything is possible. As Charles Tilly pointed out regarding the role of locally grounded studies, "outcomes at a given point in time constrain possible outcomes at later points in time."[20] This, too, suggests why a carefully grounded study of the effects of the Thirty Years' War on the local level is important. The response to unprecedented crisis obviously shaped the direction of later development in the locality.

SETTINGS

Any local study must begin with an understanding of the specific qualities of the locality being investigated, both its physical features and its political and historical frameworks. The villages investigated in this book lay near the Werra River in the landgraviate of Hesse-Kassel, one of the numerous midsize principalities of sixteenth- and seventeenth-century Germany, located fairly near the geographical center of the newly unified modern Germany. Fynes Moryson, an English traveler to the continent in the late sixteenth century, cited a common doggerel of the era, which captures some of the impressions that visitors to Hesse-Kassel must have had: "High Mounts and Valleys deepe, with grosse meates all annoide / Sowre wine, hard beds for sleepe: who would not Hessen land avoide?"[21] A traveler passing through the Werra region would have seen much that confirmed this image. It was indeed a land of high hills and steep valleys, dominated by the 750-meter-high Meißner. The region was characterized by rushing streams such as the Berka, Ulfe, Sontra, and Netra, which cut through wooded, sometimes chalky, plateaus and ridges as they flowed toward the Werra. Many of the villages of the Werra were nestled in the narrow valleys cut by the streams, often aligned neatly in rows as the valley ascended to the level of the hills. Around the town of Eschwege, the Werra formed a small plain with richer soils. The villages of the plain were distributed more evenly and in a denser concentration, and a few vines on the small hills of the plain produced the local sour wine.

Contemporaries viewed the region along the Werra as a distinct region within the territory of Hesse-Kassel, sometimes referred to as the "old Hessian landscape on the Werra." Hesse was divided up into four military districts based on the major rivers that flowed through the territory: the Werra, Fulda, Diemel, and Schwalm. The Werra military district ranged from Witzenhausen in the north to Sontra in the south. The town of Eschwege and its surrounding land served as the axis for the region.[22] The plain of the Werra was widest where the summit of the Meißner was highest. The combination of the broad plain and barrier mountain divided the Werra into northern and southern subregions—the one extending along the banks of the Werra toward Hannoversch Münden and the confluence with the Fulda, and the other moving inland along the smaller streams to the south. This book focuses on the southern subregion, encompassing about thirty square kilometers and marked by the villages of Orferode and Cammerbach in the north, the district of Wanfried and the Werra River in the east, the village of Rauttenhausen and the cloister of Cornberg in the south, and the villages of Königswald and Bischhausen and the Meißner in the west.

The Werra was a border region. The ruling houses of Hesse and Thuringia had vied for control of this area during the Middle Ages, but by the sixteenth century, Hesse was firmly established as the ruling house of the region. Thuringian customs persisted, however, so that the Werra became a mixing ground of Hessian and Thuringian practices.[23] The border character of the Werra was enhanced by its geography. The Werra River flowed from Saxon territory to Hannoversch Münden and hence to Bremen. It provided easy access to Lower Saxony, but it did not tie the region to the princely residence at Kassel, which was located in the valley of the Fulda region, on the other side of the Meißner and Kaufunger forest. Two major trade routes passed through the region: a north-south route connecting Hamburg and Nuremberg, and an east-west route connecting Leipzig and Cologne.[24] The former route failed to link the Werra with the rest of Hesse but connected it with the important trading centers of Hannoversch Münden and Göttingen; the latter passed through very hilly and wooded country on its way toward Kassel and connected the region with the Saxon town of Eisenach.

Hesse-Kassel was always a poor country. Moryson disparaged the towns of the territory: "The houses were of timber and clay, each one for the most part having a dunghill at the doore, more like a poore village, then [sic] a city; but such are the buildings in the cities in Hessen."[25] There were six towns in the immediate area of the Werra—Eschwege, Allendorf, Sontra, Wanfried, Treffurt, and Waldcappel—but with the exception of Eschwege, they were barely larger than the largest villages of the region and must have lived up to Moryson's generalization. But the Werra region was far from marginal in the financial and political calculations of the landgrave. Eschwege was the third largest town in the territory (after Kassel and the recently acquired Hersfeld), with 733 households in 1583. The region featured coal and copper mines near the Meißner and Sontra,[26] and a center for exporting pottery in Wanfried. With the exception of the potteries in Wanfried and the saltworks in Allendorf, just to the north of Eschwege, none of the industries of the Werra possessed more than local importance, but these resources were supplemented by the primary source of local prosperity: farming. Moryson complained of the poor housing of the towns and villages, but he admired the "fruitful hils of corne."[27] Hesse was a land of villages, where agriculture predominated. The six towns—the smallest of which was Wanfried, with 177 households—were surrounded by seventy-eight villages. Some villages were tiny, consisting of no more than ten households; others were as large as a small town, with as many as 150 households, but most ranged from about thirty to seventy households in size.

The villages of the Werra attained their specific character not only from these facts of geography and economy but also from the political evolution of the territory of Hesse-Kassel from the medieval period to the seventeenth century.[28] The landgraviate of Hesse-Kassel was an imperial Estate and was free from meddling by the empire in its internal organization. Most midsize principalities had a territorial nobility, linked to the territorial prince through feudal grants called *Lehen*. In the fifteenth century, the Hessian nobility formed itself into a territorial Estate; this established the dualistic constitution that was characteristic of most midsize states of the early modern era, in which the nobility served as a counterweight to the centralizing tendencies of the prince. The source of the nobility's strength in the dualistic *Ständestaat* was its local power base on its own hereditary lands and its right to regulate taxation within the territory. The Werra region was one in which local nobles held particular strength. Three of the most active families in the territory had their primary seats in the region: the von Boyneburg, von Baumbach, and Treusch von Buttlar. The von Boyneburg and Treusch von Buttlar lands were so extensive that they were recognized as distinct districts, called *Gerichte*. Several other less prominent families were also active in the region: the von Keudel, von Eschwege, von Meisenburg, Diede zu Fürstenstein, Trott zu Solz, von Harstall, and von Biedefeld. The noble presence was accented by the castles and palaces that dotted the countryside, most notably the Fürstenstein of the Diede, the Tannenberg of the von Baumbach, and the Boyneburg, all of which stood at the top of highly visible hills.

The tensions between the aspirations of the landgraves for centralized administration and the dualistic rule of the estates came to a head in the early sixteenth century, as Hessian landgraves began to seek new sources of financing for more ambitious foreign and domestic policies. Landgrave Philipp made Hesse one of the major powers of the Holy Roman Empire, and his successors tried to follow his path by modernizing and consolidating fiscal administration. One historian interpreted this new financial policy as the transition from a medieval "domain state" (*Domänenstaat*) to a "financial state" (*Finanzstaat*), which led to the modern "tax state" (*Steuerstaat*).[29] The efforts of the Hessian landgraves to become a permanent power in the empire were hampered by the division of Hesse into four lines (one of which rapidly died out and was incorporated into the other three) by Philipp in 1567. Hesse-Kassel, under Landgrave Wilhelm IV, was the primary line of succession, but the three branches were about equal in size, and each continued the policies of internal fiscal consolidation that Philipp pursued. The third line of Hesse-Marburg ended without an heir in 1604 and was redivided between the two remaining lines, Hesse-Kassel and Hesse-Darmstadt. Philipp's improvident division of his lands created a lasting tension between the two lines that was to continue until the nineteenth century.

None of the developments described above suggests that the Werra region was exceptional for late-sixteenth-century Germany. But at the same time, it would be hard to argue that the region was typical. The structure of the empire encouraged local particularity, and the Werra region possessed as much of that as anyplace else. The task of the chapters that follow is to present the local particularities while noting the underlying processes that made a village a distinct social unit. As we shall see, one of the peculiarities of the Werra region was that it was hit very hard by the Thirty Years' War in comparison with other regions. The crisis of the war was local and specific and cannot be assumed to reproduce the experiences of other regions, but the forces it uncovered were not unique. Thus, the local situation of the Werra region is an illustration of how the early modern village functioned in extremis.

Notes

1. I discussed the comparative lack of interest in the rural world of early modern Germany since 1945 in John Theibault, "Review Article: Towards a New Socio-cultural History of the Rural World of Early Modern Germany?" *Central European History* 24 (1991): 304–24.
2. H. J. C. von Grimmelshausen, *The Adventurous Simplicissimus*, trans. A. S. Goodrick (Lincoln, NE, 1962). Grimmelshausen was a regimental clerk during the war. The question whether his vivid descriptions, especially the dramatic scene of soldiers plundering a farmhouse in Chapter 4 of the book, were based on his experiences during the war has generated a considerable literature. Most scholars conclude that Grimmelshausen relied more on literary traditions than reporting from experience. See Hans Dieter Gebauer, *Grimmelshausens Bauerndarstellung: Literarische Sozialkritik und ihr Publikum* (Marburg, 1977).
3. Gustav Freytag, *Bilder aus der Deutschen Vergangenheit*, vol. 3, *Aus dem Zeitalter des Grossen Krieges* (Leipzig, 1871).
4. The literature of these debates has been reviewed many times. T. K. Rabb, "The Effects of the Thirty Years War on the German Economy," *Journal of Modern History* 34 (1962): 40–51, remains one of the best summaries of the issues. He gave the major schools of interpretation the designations "earlier decline" and "disastrous war." He sketched the progress of the debate up to the First World War on the basis of more than twenty publications, then carefully surveyed thirty-four works from the period 1910–1943 and concluded with a brief discussion of a few postwar interpretations. He determined that many more local studies supported the "disastrous war" interpretation than the "earlier decline" interpretation. The most recent work on the issue is Manfred Vasold, "Die Deutschen Bevölkerungsverluste während des Dreissigjährigen Krieges," *Zeitschrift für Bayerische Landesgeschichte* 56 (1993): 147–60.
5. See Wilfried Schlau, *Politik und Bewußtsein* (Cologne, 1971), 127–28.
6. Günther Franz, *Der Dreißigjährige Krieg und das Deutsche Volk*, 4th ed. (Stuttgart, 1978).
7. Siegfried H. Steinberg, *The Thirty Years' War and the Conflict for European Hegemony 1600–1660* (New York, 1966).
8. The classic statements of the general crisis are by E. J. Hobsbawm and Hugh Trevor-Roper, both of whose contributions are in a volume edited by T. S. Ashton, *Crisis in Europe, 1550–1650* (New York, 1965). Josef Polisensky, "The Thirty Years' War and the Crises and Revolutions of Seventeenth-Century Europe," *Past and Present* 39 (1968): 34–43, and Henry Kamen, "The Economic

and Social Consequences of the Thirty Years' War," *Past and Present* 39 (1968): 43–61, explicitly link the war to the general crisis. See also Theodore K. Rabb, *The Struggle for Stability in Early Modern Europe* (New York, 1975). For a recent statement of the importance of the German case in the debate over the general crisis see Sheilagh C. Ogilvie, "Historiographical Review: Germany and the Seventeenth Century Crisis," *The Historical Journal* 35 (1992): 417–41.

9. Compare Wilhelm Abel, *Agricultural Fluctuations in Europe from the Thirteenth to the Twentieth Centuries* (New York: 1980), especially pp. 147–57, and Friedrich Lütge, "Die Wirtschaftliche Lage Deutschlands vor Ausbruch des Dreißigjährigen Krieges," in Friedrich Lütge, *Studien zur sozial- und Wirtschaftsgeschichte* (Stuttgart, 1963), 336–95.

10. Heiner Haan, "Prosperität und Dreissigjähriger Krieg," *Geschichte und Gesellschaft* 7 (1981): 91–118.

11. Christopher Friedrichs, *Urban Society in an Age of War: Nördlingen, 1580–1720* (Princeton, 1979).

12. Ibid., 111–24.

13. Bernd Roeck, *Eine Stadt in Krieg und Frieden* (Göttingen, 1989).

14. Ibid., 334.

15. Thomas Robisheaux, *Rural Society and the Search for Order in Early Modern Germany* (Cambridge, 1989); Rudolf Schlögl, *Bauern, Krieg, und Staat: Oberbayerische Bauernwirtschaft und frühmoderner Staat im 17. Jahrhundert* (Göttingen, 1988).

16. Robisheaux, *Rural Society*, 12.

17. A recent restatement of the idea that crisis is socially determined is by Paul Hugger, "Elemente einer Ethnologie der Katastrophe in der Schweiz," *Zeitschrift für Volkskunde* 86 (1990): 25–36, who explores the "tremendous social potential" in crises. For a general statement of the impact of catastrophes on human communities, see Pitrim Sorokin, *Man and Society in Calamity* (New York, 1968). The literature on the social influence of catastrophes is small. A criticism of the literature, which explores how catastrophes are embedded in the structure of society, is Wieland Jäger, *Katastrophe und Gesellschaft Grundlegung und Kritik von Modellen der Katastrophensoziologie* (Darmstadt, 1977). Two superior case studies of a community in disaster are Kai Erikson, *Everything in Its Path: Destruction of Community in the Buffalo Creek Flood* (New York, 1976), and the historical account by Anthony F. C. Wallace, *St. Clair: A Nineteenth Century Coal Town's Experience with a Disaster-Prone Industry* (New York, 1987). One of the few recent works to study the social construction of a seventeenth-century crisis is Giulia Calvi, *Histories of a Plague Year*, trans. Dario Biocca and Bryant T. Ragan, Jr. (Berkeley, 1989). An analysis of some of the specific problems of interpreting war as an element of crisis can be found in Myron Gutmann, *War and Rural Life in the Early Modern Low Countries* (Princeton, 1980), 3–8.

18. David Warren Sabean, *Property, Production, and Family in Neckarhausen, 1700–1870* (Cambridge, 1991), 12.

19. I am not arguing for the primacy of *Verfassungsgeschichte* in rural studies. The elements that I describe are part of the practical experience of rule, not merely the formal contours of authority. For a critique of social history in traditional forms, see Josef Mooser, "Wirtschafts- und Sozialgeschichte," in Richard van Dülmen, ed., *Fischer-Lexikon Geschichte* (Frankfurt, 1990), 86–101.

20. Charles Tilly, *Big Structures, Large Processes, Huge Comparisons* (New York, 1984), 14.

21. Fynes Moryson, *An Itinerary Containing His Ten Yeeres Travell Through the Twelve Dominions of Germany, Bohmerland, Sweitzerland, Netherland, Denmarke, Poland,*

Italy, Turky, France, England, Scotland, and Ireland, vol. 3 (Glasgow, 1907), 455. William J. Wright mentions a variation of the doggerel in *Capitalism, the State and the Lutheran Reformation: Sixteenth Century Hesse* (Athens, OH, 1988).
22. There are few general histories of the region. The main works are Karl August Eckhardt, *Die Politische Geschichte der Landschaft an der Werra und der Stadt Witzenhausen* (Witzenhausen, 1928); Julius Schmincke, *Geschichte der Stadt Eschwege* (Eschwege, 1922); and Lorenz Collmann, *Geschichte der alten Bergstadt Sontra in Niederhessen* (Kassel, 1863).
23. See Karl A. Eckhardt, *Eschwege als Brennpunkt Hessisch-Thüringische Geschichte* (Marburg, 1964).
24. Herbert Krüger, *Hessische Altstraßen des 16. und 17. Jahrhunderts* (Kassel, 1963), 90–97.
25. Moryson, *An Itinerary,* 1: 72.
26. H. Strube, "Kupferschmelzhütten im Sontraer Raum—Von den Anfängen bis zum Ausbruch des Dreißigjährigen Krieges," *Hessische Heimat* 24 (1974): 199–208.
27. Moryson, *An Itinerary,* 1: 72.
28. The most recent political history of Hesse is Walter Heinemeyer, ed., *Das Werden Hessens* (Marburg, 1986). A work that focuses on the institutional framework is Kurt Dülfer, "Fürst und Verwaltung: Grundzüge der hessischen Verwaltungsgeschichte im 16.–19. Jahrhundert," *Hessisches Jahrbuch für Landesgeschichte* 3 (1953): 150–223. On Estates in general and the Hessian case in particular, see Francis Carsten, *Princes and Parliaments in Germany from the Fifteenth to the Nineteenth Centuries* (Oxford, 1959). Carsten capitalizes Estates, meaning territorial assemblies, to distinguish them from estates, the domains of landlords. I follow his practice here.
29. Kersten Krüger, *Finanzstaat Hessen 1500–1567* (Marburg, 1980).

Part I
The Village Whole

1

Lord, State, and Village:
The Strands of *Herrschaft*

What was a village? What made a village Hessian? Both questions may seem simple at first, but both raise fundamental issues of interpretation for rural society. Neither can be adequately addressed by formal, abstract definitions; instead, they must be approached through contemporary practice. Fortunately, the process of political development described in the introduction provides one means of seeing how contemporaries tried to answer those questions.

Landgrave Wilhelm IV was an administrative systematizer. From the beginning of his reign, he collected political maxims and statistical information about his territory. In 1585, this information was bound in a single volume that was later given the sweeping title "Economic State."[1] One of the centerpieces of the Economic State was a district-by-district survey of all the towns and villages in Hesse, which was called the "Village Book." The first Village Book was put together in 1568, but in 1575 Wilhelm ordered a second survey so that the structure of his territory would be represented more accurately.[2] The Village Book was a useful tool for the Hessian administration to determine the jurisdictional limits of Hessian authority. The title—indeed the mere existence—of the Village Book is a sign that the village figured in the political calculations of the central administration. The way in which villages were presented in the Village Book suggests that the village was conceived as a unit in the administrative structure. By treating villages as units, the Village Book fixed their location in the administrative hierarchy as well as in the landscape. This fact about the book helps us understand how the whole apparatus of rule functioned on a day-to-day basis. Villages were identifiable things with specific properties, not just abstract categories. They served as the location in which the more abstract qualities of legitimate rule could be exercised.

The contents of the book show which aspects of administration were deemed most central to legitimate rule by the landgrave and his agents. The landgrave and his agents saw themselves as the superiors or authorities

(*Obrigkeit*), and the practical manifestation of their position as authorities was the exercise of lordship (*Herrschaft*). The idea of *Herrschaft* is complex; although it may be interpreted as an abstract quality of rule, it was almost always used by people in the seventeenth century to denote concrete relationships, often with personal ties.[3] *Herrschaft* was not limited to, nor indeed primarily concerned with, the exercise of state authority. Instead, it found expression in multiple strands that included seigneurial exploitation and religious indoctrination. Rule through seigneurial exploitation, for example, was expressed in the idea of *Grundherrschaft*—literally, "landlordship."

Beginning with the Village Book, we can trace the various ways in which *Herrschaft* was focused and constrained by the assumption that the village was a unit, embedded in a larger political structure. It will become apparent that the fixed location of the village created tensions and opportunities in the exercise of *Herrschaft*. No matter how formalized the administrative structure was, its effectiveness rested on the local presence of agents who embodied the principles of *Herrschaft*. Tracing the channels of *Herrschaft* demonstrates the reciprocal influence of village interests and the larger political structure. The process of defining the village as a unit of administration reinforced the distinctions between villages, which contributed to the village being defined as a unit in other respects as well, which are investigated in the following chapter.

First, the Village Book defined a village by distinguishing it from other forms of settlement in the region.[4] Villages were any settlements that were not towns or farmsteads. The three terms *Stadt* (town), *Dorf* (village), and *Hof* (farmstead—though the term usually referred to a large estate where three or four households resided, rather than a single isolated house and farm)—were used to designate the three categories of settlement in the region. All the *Städte* and *Höfe* were noted as such in the Village Book, which singled out those forms of settlement by mentioning the *Städte* before the villages and the *Höfe* after the villages. The distinctions among the three were based on two main criteria: size and legal status. A village was different from a farmstead because it had more households and a more diverse landholding structure.[5] A village was different from a town because a town was usually larger and possessed distinct privileges that residents jealously guarded from encroachment by the nonprivileged. Towns usually looked different too, because of the presence of town walls and the internal organization of space.[6] Of the three forms of settlement, the *Dorf* was by far the most common in the Werra region.

In addition to defining a village by what it was not, the Village Book provided a practical definition of a village through the system it used to tabulate a village's central characteristics.[7] It specified the number of householders (*Hausgesessene*), the number of people who owed the landgrave labor service as a condition of tenure, and the size of the military baggage train

(*Heerwagen*) owed in wartime for each settlement listed. In addition to these statistics, it noted who was entitled to propose a new pastor or school-master for the parish when the post was vacant (*Collator*) and who was responsible for high and low justice in each place. The village was the place in which these items, or rights, could be located. Some revisions of the Village Book omitted the categories for labor service and military bag-gage train, which suggests that control over *Hausgesessene*, *Collator*, and high and low justice figured most prominently in determining authority in the village. These three strands—in the forms of seigneurial rights, "po-lice," and the church—are the main points of intersection between village and *Herrschaft* outlined in this chapter.

Close scrutiny of the structure of the Village Book also helps answer the question as to what made villages Hessian. The inclusion of a settlement was a statement that Hesse possessed some kind of authority over it; but mere inclusion said nothing about the nature of that jurisdiction. The "Hessianness" of villages was not based on their geographical location but on the bundle of rights and obligations associated with the land and people derived from essentially feudal or seigneurial traditions. Contiguous territo-rial boundaries were very rare, but exclaves and mixed jurisdictions were common in the sixteenth-century territorial state, so the elaboration of ju-risdictional rights had to be defined at the level of the individual village.[8] Some places might be subject to several different lords. For example, the town of Treffurt and its neighboring villages were divided into three parts among Hesse, Saxony, and Mainz, so the town and its villages were all listed as being one-third Hessian, one-third Saxon, and one-third Mainzish. This division did not rest on a pure division of the fields into three parts but involved constant recalculation in order to preserve the administrative balance among the three parts.

Although the Village Book was useful for defining Hessian jurisdiction in areas where it was in competition with neighboring principalities, most of the book was devoted to locating the internal contours of authority. Villages did not appear randomly in the Village Book; they were organized according to the administrative district (*Amt*) to which they belonged. This was a reflection of the way in which the landgrave and his administration viewed the strands of authority they exercised rather than a mere book-keeping convenience. The *Amt* was no more a contiguous geographical unit than was the territory of Hesse as a whole. *Amt* boundaries were tradi-tional, reaching back to the original feudal grant (*Lehen*) under which Hessian dominance was established, so they did not follow logical geographical bound-aries. The traditional holdings of an *Amt* sometimes extended into the fields of neighboring *Ämter*. The best illustration of this in the Werra region is the domain of the secularized monastery Germerode, which was reorganized as a district called a *Vogtei* in the sixteenth century. Its *Grundherrschaft* was built up through donations by Hessian nobles and others in the course of the Middle Ages, so when it was converted to a secular administrative district in the Reformation, it possessed land widely strewn about the Werra region. The villages of Kammerbach and Orferode were rather distant from the village of Germerode, but they were part of the *Vogtei*, while the neighboring villages of Abterode and Vockerode were in *Amt* Eschwege, which was also known as *Amt* Bilstein for the ruined castle that was once the center of jurisdiction. Germerode did have some land in Abterode and Vockerode, however, as well as land in Breittau in *Amt* Sontra, Reichensachsen in *Gericht* Boyneburg, and Lüderbach in the Treusch *Gericht*.[9] This feudal remnant in *Amt* organization meant that each *Amt* represented a distinct seigneurial jurisdiction of the landgrave, administered in traditional seigneurial fashion. Labor services and military baggage trains were obligations bound up with feudal property rights. It was the sort of information that appeared in identical form in the account books of the district, along with hereditary rents and yields from the landgrave's personal domain. Even jurisdiction over the courts had some characteristics of a seigneurial rather than a territorial administration, because fines paid by the perpetrators of crimes became revenues for the district as well.

The landgrave administered his *Amt* the same way that the territorial nobility administered their estates, which suggests the extent to which the *Amt* was conceived as a seigneurial jurisdiction. Both used a document called a *Salbuch* to keep track of fees in money and in kind as the condition of tenure of individual peasants in the sixteenth century.[10] Both were constrained by the customs of the territory from changing the conditions of tenure for most of their land. This chapter focuses on the lands owned by the landgrave or in which the landgrave had a concrete jurisdictional role, in part because the records of the local nobility are too chaotic to make a thorough analysis possible, but also because the landgrave was by far the leading *Grundherr* of the territory.[11] However, many elements of the landgrave's jurisdiction can be carried over to the estates of the nobility without qualifications.

One advantage that the landgrave had over his nobility in his efforts to modernize seigneurial administration, besides his position as territorial ruler, was that he controlled a great many distinct manorial jurisdictions, which he set about running in a uniform manner. All the manors of the landgrave, including those confiscated from the monasteries during the Reformation, were administered the same way. The structure of authority embedded in the *Amt* also served as a means of exercising a slowly unfolding centralized state authority. Kersten Krüger noted how the effort to exploit every potential source of traditional seigneurial revenues within the *Amt* was the first step toward establishing regular tax revenues to support more ambitious administrative structures; thus the seigneurial character of *Amt* administration melded into emerging state administration.[12] In the sixteenth century, taxes were treated as distinct from seigneurial revenues, but they were grafted onto existing *Amt* institutions.

TABLE 1.1

Total Assessed Value of Property in *Ämter* of the Werra Region
According to the Treysa Assessment

PLACE	VALUE IN RTHLR
Landgravial jurisdictions	
Town Eschwege	287,825
Town Sontra	43,700
Town Wanfried	65,850
Amt Eschwege/Bilstein	27,475
Amt Sontra	67,700
Amt Wanfried	48,140
Kloster Cornberg	5,600
Noble jurisdictions	
Gericht Boyneburg	63,250
Gericht Treusch	66,700
von Diede	7,000
von Eschwege	19,000
von Keudell	9,350
von Baumbach-Tannenberg	3,000
Total for all of Hesse	6,151,400

Source: StAM Kop 57.

The clearest example of how state interest and seigneurial administration began to intersect is in the general agreement between Landgrave Wilhelm IV and the Estates of Hesse on the apportionment of future tax burdens, which was called the Treysa Assessment of 1586.[13] The Treysa Assessment was a survey of the estimated taxable wealth within each *Amt* (Table 1.1). The assessment distinguished between urban and rural wealth within each *Amt* but otherwise left the internal apportionment to local officials. When taxes were granted by a meeting of the Estates, a fixed sum was asked for, and its distribution was apportioned according to the assessment.[14] It was assumed that a similar principle would be used within the *Amt*, but there were no mechanisms to ensure that it would be. The *Ämter* had an estimated property value, but the individual villages within the *Amt* did not. The assessment of the amount due from individual villages had to be worked out in negotiations within the *Amt*—and the amount due from individual villagers was worked out within the village itself. Prior to the Thirty Years' War, villages subject to the jurisdiction of the nobility were exempted from taxes, but the value of noble estates was still estimated in the Treysa Assessment. After the war broke out, one attempt to assess an equitable distribution of taxes within the *Amt* Sontra produced a very rough proportion of one-third for the town of Sontra, one-third for the villages under the jurisdiction of the landgrave in the *Amt*, and one-third for the villages under noble jurisdiction in the same area.[15] Predictably, this led to a feeling that the burdens were apportioned unfairly. The Treysa Assessment and the Village Book emerged almost contemporaneously, and both reflected the tension between traditional seigneurial authority and the expanding "finance state" resting on *Amt* administration.

All attempts to locate jurisdictional authority and *Herrschaft* within the village were merely formal unless there were agents available to exercise that authority. *Herrschaft* connoted reciprocal relationships that had their ideological underpinnings in the phrase *Schutz und Schirm*, which suggested that obedience was due only so long as the ruler offered protection to his subjects. In day-to-day matters, the exercise of *Schutz und Schirm* that legitimated the landgrave's rule was in the hands of the same agents who tried to enforce his will at the local level. The figures who held together the landgrave's multiple-stranded practice of *Herrschaft* through *Amt* organization were the *Amtmann* and the *Rentmeister*. Originally, the *Amtmann* was the chief agent of the landgrave, with administrative authority, and the *Rentmeister* was the fiscal officer of the *Amt*. By the seventeenth century, the duties of the two offices had begun to blur somewhat.[16] The centrality of a seigneurial conception of the officials of the *Amt* can be seen in the formal commission of Henrich Pfeffer as *Rentmeister* in Eschwege in 1633.[17] Nine of the fourteen specifications of the commission mentioned the protection of traditional sources of seigneurial revenue. Two others were concerned more explicitly with the format for presenting those revenues. The other specifications concerned overseeing the work of the forester, marking the boundaries of the district, and a general admonition to protect the subjects from unseemly labor services and the like. The letter concluded with a formulaic expression that the *Rentmeister* "be true, steadfast, obedient and ever-available to us ... to warn truly of dangers, to promote the pious and best and to do all that which a true *Rentmeister* and servant is obligated and responsible to do for his lord."[18] The term "servant" is significant in this case. Agents of the landgrave were his servants, not merely his salaried officials. Servants included gardeners, winemasters, and ass-drivers as well as the *Amtmann* and *Rentmeister*, which underscores the extent to which the landgrave conceived of his servants as helping him run his seigneury rather than his state. Within the *Amt*, the number of servants varied from two in Cloister Germerode to sixty-four in *Amt* Kassel.[19]

The leading noble families of the region had comparable servants, who went by the titles *Verwalter* or *Gerichtsschreiber*. As the discussion of *Vogtei* Germerode showed, some villages had two or more lords who owned enough land to claim jurisdiction over individuals within the village. The political structure within the village often reflected the tensions between manorial lords. For example, the village of Frankershausen was assumed to be part of the landgrave's seigneurial jurisdiction, but fifty-five inhabitants were subject to the noble von Dornberg. The village of Netra belonged to the noble administrative district of the von Boyneburg, but eighteen inhabitants were subject to the landgrave's seigneurial authority.[20] Serving as the judicial lord in high and petty cases, having the right to suggest a new pastor, and being the principal landlord in the village were distinct, concrete strands of authority in each village. In some villages, the same lord, and thus the same agent, held all the authority in his own hands; in others, one lord would highlight his particular strand in competition with a different strand from another lord. The landgrave's officials and agents of the nobility often disputed the extent of each other's authority in those villages. This meant that the tensions of local office were inherent in the structure of *Herrschaft* at the local level.

Despite some attempts to rationalize local administration through the imposition of a uniform format of *Amt* accounts, a tradition of noninterference in local administrative practices persisted. There was still no conceptual separation of administration from adjudication either in the highest bodies of the territory or in the local administration.[21] The same officials collected revenues and administered justice. Indeed, administration of justice frequently meant collecting or protecting revenue. The twin strands of fiscal and judicial administration were carried out within the framework of the *Amt* by officials who ultimately reported to the landgrave or his council.

The landgrave had to rely on those same officials for any information about the local level, because the Village Book was too general to handle all the complications of *Grundherrschaft*. For one thing, *Grundherrschaft* controlled people through control of the land, but the Village Book did not discuss the land of the village at all. Thus, the local knowledge of the landgrave's agents was an essential means of connecting formal structures with day-to-day action. The *Amtmann* had to get the villages to fit into his own administrative practice.[22] The *Amtmann* used his local knowledge to bridge the seigneurial interest in landholdings with the administrative conception of villages as units. To carry out their work, *Amtmänner* needed other agents with even more extensive local knowledge. The reason for this becomes clear if we look at the *Amt* account books. Information within the books was organized by village, but only after it was organized according to form of payment and formal basis of the payment. For example, landholders in both Rockensüß and Königswald paid dues for their lands in the forms of cash for *Dienstgeld* and *Rodgeld* and rye for *Rodzehend* in *Amt* Sontra.[23] One could not locate this information by looking for Rockensüß and Königswald in the accounts. Instead, one had to look first at money for *Dienst*, next at money for *Rodacker*, and then at rye for *Rodacker*. The entries for the two villages were within each of those categories.[24] It would have been impossible for the *Amtmann* to keep track of these revenues if this was the only information he had to go on. In practice, he did not divide payments in this way. Instead, he relied on local agents within each village who were responsible for the variety of payments. The best way to locate the people who were supposed to pay was through their places of residence in the village. Other seigneurial agents, such as winemasters and ass-drivers, were obviously unsuited to this task. Only inhabitants of the villages themselves could provide the necessary qualities. For that reason, the final cog of the administrative apparatus was the village heads and auxiliary officers.[25] They were essential links in creating a chain of legitimacy. Heads of villages were more familiar with the agents of the landgrave's *Herrschaft* within the *Amt* than ordinary villagers were. In order to make sense of the administrative view of the village, therefore, we must examine the ambiguous position of the village head within the administration.

The most common name for the village head in the Werra region was *Schultheiß* or *Schulz*, but the office was common to almost every village in Germany under a wide variety of names, such as *Greben*, which was also used in the Werra region. Almost every village had additional auxiliary officers who worked with the *Schultheiß* to administer the village. Auxiliary officers also went by a variety of names—the most common in the Werra region were *Vormunder*, *Vorsteher*, and *Heimbürge*. There is little information about how the village head and *Vormunder* were selected. Herbert Reyer gathered considerable evidence that they were usually appointed by the landgrave's officials.[26] But, as he notes, one of the sources that suggests the opposite is the court instructions for *Amt* Bilstein, which specify: "From this point on the villages will not be allowed to install or depose a village head without the foreknowledge of the *Rentmeister* and the *Centgraf* or *Amtschultheiss*."[27] This implies a process of internal recommendation, over which the *Rentmeister* could exercise a veto, rather than an administrative appointment.

It is likely that the office of *Schultheiß* was initially created by *Herrschaft*, and the office of *Vormunder* was created by the villagers. But by the sixteenth century, the functions of the two offices had converged. Neither was a coveted office. Hermann Hiebethal was fined "because when the *Schulz* said to him that he would be *Vormunder* from then on, he gave him a punch in the mouth so that it bled."[28] Leaving aside why Hiebethal found the prospect of being *Vormunder* so unappealing, two features of this brief incident stand out. First, it was the village head who informed him of the decision to make him *Vormunder*, suggesting that the process of selection may have been internal. The second revealing feature of the incident is that Hiebethal was selected as *Vormunder* despite his obvious dislike for the position. This indicates that Hiebethal was not involved in the decision-making process.

Because of the gaps in bureaucratic authority that went with seigneurial *Amt* administration, the village head and auxiliary officers had to carry out a wide range of administrative tasks. The village head was responsible for ensuring that all crimes in the village were reported to the court. He also called together villagers for labor services on the lands of the landgrave and collected, or at least apportioned, taxes and communal fees. In some instances, the village head could be viewed as the subordinate official of the *Rentmeister*. Village heads were sometimes called upon to sign the official *Amt* account books, testifying that information on the number of sheep in the village or other such details were accurate.[29] Those who could not sign their names asked the pastor to sign in their names. This procedure directly associated the village heads with the activities of the *Rentmeister* in one of the more oppressive manifestations of *Herrschaft*. Indeed, the administrative functions of the village head often made him a target of opposition and abuse within the village, which might explain why Hiebethal reacted as he did. Sometimes, the opposition was a direct challenge because a villager believed that he was being unfairly burdened, such as the villager in *Amt* Bilstein who claimed that "a rogue had written him in under those who had to carry mortar."[30] Often, though, the charges of unfairness were vaguer and showed a general discontent with how *Herrschaft* was practiced. For instance, the record of a fine that was levied in *Amt* Sontra stated that "as the *Vormunder* and village head were working out an agreement to deal with the cavalry, Hans Bohne Wezell and Stoffel Scheffer insulted the village head and *Vorsteher* while drinking and said that they never acted aboveboard . . . and they considered the village head and *Vorsteher* to be rogues."[31] The antagonism between villagers and the village head was seen as axiomatic by Otho Melander, a compiler of parables from the Werra region, who described how a clever peasant tricked a village head into indicting himself for a substantial punishment when his animals did damage to the villager's crops.[32]

Although the village heads had official responsibilities on behalf of the landgrave, they were not counted as state agents.[33] Only occasionally were village heads paid by the *Amt* for their services. Sometimes, but again rarely, they were exempted from paying trivial seigneurial dues, such as the "hearth chickens" that were due every year for their homesteads. Village heads were thus not so much employed as taken advantage of by the landgrave's administration. The advantage of using the village head was that he could be a concrete expression for the otherwise amorphous village. The next chapter shows that the village head could also serve as a focus for village solidarity. The central administration expected the village head to represent the village, so the village used him as its representative. This took concrete form in the formulation that frequently appeared in letters from the village to the landgrave: "*Schultheiß, Vorsteher und ganze Gemein.*"[34] In early modern Europe, it was not always clear in whose interest the political village acted. One determining factor of the village was the administrative role that the central administration demanded of it. Another was the way in which individual inhabitants acted to assert village unity. The village heads were caught between these two, often contradictory, expressions of the village.

Although the landgraves of Hesse-Kassel followed the contemporary ad-
age that financial means are the nerves of the state, they were aware that
the Amt was not solely a fiscal unit and that their authority had to rest on
more than just Grundherrschaft in the narrow sense. The principle of Schutz
und Schirm suggested that the landgrave had to maintain public order and
prevent both external and internal disruption. The Amt, with its concentration of local knowledge and empowered agents, was the logical unit from
which to direct public order. Here too, the seigneurial and state interests of
the landgrave intertwined. The landgrave issued ordinances (Landesordnungen)
in his capacity as territorial ruler to regulate actions within the territory.[35]
It was difficult to compel the nobility to enforce the decrees on their lands,
where the landgrave did not have direct forms of Herrschaft to exert. Indeed, it was difficult enough for the landgrave to get his own tenants to
obey his ordinances. The ordinances were printed up and sent to the
Amtmänner, who were instructed to have the ordinances read in all the
villages.[36] They could only be as effective as the emphasis applied by the
Amtmänner in enforcing them. The repeated promulgation of some ordinances shows that they were not always enforced effectively. For example,
Landgrave Philipp began issuing ordinances against the partibility of inheritances as early as the 1510s, yet partible inheritance was still being practiced in the Werra region in the eighteenth century.[37] Many ordinances
regulated behavior in the village. The landgrave and his officials used ordinances to give some system to the otherwise arbitrary assortment of local
customs that made up the law in the individual villages. The ordinances
should not be dismissed as wholly ineffectual, but the existing customary
administrative structure limited the extent to which decrees could be enforced.

The result of these multiple obligations of Herrschaft was to create tremendous tensions in the office of the Amtmann, who had to serve as both
seigneurial representative and administrator of police. The range of tasks in
the hands of the Amtmann opened up a debate over how the authority of
the landgrave should be applied to the village. The source of most disputes
between the village and the Amtmann was the ambiguity of local customs
or the difficulty of accommodating both the desire for a centralized, uniform administration and the diversity of local customs that dominated local
affairs. Custom was determined in a number of ways, but its primacy in
those cases that were disputed in Kassel was never questioned. A perfectly
legitimate defense of an action was to state that it had been done that way
"since time immemorial" (seit undenckliche Jahren herkommen).[38] Indeed, one
of the most common ways of arguing a case was to talk to the oldest members of the community to determine how things had been in the past. The
Eltisten were not always the most competent elders but simply the oldest
who could best remember the way things used to be done.[39] Only if some
sort of documentation could be produced would an existing habit be changed,
and any innovation had to be proved to be legitimate. This system of legal

decision making extended to disputes between the landgrave and local nobles. When the von Baumbach family claimed that they should install the new pastor in the parish of Herleshausen, the Village Book noted that they had asserted this right by force; since time immemorial, the village church had been a filiate church of Offenau, and the Baumbachs could produce nothing to prove their claim.[40]

It was in the interest of the central administration to gain an overview of local customs so that it did not have to rely on inhabitants of the village to assess what was customary. The frequent appeals to "old custom," as interpreted by the common people in the Peasants' War of 1525, indicated to the lords that there was some danger in having villagers serve as the final arbiters of what was customary. Well before the sixteenth century, there were attempts to codify local customs, of which there were a bewildering variety.[41] The most notable of these codifications were the *Weistümer*, which nineteenth-century historians sometimes mistook for expressions of communal practice without elite interference. By the seventeenth century, the *Weistümer* were superseded by new forms of legal practice. Instructions for holding court, explicitly created by the central administration but derived from local practice, were among the devices that took their place.[42] The instructions served a twofold purpose: They described the punishment for each transgression and prescribed the behavior of both judge and jury.[43] Like the earlier *Weistümer*, they codified traditional practices so that they became fixed and predictable for the administration in a way that emphasized the police function embodied in *Grundherrschaft*. The villages of *Gericht* Boyneburg were covered by a forty-two-point instruction in 1604, created by the several branches of the von Boyneburg family. The words with which court was convened show that judicial procedure involved the complex interplay of the territorial nobility, the landgrave's manorial and state authority, and local particularism:[44]

> Judge says: You jurors / I ask you according to law / if it is time / that I convene the court of my benevolent lord?
> Jurors answer: The jurors recognize / when the lords desire it / that is the time.
> Judge says: You jurors / I ask you further according to law / how shall I proceed / that I do right and avoid injustice?
> Jurors speak: According to the customs of the land and their old law.

The exchange of statements between judge and jurors was, in practice, an exchange between *Amtmann* (in this case, the seigneurial agent of the von Boyneburg) and villagers over the legitimate exercise of *Herrschaft*. It is important to recall that *Herrschaft* involved constant interaction between agents of authority and villagers, in which the expression of legitimacy had to be confirmed repeatedly.

At the same time that ordinances and court instructions attempted to impose conformity on the village through decrees from above, the landgrave's administration left opportunities for the locality to voice its interests to the landgrave. It was always possible for villagers to appeal directly to the landgrave and his counselors. The ability to appeal to the landgrave was an essential component of *Schutz und Schirm*, which served as part of the legitimation of the landgrave's rule. In addition, in cases of dispute—of which there were many in the sixteenth and seventeenth centuries—the council in Kassel (Räte) was the last instance of appeal for any subject.[45] This route could be used in disputes between individuals or between villages and in cases in which a village or individual believed that customs were being threatened by some action of an *Amt* official.[46] This could be an effective check on the activities of the *Amtmann* whenever he tried to take advantage of his position for gain at the expense of the villagers. It left the *Amtmann* in an ambivalent position: He was responsible for enforcing the landgrave's will at the local level, but his actions could be exposed by villagers who resented his authority. The central administration was left to decide whether the peasants' claims that the *Amtmann* placed inordinate burdens on them were true or whether they were just trying to avoid paying their fair share.

We can see the problems built into the application of *Herrschaft* by investigating the interactions of one *Amtmann* with the villages of an *Amt* in a long dispute over the limits of his authority. In July 1621, Landgrave Moritz of Hesse-Kassel and his council received a supplication from all subjects of *Amt* Sontra.[47] The complaint alleged that the *Amtschultheiss*, Christoffel Gude, oppressed them by demanding excessive payments for the maintenance of the militia and had pocketed part of that payment for his own use.[48] The landgrave's council responded to the supplication by convening a special commission to hear testimony from both sides of the controversy. Gude began his defense by asking that the commission interrogate all the heads of the villages of the *Amt* to determine "whether they will admit . . . that he had had to march with the militia to Friedewald on orders from the landgrave"[49] and, by implication, that his exactions for the militia were justified. The commission duly brought the heads of all twelve villages, plus two small isolated settlements, to Sontra to testify. The decision of the commission to begin its investigation by interrogating the village heads rather than by convening village assemblies or questioning individual villagers imposed a specific administrative definition on the village that was consistent with the idea of a chain of legitimacy. The procedures of the inquiry were not spelled out in detail—like so many other administrative tasks of the era, they seemed to be based on custom—but there is sufficient internal evidence in the testimony to provide a basic outline of events.

The commission consisted of three officers of the town of Sontra and the *Rentmeister* of *Amt* Sontra, Heinrich Rodingus. The inquiry must have taken place in the town hall of Sontra, a place with strong administrative associations for the villagers. One can imagine the commissioners sitting on a dais while the village heads who gave testimony stood, facing them.

The commission asked questions initially proposed by *Amtschultheiss* Gude, the object of the supplication. The transcript reports that Gude was not satisfied with the answer when "the village heads and auxiliary officers (*Vormunder*) . . . were all asked together and gave their answer together uniformly" so he "requested that each village head who was present give his answer himself.[50] The village heads may have testified together at first because the initial claim was on behalf of all subjects. Apparently, the uniform response was that they persisted in their complaint.

When the village heads testified separately, a different picture began to emerge. The first village head to respond was from Hornel, a tiny village of just thirteen households located nearest to Sontra. It was unlikely that he was chosen first because he had particular insight into how the supplication was made. His testimony clarified little about that, though it revealed something about how news of the supplication spread. He claimed that his village first heard of the supplication when he was in Heringen, a small town on the Werra about twenty kilometers from Sontra. He had not participated in drawing up the supplication; he had not even been asked if he wanted to join the complaint. However, when the villagers ("*Nachtpahrn* [*sic*]")[51] of Hornel heard about the supplication, they told him to hold off on collecting the money "until they see what other villages are going to do; what they do, we will do too."[52] Although brief, this testimony introduced many of the themes that later testimony elaborated. The village head played no role in drafting the initial complaint. This was a common refrain in subsequent testimony. The village heads of Rauttenhausen, Weissenborn, Krauthausen, Breittau, Dens, Hübenthal, Wölfterode, and Lindenau all denied participating in the drafting of the supplication. Although there may have been an element of fear that prompted these village heads to deny that they had participated, it is also likely that the drafters of the supplication had not bothered to consult with those village heads and had made their claim on behalf of all subjects based on their own sense of what was right. Indeed, one of the striking features of the testimony is that six of the village heads claimed to have no knowledge at all about the supplication. Most simply said that they "know nothing about it,"[53] though the head of the village of Dens claimed that "he was not there as the complaint was made and gave neither advice nor aid to it since he was at [the village of] Wommen at that time,"[54] thereby providing himself with an alibi to distance himself still further from the complaint.

The wait-and-see attitude adopted by the village of Hornel was an astute way of maneuvering within *Herrschaft*, but most of the eight villages that disassociated themselves from the process of supplication did so in a way that highlighted obedience to the dictates of *Herrschaft*. The head of the village of Dens did not merely deny that he had participated in drawing up the supplication but also assured the commission that he had complied with the request for payments. The money had already been collected and delivered to the *Stadtschreiber* in Sontra. The head of the village of Weissenborn also underscored how far removed from any course of resistance he was by explaining that he was never asked to join in any complaint. He too had already collected and delivered the first payments—he even specified the amount delivered—and had collected but not yet delivered the second round. Most of the villages that claimed to have no knowledge of the supplication were among the smallest in the *Amt*. Of the villages in the *Amt* with more than thirty households, only one, Breittau, claimed complete ignorance of the supplication. More than half of the villages with fewer than thirty households claimed not to have participated. As the head of the village of Rauttenhausen—which had just seventeen householders—noted: "they probably did not pay any attention to it because we are such a tiny little village."[55] These acts of obedience must have put added pressure on the heads of those villages that had produced the supplication to justify their recalcitrance. It also makes one wonder all the more at the "uniform" response the village heads supposedly gave when testifying as a group. They clearly hedged their bets in the complex strands of *Herrschaft*. We cannot know whether there was a tone of submission in the voices of those who claimed to have no knowledge of the supplication or if there was defiance in the voices of those who had sent it. But the interrogation broke down the apparent solidarity of the initial testimony.

The decision of the special commission is not extant, so it is unclear whether the supplication was successful. But for all its mundane qualities, it shows how the multiple strands of *Herrschaft* allowed villages to adopt different strategies to circumvent the coercive force of the landgrave's agents. Village heads were able to use supplications to associate themselves with a strand of legitimate authority in order to challenge a different strand of legitimate authority. As the next chapter illustrates, in adopting this strategy, they also contributed to the definition of internal unity in the village. But the relationship between *Amt* officials and villages was not always adversarial. It was possible for the village head to work in concert with the *Amtmann* to achieve some mutually beneficial goal. Jurisdictional disputes between agents of the landgrave and agents of territorial nobles could be vehement, and villagers could be useful allies in justifying one's position to the landgrave.

The conflicts between the lords' agents in the villages of *Gericht* Boyneburg illustrate the difficulties of administering a village as a unitary body when the strands of *Herrschaft* were so diverse. Despite repeated negotiations between the landgrave and the von Boyneburg, culminating in a general agreement in 1602, the von Boyneburg complained continually that agents of the landgrave were usurping their prerogatives.[56] Often, the disputes centered on seemingly empty rights, such as who was allowed to impound (but not confiscate) property in a village, but the process of disputes led to a forging of alliances between the agents and "their" villagers in opposition to encroachments by the agents of others. In their complaints to the landgrave, the von Boyneburg family emphasized that jurisdictional interference by the landgrave's agents led to "disobedient and contrary" villages.[57] But in these cases, at least, the *Amtmann* claimed that there was nothing disobedient in the actions of the villages. They were merely protecting the legitimate rights of the landgrave as his loyal subjects. The reciprocity of *Herrschaft* thus permeated all jurisdictional issues that were at the heart of public order in the village.

Schutz und Schirm was essentially a secular notion, which relied on secular agents to negotiate the legitimacy of *Herrschaft*. But public order involved more than just the ability to extract resources from the village and the legitimacy of police. The organization of the church at the local level was also defined as part of the village in the Village Book, through the identification of the *Collator* of each village. Its presence in the Village Book indicates that the church was conceived as part of the apparatus of *Herrschaft*. The practice of *Collator* was a remnant from the days before the Reformation; it persisted because those groups that possessed the right did not wish to see their privileges diminished. The right of *Collator* was almost always held by the noble family that administered high and low justice in the village, which meant that it was usually in the hands of the landgrave himself in the Werra region.[58]

Just as we traced the structure of *Amt* administration within the secular administration, we must understand how ecclesiastical *Herrschaft* was embedded in the religious development of Hesse.[59] Landgrave Philipp was one of the earliest princely converts to the Lutheran Reformation, and subsequent landgraves followed in his tradition of aggressive political Protestantism. As in other reformed principalities, the territorial church was administered from within the territory under the purview of the landgrave and subject to his approval. Landgrave Moritz built on the institutions of the territorial church to make it conform more closely to his own vision of effective ecclesiastical organization. He was determined to have his will carried out throughout the territory. He began "reforming" the Hessian church by reviving the institution of the consistory in 1599.[60] The consistory was made up of the superintendent and other church officials from Kassel plus members of Moritz's own chancery in an effort to bind it as closely as possible to the secular administration. The interests of Moritz as head of the territorial church were thus represented in the highest administrative body of the church in the territory. The consistory served much the same purpose in the ecclesiastical administration as the *Räte* did in the secular administration. It was the final instance of appeal for any decision concerning church affairs. It answered only to the landgrave and God.

There were strong parallels in the formal structure of the secular administrative hierarchy and the ecclesiastical hierarchy in Hesse-Kassel due to how *Herrschaft* was exercised in each. As in the case of the secular administration, there were intermediate levels of administration between the villagers and the supreme religious decision-making body that were responsible for the day-to-day decisions affecting the village.[61] Between the parish and the consistory were urban metropolitans and district superintendents who watched over the pastors in the parishes and protected the local interests of the church against encroachment by the secular hierarchy. They derived their authority over the villages from their more immediate contact with the consistory. Only if an issue was too delicate or fundamental for intermediate officials to handle would it be referred to the consistory.

The similarities between the secular and ecclesiastical hierarchies left the church open to the same claims of jurisdictional partisanship that complicated the secular administration. The noble family von Boyneburg claimed in 1608 that the pastor in Röhrda, in collusion with the *Beamte* (official) in Eschwege, let a child murderer go free simply because her father's land was subject to the church rather than to the von Boyneburg family.[62] As the letter made clear, the jurisdiction of the courts was at issue, since the von Boyneburg went on to claim that the villagers "are no longer obeying our ordinances and commands, but rather attach themselves to the pastor."[63] The von Boyneburg were irritated by the pastor, whom they described as "unruly" and "quarrelsome." They appealed to the landgrave to redress their grievances with repeated reference to a Recess of 1602 between the landgrave and the von Boyneburg, which ostensibly regulated the jurisdiction over church land. The landgrave's decision in this case is not available, though he probably decided in favor of the pastor, since the conflict was connected to a still more fundamental fight over religious practice in Hesse as a whole. In fact, the fate of the woman accused of killing her child is not clear either, though members of the ecclesiastical hierarchy did not look upon crimes of this sort any more favorably than the nobility did. The incident illuminates, however, how conflicts between secular and ecclesiastical authority were appealed to the landgrave and how overlapping jurisdictions complicated the policing of morals.

Despite the many layers of ecclesiastical administration, it was the parish, especially as personified by the pastor, that integrated individual villagers and villages as a whole into the church. A rural parish in the Werra region usually consisted of two or three villages. Village and parish were separate institutions, but they were joined by the pastor's participation in both. The pastor tended to the spiritual needs of the parishioners and acted as the chief administrator of the church's properties. The primary task of the pastor in the village was to preach the word of God to the parishioners, but preaching the word of God brought administrative responsibilities. In some respects, the administrative position of the pastor was comparable to that of the village head, because he actually lived in the village. But the pastor was not "of" the village, and his primary loyalty had to be to the word of God and the way it was interpreted outside the village.

The process of selecting a new pastor for a village indicates the complicated character of the tie between village and church. As already noted,
the right of *Collator* supposedly kept the choice of pastor out of the hands
of the parishioners and put it in the hands of an outside authority. As we
shall see, this was not the only ecclesiastical remnant in a Protestant territory that appeared to contradict the ideas of the Reformation. In this case,
however, the actual practice of the region allowed more local choice than
the formal rights would suggest. Frequently, villages requested a pastor on
their own. Such a request was usually enough to sway the landgrave or
local nobles to choose that pastor through their right of *Collator*, thereby
preserving both their ancient privileges and the idea of selection by the
parish.[64] When the village did not request someone, a proposed pastor was
required to give a sermon before the village prior to his confirmation as a
way of testing his acceptability.[65] This process did not guarantee a peaceful
relationship between the pastor and the parish, but it did give the villagers
a chance to participate in the selection process and to voice an objection if
the proposed candidate seemed unacceptable. The landgrave's consistory also
kept watch on ecclesiastical appointments through the superintendent, who
tested all potential candidates for their competence and, by extension, for
their orthodoxy.[66] The superintendent blocked all attempts by the nobility
to install preachers or practices that would undermine the landgrave's vision
of the territorial church. In practice, therefore, the right of *Collator* allowed
the villagers' active participation in the selection process but reserved for
both the lords who were *Collators* and the territorial church administration
the power to veto unacceptable candidates.

Once a pastor was selected, his primary duty was to minister to the spiritual needs of his community by preaching. He was required to give a fixed
number of sermons in each village of the parish. Baptisms, marriages, and
burials were services that the church was expected to render, but they required
an additional payment (*Accidentien*) on the part of the individual peasant.[67]
These were not ordinary duties of the pastor, but they were traditional activities that tied the parish to the church and its pastor. Of the three, only
baptism remained a sacrament, but all three continued to be important to
the religious identity of the parishioners. The pastor would not refuse to
participate in a ceremony unless there was something objectionable about
it, especially since church policy demanded that marriages take place in the
home parish of the participants rather than in some suspicious foreign locale.
In fact, collecting *Accidentien* was a simple privilege that went with the
office. Though the payments varied according to the custom in different
villages, the secular and ecclesiastical authorities endeavored to standardize
them. The pastor in Niederhona noted of his *Accidentien*: "At baptisms I
and my wife receive two days free meals, but nowadays in accordance with
the newly published *policey ordnung*, I receive one local *thaler* and forget
the meals, because my bodily condition does not allow me to be at all such

things, but I certainly do not wish to weaken the old tradition by my example, nor do I wish to give away anything for the successor to my office."[68] The pastor's concern that he not take any action that might be detrimental to his successors shows that pastors recognized their office as a pragmatic as well as spiritual one.

The pastor was not the only official of the church who was present at the local level and ministered to spiritual needs. Often he was assisted by a schoolmaster. The *Accidentien* of the schoolmaster were similar to those of the pastor. The schoolmaster also received the payments in exchange for performing traditional services of the church. Aside from teaching children as many as five hours a day, the schoolmaster also led the singing in the church and rang the bell to call the villagers to worship. He was responsible for filling in whenever the pastor was away, so he had to be versed in the rudiments of preaching and administering sacraments. Besides this, he had more prosaic tasks such as setting the clock on the church tower and cleaning the church interior and grounds.

In most cases, the pastor and schoolmaster were not from the village they served. There were other church offices that were designed to forge a closer tie between ecclesiastical authority and local legitimacy. The parish of Abterode, for example, had four officers as official servants of the church: pastor, elder, treasurer, and schoolmaster.[69] Two of these officers—the pastor and schoolmaster—came from outside the village and were responsible for the actual transmission of the word of God, as well as for seeing that it was obeyed. The other two offices were filled by members of the parish, which gave villagers a role in their spiritual management that was similar to the roles of village head and *Vormunder*. They were responsible for the regular tasks of church administration, which included enforcement of the word as preached. In these activities they acted as the adjunct of the pastor. Whereas the elders held office for long periods, the treasurers served for short terms before handing the office over to someone else.[70] Their task was to keep track of the money collected by the church and to check the purposes for which it was spent, though the final responsibility for this fell to the pastor himself. The purpose of the treasurer was as much to ensure that the pastor committed no improprieties with the church funds as it was to enable the parishioners to administer their church to a small extent. This supervision must have been reassuring to villagers who were habitually suspicious that their superiors were trying to take financial advantage of them.

The elders were village members of good moral repute who were called on to judge cases involving moral delinquencies on the part of members of the parish. They were responsible, along with the pastor, for the maintenance of discipline in the parish. For example, when the pastor in Abterode discovered one of his parishioners with an unidentified woman in the fields, the superintendent in Eschwege recommended that the pastor "cite Braumuller [the villager] before the elders, examine him about the circumstances and after determining whether he admits or disavows, arrive at a judgement."[71] The elders were expected to contribute to the pastor's investigation of the case. Perhaps they passed judgment as well. At the same time, the elders acted as spokesmen for the parish in cases of complaints about the actions of the pastor. The elders of Datterode complained to the superintendent when their pastor failed to hold services for two Sundays prior to Christmas in 1639.[72] This dual role made elders of the parish a part of the church hierarchy and thereby integrated the church into the village. The selection of elders was regulated by *Kirchenordnung* (church ordinance),[73] which ensured the authority of the pastor and the superintendent over village participation in the ecclesiastical structure. The effectiveness of this system depended on the respect the villagers accorded to the elders, but the general result was the creation of a force for policing morals within the village; it carried the weight of the pastor's religious authority but was implemented by members of the parish.

Police and revenues were closely linked in the secular administration, so it is not surprising that the spiritual supervision of the pastor was linked to fiscal controls as well. The pastor had to keep track of the various accounts that accompanied control over church land and local bequests to the church, which often put him at odds with the villagers.[74] An even greater tension within his office was that he had to collect revenues from the villagers, since the church was the overlord of some property. These holdings were almost always very small, especially in comparison with the holdings of the landgrave, but they were a source of income for the parish that the pastor collected directly from the villagers. The pastor was, therefore, associated with the entire apparatus of *Grundherrschaft*. Peasants were no more willing to hand their money over to the pastor than they were to hand it over to the landgrave or his officials. In contrast to the relationship between the peasant and the landgrave, however, the pastor and the peasant were in constant personal contact. The result could be exasperation on the part of the pastor at the intransigence of the peasants and an exchange of insults.[75]

The pastor's position was all the more uncomfortable because he was not free to dispose of the money he collected as he wished. Instead, it was subject to scrutiny by both his superiors in the church hierarchy and members of the village who acted as church treasurers. The traditions of his office constrained the pastor's disbursement of church funds. The money from the lands could be a source of the pastor's salary, but that was not its only application.[76] The church itself was the true *Grundherr* over the lands. The revenues were not tithes that were due to the church by some ecclesiastical law but were claims on revenue backed by the secular guarantee that the overlord of land would receive payment for a tenancy.

The pastor of Reichensachsen, Lorenz Ludolph, commented directly about the frustrations caused by the administrative tasks of his office and the sort of administrative tasks that would be more appropriate. As a preface to his "*Seelenrechnung*," Ludolph noted: "as it is a *sordidum* [unseemly thing] to burden a pastor with accounts of money, income and expenditures, so it is on the contrary a *decorum* [fitting thing] and *iustum* [proper thing] to demand of a pastor an account of souls."[77] Though this passage indicates that Ludolph found the fiscal responsibilities that went with the office of pastor to be burdensome, there is no indication that he was ever negligent in carrying out those tasks. In fact, Ludolph was prepared to exercise administrative authority in a form that would have been quite familiar to a secular administrator. He turned up frequently as a complainant to the superintendent in Eschwege when the income from church land was at stake.

But, as Ludolph pointed out, the moral and spiritual sphere of the village was central. The pastor officiated at marriages and baptisms, which made him responsible for overseeing the sexual conduct of his parishioners. This role of moral policeman connected him with the rest of the ecclesiastical administration. Among the most frequent police issues that were brought before the superintendent were extramarital pregnancies and inquiries as to whether two individuals were too closely related to be married. Violations of marriage morals were tried and punished by the consistory. The policing of morals in general was conducted by both secular and ecclesiastical authorities. The ambiguities of jurisdiction in these sorts of cases made the policing of morals the object of great controversy. In most cases, illegitimate pregnancies were subject to both secular and religious sanctions, and thus to competing jurisdictions. The account books of the *Amt* kept a separate account of fines for such violations. Illegitimate pregnancies were almost invariably punished much more severely than the more ordinary crimes of fighting and insulting.[78] Similarly, violations of the Sabbath were punished by the secular authorities, though not with quite the same alacrity. The account book for Eschwege contained a section for Sabbath violations, but violations were listed only beginning in 1659, when the authorities were admonished to do so by the *Räte* in Kassel. The enforcement of morals was of great importance to the ecclesiastical hierarchy, however. The work diary of the superintendent of Eschwege is filled with cases of local pastors reporting moral violations to the superintendent. Some of these reports were simply to inform the superintendent of deficiencies in the moral character of the villagers or to point out a particularly obstreperous villager, but others were direct appeals to the authority of the superintendent for help in enforcing a decision when there was a conflict of jurisdiction.

Pastors such as Ludolph saw it as their responsibility to punish transgressions sharply. They took personal pride in being pastor to a parish that acted morally. Ludolph was fond of the image of the pastor as the true shepherd of his flock. He reacted with both anger and personal disappointment when his record of moral leadership was broken by the immoral behavior of one of his parishioners. In his parish register, he noted the birth of an illegitimate child in his parish in 1653 with the comment: "if this whore had not come by I could have said that I had served in Reichensachsen for 20 years and not baptized a single whore-child; God, however, has taken this glory away from me."[79] Although a violation of this kind was subject to a public church punishment and an investigation by the village elders, the secular administration collected the largest share of the fines. In the end, the pastor had to rely on secular officials for practical sanctions against the recalcitrant. The superintendent was inclined to resolve disputes over ecclesiastical and secular jurisdictions by a process of negotiations that located precedents in the written record.[80] This meant that the limits of ecclesiastical jurisdiction were determined by secular territorial law, which was ultimately determined by the landgrave and his immediate advisors.

The preoccupation of church officials with moral policing had another, more consequential, meaning in the first two decades of the seventeenth century. In the sixteenth century, the word of God preached in the villages was Lutheran. Early in the seventeenth century, that changed. Landgrave Moritz used his considerable intellectual skills to try to arrive at a compromise doctrinal position between the factions of Protestantism in Germany.[81] In consultation with his religious advisors, Moritz devised a plan to introduce a modified form of Calvinism that he hoped would unify the Protestant movement in a single faith. That effort was to prove abortive, and the resistance Moritz faced in his own territory when he tried to implement his reforms suggests how unrealistic his expectations were.

The founding of the consistory was the first step in Moritz's reform. Shortly thereafter, Moritz began to implement his plan in earnest, with the introduction of the so-called Verbesserungspunkte (literally "points of improvement" in religion) in 1604.[82] In 1605, Moritz introduced the breaking of bread in communion in his own chapel and in the towns of Kassel and Marburg, but the innovation met resistance in the rest of the territory. Only after diocesan synods and a general synod were held in 1607 was Landgrave Moritz confident that his changes—which revolved around the breaking of bread, a strict interpretation of the commandment forbidding graven images, readings from the Bible and Psalter, and adherence to a new Kirchenordnung (church ordinance)—could be implemented for the territory as a whole. Three of the diocesan synods, Kassel, Marburg, and St. Goar, showed only insignificant resistance to the changes. The fourth, Eschwege, proved more recalcitrant.

Office for a pastor meant something different from office for a servant of the landgrave. Service to God meant that a pastor could never be an unambiguous agent of the landgrave. Moritz's Verbesserungspunkte opened up a direct confrontation over the limits of a territorial church as an active force in extending the landgrave's will. Several pastors from the diocese of Eschwege were determined to resist the changes in religious practice. For the most part, these pastors served in villages where subjects of the nobility predominated, so the religious struggle over the *Verbesserungspunkte* immediately converged with the political struggle between the landgrave and his Estates over the range of central authority. It was, above all, the nobility who were unsympathetic to the changes in religious practice. In *Amt* Sontra, which was predominantly subject to the landgrave, the *Verbesserungspunkte* were accepted with little opposition. The pastors of Nentershausen and Wichmannshausen, which bordered on Sontra but were subject to the von Boyneburg and von Baumbach, expressed personal sympathy for the changes but were slow to administer them because of the opposition of their noble patrons.[83] The pastor of Wichmannshausen complied with the changes by removing all pictures from the church in Hoheneiche, but these were replaced by the von Boyneburg. In those areas where the nobility predominated, then, there was little compliance. Even some pastors who had been installed by the landgrave refused to introduce the reforms out of fear of revenge by their angered parishioners.[84] Although proponents of the reforms made some progress in convincing reluctant pastors to introduce the changes in head-to-head meetings with the superintendent and the landgrave, the last resistance could be broken only by deposing the recalcitrant pastors and replacing them with Calvinist pastors. This was done in a number of villages in the area of the von Boyneburg.[85]

The date of the infanticide case in Röhrda mentioned above helps explain the sharp conflict of jurisdictions and the importance of the landgrave's role as arbiter. It took place just one year after the landgrave had deposed several Lutheran pastors in the region in favor of Calvinist adherents to the *Verbesserungspunkte*. Seen in this light, the actions of the pastor in Röhrda can be better understood. The pastor was trying to exert his authority in an area dominated by a Lutheran nobility, who were trying to protect their religious practice while opposing the encroachment of the landgrave on their political position. This was tricky in a village such as Röhrda, where the landgrave had the right of *Collator*, yet the majority of villagers were subject to the von Boyneburg.[86] It is noteworthy that the pastor, acting on the side of the landgrave, was able to find allies in the village despite the fact that the peasantry purportedly did not welcome the changes.

The landgrave and the consistory eventually overcame the local clergy's resistance to the reforms and achieved confessional unity in the ecclesiastical hierarchy if not always in local practice. Initially, the pastors of some villages complained of the parishioners' unwillingness to accept the changes and pleaded that the dying and the newborn be given the chance to receive communion in the old style.[87] The landgrave was adamant in his program, however, and brought the entire weight of the ecclesiastical establishment to bear on individual pastors, forcing them to administer the sacraments in the reformed style only. Both the consistory and the superintendent actively visited the parishes to help bring about the transition. The removal of those pastors who opposed the changes was resisted, but the complaint by the von Boyneburg to the *Reichskammergericht* was not heard until 1622, by which time the reforms were firmly entrenched.[88]

The effect of the *Verbesserungspunkte* on the religious experience of individual villagers is difficult to determine. When rites in the parish church were first reformed, there were few communicants for the sacraments. The Werra region was near both Lutheran Saxony and Catholic Mainz. It was apparently possible to walk to Saxon territory to receive the sacraments in the old style. In fact, even into the 1630s, the superintendent was forced to threaten the congregation of Lüderbach with a 100-fl [*Gulden*] fine if they let any Saxon preachers in their church.[89] His threats were necessary, because Lüderbach was under the jurisdiction of the Treusch von Buttlar rather than the landgrave himself, so there were no local agents to enforce conformity. Lutheran nobles posed a constant obstacle to uniform administration. The pastor of Reichensachsen reported in 1639 that he had brought legal action for a fine of 2 gulden against some individuals with Reinhard von Eschwege concerning abuse of the baptismal font. "The junker [von Eschwege] responded, however... that this may well be how things are done in the princely villages [i.e., those in which the landgrave is the sole *Grundherr*], but he did not acknowledge the right of the church to this punishment."[90] Reinhard von Eschwege was a Lutheran who tried to defend his religious practice behind a shield of jurisdictional claims. The nature of the alleged abuse was not specified, but the font was probably used to baptize a child in a Lutheran rite.

Despite the opposition of the local nobility, most of the population began to accept the reformed rites, once the initial shock wore off. In 1645, the pastor of Reichensachsen, one of the villages at the forefront of resistance in 1608, reported that 52 out of 419 souls had failed to attend communion.[91] The pastor considered this a distressing figure, a sign that there was too little fear of God among his parishioners. There are, unfortunately, no figures for comparison with attendance at communion at Lutheran services before 1604, but this number does not seem high enough to argue that there was ongoing strong resistance to the reformed rites. It is plausible that the nonattenders were "epicureans" rather than Lutherans.[92]

The inventories of church paraphernalia made in the 1630s and 1650s indicate that the teachings presented in the church had been thoroughly Calvinized. The characteristic Psalter in the villages was the Lobwasser *Gesangbuch*, which had been explicitly recommended when the *Verbesserungspunkte* were first published. In some villages, the Zwingli translation of the Bible was used, but in others the arch-Calvinist Herborn translation was used.[93] Thus, the readings that the peasantry heard emphasized a reformed interpretation of the scripture, complemented by the Calvinist commentaries that also appeared on the shelves of some parish houses.

The integration of this teaching into the village was accomplished by all local organs of the church. The pastor preached the reformed position in the church, and his subordinate, the schoolmaster, instructed the children of the village in the reformed teachings. Both the pastor and the school-master were required to conform to the reformed religion and were tested by the superintendent to ensure that they did. The intent of the ecclesias-tical hierarchy was to make the Calvinist teachings of Moritz's reform present in every aspect of church life while still accepting the regional peculiarities and privileges of the pastor and the parish church whenever necessary.

Moritz's reform was a key event at the beginning of the seventeenth cen-tury and had repercussions throughout the century. It precipitated jurisdic-tional conflicts as it tried to bring the ecclesiastical administration into closer alignment with the landgrave's own secular central administration, which was also trying to subvert the traditional jurisdictions of the nobility in the secular realm. Documents suggest that Moritz succeeded in achieving at least the formal acceptance of his doctrinal goals in the ecclesiastical administration. Much of church life remained the same, however, especially in those area that affected the villages most immediately. Traditional ways of doing things did not die out. Even practices that predated the reform adapted to the new doctrine. The village of Rockensüß reported in 1635 that every house in the village continued to donate bread to the pastor at Christmas because of an old Catholic custom: "the priest in papist times had to go around on Christmas eve and anoint the houses with holy wa-ter.... But nowadays he [the pastor] has to hold a sermon every Christmas morning."[94] The offices of the church looked much the same in the parish, though the elder's participation in church life was enhanced by reform. The parish remained the ecclesiastical administrative district, and its rela-tion to the village as an institution was unchanged. The church continued as an administrative and fiscal system in competition with both the village and the manorial systems of the landgrave and the nobility. Individual vil-lagers had many dealings with the church that could lead to tense relations with church officials. But the villagers could more easily see the service being provided by the church, which at least partially justified its intrusion into village life.

The pastor tried to ensure that church rituals and the messages they con-tained possessed enough force to bring about adherence to Calvinist beliefs. As late as 1639, there were still villagers who had not assimilated Calvinist teachings. The village head of Burghofen was caught reading "suspicious devotional literature" to a congregation outside the church.[95] Burghofen's deviation from doctrinal orthodoxy was striking, but more striking is the singularity of the case. The behavior of the majority of villagers indicates that the Calvinist message was not being rejected. As villagers were exposed to more sermons and songs, they may well have come to accept and adhere to the judgment and biblical allusion of pastor Ludolph of Reichensachsen: "How much security is here? How many fail to do penance to God? How few pray? believe? obey?... Wake up and pray, so that you do not fall into temptation. And be sober and watch, because the devil goes among you like a growling lion and searches out which of you he would devour."[96]

The successful imposition of the *Verbesserungspunkte* was a victory for secular administration as well as for ecclesiastical organization. *Herrschaft* was exercised through many institutions, which sometimes competed with and sometimes supported one another. The links between obedience in the public realm and obedience to God's order were part of the message conveyed by Ludolph. His warning was that of an outsider who had a better view of the inner workings of the village. The church was the sphere of administration that the villagers themselves were most prepared to integrate into the everyday rhythms of village life, though they continued to attach their own meanings to (and even outward forms on) many church practices, such as the Christmas sermon. The demands of all the strands of *Herrschaft*, as manifested in the seigneurial and state functions of the *Amt* and its chief officials, the ambivalent administrative role of the village heads, and the spiritual supervision of the church, were translated only imperfectly into the realm of the village, but their cumulative effect was to encourage at least outward conformity to a vision of "social discipline." The final instance of social discipline had to come from within the village, however, where the meanings attached to the village were quite different.

Notes

1. Ludwig Zimmermann, *Der Hessische Territorialstaat im Jahrhundert der Reformation. Der Ökonomische Staat Landgraf Wilhelms IV*, vol. 1 (Marburg, 1933), 128. The most recent comprehensive history of Hesse in this era is Walter Heinemeyer, ed., *Das Werden Hessens* (Marburg, 1986).
2. Ludwig Zimmermann, *Der Ökonomische Staat Landgraf Wilhelms IV. Nach den Handschriften bearbeitet*, vol. 2 (Marburg, 1933). The statistical work was supported with a cartographic record, begun by Arnold Mercator and completed by Wilhelm Dilich. See Edmund E. Stengel, *Wilhelm Dilichs Landtafeln hessischer Ämter zwischen Rhein und Weser* (Marburg, 1927).
3. See "Herrschaft" in Otto Brunner et al., eds., *Geschichtliche Grundbegriffe*, vol. 3 (Stuttgart, 1982), 1–102, especially 14–48. A sign of the complexity of the term is that five different authors contribute to the definition. I treated this problem in greater detail in John Theibault, "Community and Herrschaft in the Seventeenth Century German Village," *Journal of Modern History* 64 (1992): 1–21. David Sabean, *Power in the Blood: Popular Culture and Village Discourse in Early Modern Germany* (Cambridge, 1984), 20–27, and Robert Berdahl, *The Politics of the Prussian Nobility* (Princeton, 1988), 10–13, also offer important approaches.
4. Zimmermann, *Der Ökonomische Staat*, vol. 2, passim.
5. On the *Hof* as a settlement form, see Martin Born, "Siedlungsgang und Siedlungsformen in Hessen," in Martin Born, *Siedlungsgenese und Kulturlandschaftsentwicklung in Mitteleuropa* (Wiesbaden, 1980), 239.

6. Compare Mack Walker, *German Home Towns: Community, State and General Estate, 1648–1870* (Ithaca, NY, 1971).

7. Jacob Grimm and Wilhelm Grimm, *Deutsches Wörterbuch*, vol. 2 (Leipzig, 1800), col. 1276–79. The Grimms give five definitions of the term that cover the physical appearance and the inhabitants, including the full range of rights and powers concentrated in the village.

8. Peter Sahlins, *Boundaries: The Making of Modern France and Spain in the Pyrenees* (Berkeley, 1989).

9. See Hessian State Archives, Marburg (StAM) 40d Germerode Lfd. Nr. 151.

10. For example, StAM S 240 was a *Salbuch* for the landgrave's estates, and S 494 was for the von Baumbach family in Nentershausen, yet both listed obligations for the land in a similar manner.

11. Hugo Brunner, "Rittergüter und Gutsbesitzer im ehemaligen Kurhessen," *Jahrbücher für Nationalökonomie und Statistik* 115 (1920/21): 51, estimates that three-quarters of the land in Hesse was directly subject to the landgrave.

12. Kersten Krüger, *Finanzstaat Hessen, 1500–1567* (Marburg, 1980).

13. StAM Kop. 57 gives the breakdown for the assessment for each *Amt*.

14. An example of this procedure can be found in a *Landtagsabschied* of 4/8/1609, which apportioned a tax of 150,000 fl. in six installments on the basis of the Treysa Assessment. See StAM 340 von Baumbach-Nentershausen II, 149.

15. StAM 4h, 3657.

16. See, in general, Carl-August Agena, *Der Amtmann des 17. und 18. Jahrhunderts* (Göttingen, 1973).

17. StAM 17e Eschwege 230, 1/1/1633.

18. Ibid.

19. StAM S 78.

20. Zimmermann, *Der Ökonomische Staat*, 2:78–79.

21. Kurt Dülfer, "Fürst und Verwaltung: Grundzüge der Hessischen Verwaltungsgeschichte im 16.–19. Jahrhundert," *Hessisches Jahrbuch für Landesgeschichte* 3 (1953): 163. Also compare the case in Kersten Krüger, "Frühabsolutismus und Amtsverwaltung: Landgraf Wilhelm inspizierte 1567 Amt und Eigenwirtschaft Trendelburg," *Hessisches Jahrbuch für Landesgeschichte* 25 (1975): 117–47.

22. There is a good analysis of the increasing presence of the administrative side of the village community over the course of the sixteenth and seventeenth centuries in Heide Wunder, *Die Bäuerliche Gemeinde in Deutschland* (Göttingen, 1986).

23. *Dienstgeld* was a cash payment to substitute for labor services owed for properties in the main fields of the village. *Rodgeld* and *Rodzehend* were both paid on lands that had been cleared in the late medieval clearings.

24. See StAM Rech II Sontra 3, passim.

25. On the roles of village heads, see Herbert Reyer, *Die Dorfgemeinde in Nördlichen Hessen* (Marburg, 1983). See also Manfred Reißner, "Bauern als Inhaber öffentlicher Ämter im Spätfeudalen Dorf Kursachsens," *Jahrbuch für Geschichte des Feudalismus* 7 (1983): 298–325.

26. Reyer, *Die Dorfgemeinde*, 52–54.

27. H. A. Geise, *Teutsche Corpus Juris* (Hanover, 1703), 539.

28. StAM Rech II Germerode 5, 1634.

29. StAM Rech II Sontra 3, 1660.

30. StAM Rech II Eschwege 10, 1630.

31. StAM Rech II Eschwege 10, 1665.

32. Otho Melander, *Joco-Seria / Das ist Schimpff und Ernst / Darin nicht allein nützliche und denckwürdige / sondern auch anmühtige und lustige Historien erzehlet und beschrieben werden* (Darmstadt, 1617) 188.

33. StAM S 78 presents a survey of all the officials (*Beamten*) of the landgrave in each *Amt*. The list includes officials such as the gardener, the winemaster, and the ass-driver, but no mention is made of village heads.

34. See Reyer, *Die Dorfgemeinde*, 42–43 and Karl Siegfried Bader, *Dorfgenossenschaft und Dorfgemeinde* (Weimar, 1962).

35. These are collected in Christoph Ludwig Kleinschmidt, ed., *Sammlung fürstlich hessische Landesordnungen und Ausschreiben*, 7 vols. (Cassel, 1767).

36. StAM 5, 7179.

37. Kleinschmidt, *Sammlung fürstlich hessische Landesordnungen*, vol. 1. There are five ordinances concerning the breaking up of Hufen.

38. StAM 17e Rittmannshausen 6, 12/3/1618.

39. In StAM 23a Landvogt an der Werra, 28/4/1626, the village distinguished between *Heimburgen* and *Eltiste*. The former were the most competent spokesmen for the village, and the latter were the oldest and therefore most knowledgeable about the old customs. The use of the oldest members of the village as legal witnesses to old customs is seen in StAM 4c Hessen-Rheinfels-Rotenburg 836; this case also exhibits some of the pitfalls of the practice, since of the seven elders asked to remember where an oath had taken place thirty-one years before, one could not remember, three said at the castle, and three said at the cloister. The term *Eltisten* also referred to church elders, who were rarely the oldest members of the community.

40. StAM S 98.

41. Walker, *German Home Towns*, noted that this differentiation of form with similar functions was one of the ways in which home towns shielded themselves from penetration by the "movers and doers." A similar diversity made it difficult to systematize rule over villages. Sheilagh Ogilvie, "Coming of Age in a Corporate Society: Capitalism, Pietism and Family Authority in Rural Württemberg, 1590–1740," *Continuity and Change* 1 (1986): 287, notes the same multiplicity of forms and local customs in villages that hampered systematization.

42. See Geise, *Teutsche Corpus Juris*, 532–57.

43. It was obviously closely related to the *Weistümer* as a legal document. See Richard Schroeder and Eberhard v. Künssberg, *Lehrbuch der deutschen Rechtsgeschichte*, 6th ed. (Leipzig, 1919), 760–63. In the *Weistümer*, these regulations have the air of being a mutually agreed upon decision by members of the village. In the court instructions, there can be no doubt that the authority emanates from the landgrave.

44. Geise, *Teutsche Corpus Juris*, 531.

45. Dülfer, "Fürst und Verwaltung," 180.

46. There are numerous examples of each in the archives. A characteristic appeal between individuals can be found in StAM 17d v. Baumbach, 2d packet, 11/12/1629, Samptdiener Heinrich Bruckmann's widow vs. the von Baumbachs.

47. StAM 17/I 1173.

48. Christoffel Gude has been the object of extensive genealogical research by one of his descendants. See Philipp Georg Graf Gudenus, "Amtliche Schriftstücke von Christoffel Gude, Leutnant und Amtschultheiss in Sontra (1607–1626)," *Hessische Familienkunde* 18 (1986), col. 165–68; "Gude(nus) korrupt," *Hessische Familienkunde* 18 (1987), col. 333–40; "Auf Regimentsunkosten (1620)," *Genealogie*, 1990: 10–15. These works reprint several documents concerning Gude's activities as an administrative official, including some concerning the supplication against him by the villages of the *Amt*. For more on the organization of the territorial militia, see Gunter Thies, *Territorialstaat und Landesverteidigung Das Landesdefensionswerk in Hessen-Kassel unter Landgraf Moritz (1592–1627)* (Darmstadt and Marburg, 1973).

49. StAM 17/I 1173.
50. Ibid.
51. "Neighbors" was often a way of referring to members of the village community who had access to the communal resources of the village and thus participated in the village assembly. See Reyer, *Die Dorfgemeinde*, 23, and Karl-Sigismund Kramer, *Die Nachbarschaft als bäuerliche Gemeinschaft* (Munich, 1954).
52. StAM 17/I 1173.
53. Ibid. Typical of this is the brief testimony of the head of the village of Krauthausen.
54. Ibid.
55. Ibid. The reference to "they" in the testimony is somewhat ambiguous. The logic of the village head's testimony makes me think that the village was ignored by the villages drafting the supplication, though one might interpret the statement as claiming that the village of Rauttenhausen deliberately ignored what was going on around it because it feared that, as a small village, it might suffer unduly.
56. StAM 17e Boyneburg 6.
57. StAM 340 von Baumbach-Nentershausen III, 167.
58. Compare the Dorfbuch of 1587. StAM S 98.
59. The most comprehensive ecclesiastical history of Hesse-Kassel continues to be Heinrich Heppe, *Kirchengeschichte beider Hessen*, 2 vols. (Marburg, 1876). See also the shorter survey by Heinrich Steitz, *Kirchengeschichte von Hessen und Nassau* (Marburg, 1977).
60. See Heppe, *Kirchengeschichte*, 1:143, passim; 2:4.
61. See Heppe, *Kirchengeschichte*, 1:413ff.
62. StAM 22a, 8.8 Eschwege, 23/6/1608.
63. Ibid.
64. Dekanatsarchiv Eschwege, Tagebuch Hütterodt. This document has been transcribed in an abridged version with modernized spelling and punctuation in Wilm Sippel, ed., *Forschungsberichte der Stiftung Sippel*, vol. 5 (Göttingen, 1981), 173, from which I cite whenever it is complete.
65. Ibid., 21.
66. Dekanatsarchiv Eschwege, Tagebuch Hütterodt, has fascinating examples of the spontaneous writing tasks that the superintendent gave to prospective schoolmasters.
67. StAM 318 Niederhona. These reports distinguish clearly between "ordinary duties" and "*Accidentien.*"
68. Ibid.
69. StAM 318 Abterode.
70. StAM 319 Abterode.
71. Dekanatsarchiv Eschwege, Tagebuch, 28/3/1639.
72. Sippel, *Stiftung Sippel*, vol. 5, 27.
73. StAM 318 Niederhona.
74. The position of the church in the internal life of the village has been considered for many parts of early modern Europe. A good survey of the role of the parish priest in the village can be found in Jean Pierre Gutton, *La Sociabilité Villageoise dans L'Ancienne France* (Paris, 1979), 185–252. The role of the pastor in the life of the village in Germany has been touched on by Sabean, *Power in the Blood*, and by Thomas Robisheaux, "Peasants and Pastors: Rural Youth Control and the Reformation in Hohenlohe, 1540–1680," *Social History* 6 (1981): 281–300.
75. Thus, the pastor of Breitau reported to the superintendent that the pastor of neighboring Ulfen "in forderung seines lohns... sich gegen die Arme leute

mit Schmähworten und Gewalt (angefahren) ("approached the poor people with insults and violence when collecting his wages"). See Dekanatsarchiv Eschwege, Tagebuch, 7/12/1638. On the other side, "An 9/3/1639 klagt Paul Reuterus, Pfarrer in Oberelnbach, daß die Bauern die 'Heiligenländer' weder bebauen noch Zinsen dafür abführen" ("On 9/3/1639, the pastor in Oberelnbach, Paul Reuterus, complains that the peasants neither work the church lands nor pay rents for them"). Sippel, Stiftung Sippel, 5:27.

76. Sippel, Stiftung Sippel, 5:19. See also, in general, the Kirchenrechnungen; for instance, StAM 319, Nentershausen.

77. Walther Kürschner, "Aus dem Kirchenbuch von Reichensachsen von 1639–1653," Archiv für Hessische Geschichte NF 9 (1913): 54–55. Kürschner's source is StAM Ki Reichensachsen 1639–1653.

78. Compare StAM Rech II Eschwege 10, passim. Punishments for illegitimate births were rarely below 10 fl.

79. StAM Ki Reichensachsen 1639–1653.

80. See, for instance, Sippel, Stiftung Sippel, 5:120, where the pastor of Netra is threatened by the village watchman and the superintendent refers the case to the Vogt in Germerode, "weil der Schütze germerodische Mann ist" ("because the watchman is a Germerode man").

81. There is no biography of Moritz that gives a satisfactory explanation for his religious policy. Heppe's Kirchengeschichte continues to be a good introduction to the institutional and doctrinal changes Moritz brought about. Moritz's religious policy is closely tied to his political stance. For two contrasting assessments of Moritz's intellectual and political capabilities, compare Christoph Rommel, Geschichte von Hessen, 10 vols. (Marburg, 1820–58), vol. 9, and Franz v. Geyso, "Politik und Kriegführung im Zeitalter des Dreissigjährigen Krieges," Zeitschrift für Hessische Geschichte 53 (1921): 1–115.

82. See Heppe, Kirchengeschichte, 2:21ff., and Ernst Hofsommer, Die Kirchlichen Verbesserungspunkte des Landgrafen Moritz des Gelehrten von Hessen (Marburg, 1910). The conflict over the imposition of the Verbesserungspunkte in Eschwege has also been described in R. Po-Chia Hsia, Social Discipline in the German Reformation: Central Europe 1550–1750 (London, 1989).

83. Hofsommer, Die Kirchlichen Verbesserungspunkte, 146ff.

84. Ibid., 149.

85. Ibid., 178. Heppe, Kirchengeschichte, 2:35.

86. See StAM S 98.

87. Heppe, Kirchengeschichte, 2:35.

88. Ibid., 35n.

89. Sippel, Stiftung Sippel, 5:97.

90. Ibid., 37.

91. StAM Ki Reichensachsen 1639–1653.

92. "Epicurean" was a common epithet for people who seemed insufficiently fearful of God's judgment. The attitude was criticized from the perspective of orthodox Lutheranism in Melander, Joco-Seria, 77. Compare also the case of Lienhart Seitz in David Sabean, Power in the Blood, 37–60. Seitz refused to attend communion because of his own interpretation of forgiveness and its connection to absolution.

93. StAM 318. On the Calvinist qualities of the Herborn translation, see Gerhard Menk, Die Hohe Schule Herborn in Ihre Frühzeit 1584–1660 (Wiesbaden, 1981).

94. Kopialbuch Amt Sontra.

95. Sippel, Stiftung Sippel, 25.

96. StAM Ki Reichensachsen 1639–1653.

2

Inside the Village:
Space and Solidarity

The Village Book and other administrative documents viewed the village from the perspective of the central administration. Their view was necessarily limited to what was deemed important to the administration and took its particular shape from the process of negotiation between the landgrave's agents and village inhabitants. But administration was not a daily activity and thus could never provide a complete definition of the village. Inhabitants of the village spent more time in contact with their fellow villagers than they did with representatives of administration, and the way in which fellow villagers interacted also had the potential to hold the village together as a unit. This is not to say that it created village harmony. The solidarity of the village came from the realization that it could be defined from within as a unit, not from any shared sense of what unity ought to be. The internal process of defining the village was different from, though not always in conflict with, the process of external definition promoted by the administration.

It is notoriously difficult to study how ordinary people perceived their world and defined the space around them.[1] The perception of village solidarity could come from several different sources. First, the fact of living side by side with other people in a specific area helped define the internal contours of the village. People who lived near one another could define their space as something distinct from that of other villages. A sense of location is a necessary element of any definition of the village. That sense came from the physical qualities of the village—its landscape and internal architecture. Recognizing the physical qualities of the village also helped define the village as a cultural space. One must look at how people dealt with their physical proximity to understand how the village functioned. The two terms that emerge most prominently in the villagers' own understanding of their villages are *community* and *neighborliness*. Of course, not all inhabitants of the village could contribute equally to defining the terms of interpersonal relations. It is now well understood that an expression of communal solidarity could mask many internal divisions, and this must have affected the view of the village from within.[2] This problem is examined at the end of the chapter in a discussion of the coercive nature of "belonging" to the village and the definition of who did not "belong" even though they might live within the space of the village.

The situation of the villages in the Werra region in the late sixteenth century was the product of a long evolution. There were limits to how villagers organized life in their villages, based primarily on the legal perquisites of Herrschaft and the powerful force of long-standing customs. But villages were inhabited by active people, and the way in which those people lived contributed to the outward forms of the villages. The village was not "reinvented" every generation, but neither were internal perceptions unchangeable. Even the most fixed quality of the village—its location—could have different meanings for the inhabitants, depending on changes in climate, market integration, trade routes, and exploitation of natural resources. This means that an understanding of the internal qualities of the village must include an understanding of how outward influences affected life within.

In the previous chapter, I argued that the geographical location of the village and the location of the village in the administrative hierarchy placed constraints on the exercise of Herrschaft. Local knowledge and a sense of the contours of individual villages placed comparable constraints on how villagers could express their interests. No two villages were exactly alike, but most shared common characteristics that provided the repertory from which the internal definition was constructed. The most obvious definition of the village available to villagers was the physical presence of buildings and fields together. These were concrete manifestations of the individual plots of land described in the account books. Villagers saw the ensemble of buildings that made up the village from the surrounding fields.[3] This helped make them conscious of the distinctiveness of each village.

The village was visibly unified by the way it was organized on the land. The villages of the Werra were not made up of scattered homesteads. Rather, they consisted of houses clustered together with fields surrounding them. Most of the villages along the Werra were arranged in rows along a street or around a central place. The buildings were concentrated in a small area and there were few structures detached from the main cluster of buildings, so villagers lived in close proximity to their neighbors.[4] Outlying settlements were rare. Natural terrain and village social life worked together to determine the size of the cluster. Although most villages of the region had between thirty and seventy households in the 1580s, there were some villages as large as the towns of the region and others with fewer than twenty households. For some features of village life, the differences between small and large villages were probably sufficient to create a distinct atmosphere in each; for others, the differences were inconsequential. Even the largest villages of the region were small enough for any inhabitant to have a reasonable overview of the whole and to have contact with everyone who lived there.

The form and appearance of the villages of the Werra were the product of centuries of settlement patterns. Thuringian influence was often stronger than Hessian influence in the traditions of the inhabitants of the region, such as the forms villages took. Both "linear" and "closed" villages were common.[5] Early settlements were influenced by forms of landlordship and natural features as well as folk customs of the settlers. By the seventeenth century, however, the appearance of the village had more to do with the way in which the villagers lived in it at the time than its earliest settlement. Villages were designed primarily for agricultural production. Houses were built in the characteristic style of western Thuringia and eastern Hesse. Like almost all German farmhouses, they were constructed of timber frames and wattle, and the largest included courtyards—some of which had stone gates—where animals and farm implements could be kept in relative security. The population increase in the sixteenth century restructured the core of some villages. Houses became crowded together, and they were sometimes built on common land in the center of the village in exchange for a small rent. The general style of buildings in each village was the same, but the exact configuration was different. Many houses were distinguished by intricate carvings and occasionally inscriptions that lent an additional character to the inhabited core.

There were few public buildings in the villages—and some of them were "public" only because they were reserved for use by officials within the village, such as the parish priest, who was given use of the parish house.[6] The church, with its churchyard, was the centerpiece of the village and the largest public space. Its symbolic and practical importance extended far beyond its role as the site of religious observance. The presence of a church in each village contributed to the separation of one village from another. Although two or even three villages might belong to a single parish, each affiliate of the parish generally had its own church building. The pastor came into the confines of the village rather than having the villagers leave their own village and walk to another. As the largest structure in any village, the church acted as a landmark by which the village could be recognized. Church architecture did not vary greatly in the region, but the profile of each village was made distinct by the position and style of the church within the cluster of less impressive village houses shielding it from contact with the fields and the world beyond. If any structure in the village were made of stone, it would be the church, although many churches had timbered towers placed on a stone base. The building history of the village church often extended beyond the memory of the villagers. Still, villagers touted their forefathers who had built it with the phrase, "built by the *Gemeine* [community members] alone."[7]

The church building thus acted as a focus of local identity and a symbol of the whole village. Indeed, the accoutrements of the church building were nearly as important in defining the village as the presence of the building itself. Villagers emphasized their place in the village by paying for family pews in the church. The pews defined who belonged in the village by creating specific space for them in its most sacred and most visible structure.[8] After death, a family's connection to the village could be continued in the graveyard attached to the church or on the outskirts of the village.

In good weather, villagers might congregate around the church before services, making use of a public space to foster a sense of belonging. Frequently there was a village plaza, or *Anger*, next to the churchyard, which sometimes had a linden tree. The *Anger* served as a focal point for the village as it looked inward rather than at the outside world. It was the primary place of assembly for any activity that touched the village as a whole. Public buildings and public spaces took on a number of different functions and meanings for the village and its inhabitants. Any of these structures could take on symbolic importance as a village landmark, but the linden was a particularly potent symbol of the privileges and responsibilities of the community of the village.[9] Jürgen Kuczynski described the *Anger* and linden tree as part of the "joys of life" that inspired villagers through the fears and frustrations of much of their lives.[10] A brief description of an incident that took place in 1604 indicates that the linden had additional symbolic importance. Three villagers from Münchhosbach were fined a substantial sum because they ran into Ciliax Homeister's house, took a pillow from the bed of the maid there, carried it to the linden tree, and then carried it back and threw it into the house.[11] Although the meaning of this ceremony is obscure, it seems plausible that the three villagers were making a claim about the maid's or Homeister's promiscuity. By carrying the pillow to the linden tree, they had paraded their message to the whole village, thereby involving it in the rumor. In this case, the linden represented the communal spirit of the village.

The identity of individual villages was shaped by the internal layout of buildings and public spaces and reinforced by the geographical separation between village cores. In many parts of the Werra, it was impossible to see the neighboring village because of hills or woods in between. But the village did not end where the edge of the last house ended. The economic structure of the village made the fields and woods around the core as much a part of the village as the houses themselves. Unlike the buildings, the fields of a village ran right up next to those of the neighboring village, so all land belonged in one village or another. Where one village ended, the next one started; the only neutral ground was the roads leading from one village to another, which properly belonged to the landgrave.[12] An artificial boundary had to be set to distinguish the fields of adjacent villages, though that boundary often followed natural geographical boundaries. This political boundary encompassed everything that belonged to the village; it thereby contributed to the villagers' understanding of what the village was.[13]

A political boundary was more than just a convenience for the central administration. The notion of boundedness was central to the villagers' conception of the space they inhabited. Boundaries put each object or social group in a specific place and kept neighboring or similar entities from encroaching on one another. The line that separated one village from another was as indelibly printed on the sensibilities of the villagers as were the boundaries between themselves and town dwellers or nobles, or between Calvinists and Lutherans. Boundaries provided a first definition of those who truly belonged to the village and those considered interlopers. For this reason, political boundaries were marked with stones to avoid disputes between villages. In some areas of Germany, children accompanied the men who set the boundary markers of the village, and they played games at the marking stones in order to reinforce the memory of where the boundaries lay.[14] A similar ritual may have happened in the Werra region, since local officials formally visited the boundary stones to make sure that they were properly set, and villagers who failed to participate were subject to punishment.[15]

The traditional boundaries of the village were well known to the villagers. They were based on geographical landmarks and were written into the official records. Small bits of land on the border sometimes led to fierce disputes. When the village of Heldra claimed that the boundaries had been moved to its disadvantage, the officials of the landgrave queried the oldest members of the village on where the boundary had been set traditionally. In another dispute, the villagers of Berneburg were fined for trying to incorporate a piece of land that belonged to Cornberg into their own fields.[16] The issue was so explosive because the wealth of a village depended on what lay within its boundaries. The loss of even a small parcel of meadow was a loss for the entire village. The issue was also explosive because it threatened the pride and inner unity of the village when an outsider tried to encroach upon its territory. Every village controlled access to and use of its own fields, and every village tried to keep outsiders from crossing the boundary. It was unacceptable for the residents of one village to use the land of a neighboring village without permission. Disputes over boundaries were one kind of conflict that villagers looked to *Herrschaft* to resolve, as when the village of Wolfterode was fined by the landgrave's courts for pasturing animals on land belonging to the village of Ulfen.[17] The integrity of the village was protected by the landgrave's court, showing how interwoven the strands of authority and autonomy were.

Consciousness about boundaries between villages undoubtedly went hand in hand with consciousness about boundaries within the village. Different parts of the fields had names that were familiar to all villagers. Each area inside the stone boundaries had a specific identity, based on its use and the villagers' knowledge of its characteristics.[18] Croplands were planted according to the principles of three-course crop rotation, which divided the fields into three large blocs. Each bloc had a name based on its location relative to the village buildings, but it was often referred to by the crop that was planted on it that year.[19] As crops were rotated, villagers had to return to the geographical names to identify individual parcels. Many villagers had parcels in several different areas within the village. Three large pieces of land in Grandenborn were distributed in bits among fifty-eight distinct locations with local names.[20] Some of these locations took their names from geographical features within the boundaries, such as *auf der Gangtalshöhe* (on the Gangthal heights); many others were identified in relation to man-made features, such as *am Ulfer Weg* (on the road to Ulfen). Two parts of the fields were named in reference to the buildings of the village, *hinter dem Dorf* (behind the village) and *vor dem Dorf* (in front of the village), showing how villagers used the cluster of buildings as a point of reference for the village fields.

Villagers used their local knowledge of geography and traditions to define the essential unity of the village to their own benefit. What better source of information about the internal contours of the village could there be than the collective memory of its inhabitants? An example of the confidence and determination with which the village perceived its internal boundaries can be seen in a dispute between the village of Rittmannshausen and an official of the von Boyneburg over the placement of a stone near the village street.[21] The villagers—perhaps instigated by Hans Salman and Claus Heβe, who wrote to the Hessian chancery to complain about the matter—were upset that the official had widened the street so that he could incorporate an additional *Ruten* of land into his own property. He did this even though his neighbors had warned him that the new boundaries were not traditional. The members of the village acted together to preserve the boundaries that they recognized. They removed the stone from where the official had placed it and reset it in its original location. They then called in someone who was familiar with local customs to confirm that they had placed the stone accurately. In all these actions they acted as if they were certain of the justice of their own view of internal order, even though their opponent represented *Herrschaft* itself.

Sharing space in the village led to shared experiences that fostered a sense of belonging together. Probably no man-made sound was more common in the village than the chiming of the church bell. The bell did more than just chime for church services. It was a signal for almost all activities in the village. The bell sent myriad messages to the villagers that could be deciphered from the way the bell was rung. Being within the sound of the bell and understanding its message established an individual's home. It is likely that people working in the fields could easily distinguish the tones of the bells in different villages, but the only one that mattered was the bell ringing in the individual's own village; it became another means by which the individual identified with the village. Sometimes, that familiarity was essential for survival. During the confusion of the Thirty Years' War, the village of Reichensachsen set up a special signal to call people to church when danger was nearby. The pastor noted with satisfaction that only the villagers of Reichensachsen knew how to distinguish the signals for flight or assembly.[22]

Given the symbolic and practical importance of the bell in the life of the village, it is not surprising that a great deal of attention was paid to its construction and preservation. When the combined church of St. Nicolai for Oberhona and Niederhona was torn down in the early sixteenth century to make way for new churches in each village, the village of Oberhona gladly sold its share of the stones from the old church to Niederhona to build a new bridge, but it saved the bell from the old church to put into the new one.[23] Bells were an expensive accessory, yet many villages had newly decorated bells installed over the course of the sixteenth century.[24] Many of these bells lasted into the twentieth century. They sometimes had both pictorial and written messages directed at the church community or addressed to God or the saints, in much the same way that individual houses proclaimed the beliefs of their builders in their carved facades for all the village to see. The bell in Hoheneiche, cast in 1572, informed the congregation simply that "The word of God is eternal."[25] The bells of Abterode had a more complex message. The newest of the three bells was installed in 1507 with the inscription: "holy Anna, Saint Mary, Saint Boniface, pray for me."[26] The "me" for whom the saints were asked to pray may have been the manufacturer, whose name did not appear on the bell, but it was also a request for the bell itself and, through the bell, the church and the inhabitants of the village. Next to the inscription there were figures depicting scenes in the lives of Christ and Mary. These scenes were framed by images of a bishop who carried the symbols of martyrdom of St. Boniface. The figure of Boniface was the most significant for the villagers as a symbol of their village. Named not for the scenes of Christ and Mary on its exterior but for the bishop whose martyrdom it memorialized, the "Bonifatius" bell and the church that housed it retained their identification with the saint. Although the conversion to the reformed religion initiated by Moritz cooled much of the originally Catholic imagery of the saint, the church continued to carry the name of Boniface. The image of Boniface, the man who converted the Werra valley in the eighth century, reentered the lives of the villagers in Abterode whenever they heard their church bells.

The communal role of the bell was complicated by the connection of the bell to *Herrschaft*. In a legal system in which customary practice was so prominent, the bell had a legal character that could be a source of tension between the administration and the villagers. The bell tolled to indicate internal matters, which included issues of direct concern to the central administration as well as issues that primarily touched the lives of the villagers, such as the drawing of lots to determine use of the communal brewing pan.[27] Ringing the bell was understood to be a binding summons of the villagers to deal with official matters.[28] Sometimes the official matter at hand was an attempt by the administration to exert more influence at the local level, for example, the promulgation of a new ordinance that had to be read to the entire community.

Sometimes the villagers took it upon themselves to ring the bell for their own purposes. When the bell was rung as an official warning about highway robbers, the villagers of Reichensachsen did not just go into hiding; instead, they gathered together as a posse and went searching for the robbers in order to punish them themselves.[29] This sort of vigilante activity did not suit the legal prescriptions of the central administration, but it seemed justified to the villagers, both on the pragmatic grounds of responding to an immediate need and on the symbolic grounds of unified action under the authority of the bell. Similarly, unified action by the villagers in opposition to normal legal procedures seemed justified in Berneburg when the Schultheiß rang the bell to call the village assembly together to tear down the old schoolhouse and distribute the wood among the villagers. Although the central administration disapproved and tried to punish the people responsible for tearing down the schoolhouse, the villagers believed that the ringing of the bell had rendered the activity legitimate.[30]

Although the central administration could try to dispute the meanings the villagers attached to the ringing of the bell by threatening to punish those who abused it, it had only an indirect influence on the circumstances under which the bell was rung. The bell was primarily the responsibility of the schoolmaster. He cleaned the church and kept its property in order, taking care of the bell as part of his regular duties.[31] He also rang the bell to call everyone to church and for church occasions such as vespers, though the instructions for his duties specified that he must "inform the pastor verbally beforehand." But the schoolmaster's control over the bell was not exclusive; it was "the privilege of the village Schulz to call the men to the Anger."[32] The Schulz's access to the bell granted him legitimacy and power in a form that was immediately recognizable by the villagers because the bell symbolized village identity. If a villager tried to use the bell for his own purposes, thereby subverting the authority of the village head and of the bell, he was subject to punishment.[33] Presumably other villagers occasionally had access to the bell when it was necessary to warn the neighbors, but formal control over the bell was in the hands of the two officials who were members of the village and who represented the village to the outside world as well.

Inhabitants of the village were not entirely free of the influence of the administrative definition in their own definitions of the village. Attempts by the villagers to define their space as their own and make their experience the standard for internal organization conflicted with the desire of the landgrave to define the space of the village as his, through the presence of his ordinances and the actions of his agents. In either case, however, the material presence of the village remained at issue because of how it was lived in and how it focused the experiences of both its inhabitants and lords. There were two ways in which villagers could approach this challenge from above: They could act through informal channels, relying on their superior knowledge of local circumstances to thwart any efforts by outsiders to penetrate into the experience of the village; or they could act together formally, through the legitimate framework of the corporate community, the *Gemeinde*, which had a juridical status within the territorial state. Generally they chose whichever strategy seemed most likely to succeed in a given instance. Whatever approach they took relied on internal coercion to make everyone subject to a single view of what the village should tolerate. As mentioned in the last chapter, when a village sent a supplication to the landgrave, it adopted the formula "*Schultheiss, Vorsteher und ganze Gemein.*" This represented the village to the administration in a way that was acceptable, but it also required the village to present itself as a unified community.

Who constituted the unified community? Men did. The masculinity of the community was so taken for granted that few people bothered to comment on it.[34] The brief comment about the *Schulz*'s access to the bell, which allowed him to call the "men" (*Menner*) to the *Anger*, is the strongest evidence in the Werra region that public action was assumed to be male action. But villagers did express other opinions about what kind of people constituted the community. According to the villagers, the people who belonged in the village were neighbors (*Nachbarn*). The term was both an apt description of the physical proximity of the houses in the village and a legal concept denoting those who participated in the communal activities of the village. The primary qualification for becoming a *Nachbar* was the possession of a house in the core of the village. Possession of the homesite conferred privileges that made the householder a member of the village community. The tangible manifestation of this membership was access to resources held by the village in common, such as the brewing pan or wood from the communal forest.[35] The village owned land of its own, which it made available for use by members of the village. The forests were the most important pieces of land administered corporately by the village. Custom determined at what time of year a bundle of wood could be collected by each member of the village.[36] In the cadastres of the eighteenth century, the privileges that accompanied householding were given a monetary value for tax purposes, and the value assigned to them was considerable. In Rockensüß, for example, their value was reckoned at 8 fl, which was nearly the value of a cow and half the yearly cash income of some day laborers.[37] For marginal householders, these privileges could have been a significant means of keeping themselves above the status of nonhouseholders. Although the monetary equivalence of these privileges was not calculated before the eighteenth century, their existence was noted in various village regulations and carried the authority of custom from time immemorial.[38] The fact that the village as a whole controlled access to major resources compelled villagers—especially poorer villagers—to participate in the collectivity.

The other central feature of neighborliness was participation in actions deemed to be of communal interest. Hans Rese and Hans Holzhewer of Königswald were fined in the Amt courts for failing to report that their neighbors had killed a game animal.[39] Rese's and Holzhewer's lack of action was harmful to the interests of Herrschaft but consistent with the idea of internal secrecy that neighborliness enforced. Cooperation of neighbors against the interests of the central administration thus defined the village as a body with its own interests, determined by its inhabitants. In many instances, the terms Nachbarschaft (the community of neighbors) and Gemeinde (the corporate body representing the village in the administration) were synonymous. Both were expressed as a collectivity that embodied the will of everyone in the village. Both were dominated by a few heads of households, especially those who became either village head or Vormunder. Some individual neighbors opposed actions undertaken on behalf of the Gemeinde, but their opposition rarely altered its policy. For example, Valtin Kaufmann was fined because "he insulted the entire Gemeinde of Dens."[40] The term Nachbarschaft took account of the fact that the village was made up of a number of individuals, whereas the term Gemeinde perceived the village as one body with a single will. The neighbors collectively created the will of the village through the institution of the village assembly.

There is no direct evidence for the exact meaning of participation in the village besides the advantages derived from access to the communal lands mentioned above. It is not certain, for instance, that the village assembly met at any regular interval. The use of the expression ganze Gemein at least indicated that an assembly of village members had taken place.[41] Decisions were reached in the name of the Gemeinde, but it is uncertain whether they were arrived at by majority vote, unanimous acclamation, or some other method. If the impetus behind a village assembly was the village head, the village would be convened by a formal ringing of the bell. In other cases, a group of villagers would get together and try to develop a policy for the entire village.

Dissent or independent action within the village was suppressed by villagers so as to assert the unity of the community against outside institutions. If villagers did not acknowledge the authority of the Gemeinde in their everyday activities, they were liable to be punished. The village used the courts of the landgrave to enforce its will on dissenters or people who tried to circumvent the official organs of the village. Thus, even communalism was dependent on Herrschaft. A villager in Königswald was fined because he built a fence around a garden "without the fore-knowledge of the *Gemeinde*."[42] Actions undertaken in the name of the *Gemeinde* were designed to protect the authority of that institution and had a legal character. But the authority of the village could also be asserted informally through the actions of the neighbors, without relying on legal sanctions imposed by the landgrave's courts. Neighbors enforced sanctions against any member who violated the rules of the community, even when the courts found no grounds for punishing the offender. The case of the dispute over a misplaced boundary stone in Rittmannshausen, described above, illustrates this form of collective pressure. The conflict between official and village continued even after a group of villagers reset a disputed boundary stone. The neighbors imposed a penalty of 1 fl for the official's continued intransigence, but they did so as a matter of internal village administration rather than taking the matter to the landgrave's courts. According to the villagers, the penalty was backed by tradition, which meant that it had legal force. They insisted that it was not their doing alone but was the action of the whole *Gemeinde*. The offender refused to pay, even though he and the members of the community had drunk together as a token of their agreement that the sanctions were legitimate. The failure of the offender to abide by what he had drunk to was deemed an egregious offense. In response, the villagers collectively denied the offender his portion of the communal wood.[43] The sanctions continued until the individual came to an agreement with the village as a whole. In the process of forcing a recalcitrant individual to conform to the communal will, the villagers also reinforced the notion of neighborliness as the basis of cooperation. Neighborliness was not benign for those who disagreed with the prevailing values in the village. It is likely that those in a less powerful position than the agent of a nobleman were more easily cowed by the threat of sanctions, and their disagreements with the community never reached the point of public conflict.

Collective action by villagers was not confined to coercing independent-minded or obstreperous individuals into obeying the dictates of the *Gemeinde*. The *Gemeinde* also represented the interests of the neighbors in trying to resist the intrusion of the landgrave's administration. This process linked the *Gemeinde* back into the structures of authority described in the previous chapter in an entirely different manner. Community could serve as both a prop of and a challenge to *Herrschaft*.

The response of the villages of *Amt* Sontra to the impositions by *Amtschultheiss* Gude, mentioned in Chapter 1, are a good illustration of how *Gemeinde* and *Herrschaft* became intertwined. The supplication was from "all subjects," but it quickly became obvious that the complaint was organized around the institution of the *Gemeinde*. The testimony by individual heads of villages demonstrated conclusively that the initial impulse to complain came from just two villages, Rockensüß and Königswald. The heads of those two villages had to testify in such a way as to justify their own actions and the supplication itself. They did this by highlighting the active will of the community as the motive force behind the supplication. The head of Rockensüß reported that, when he read the note announcing that the villagers had to pay the expenses of the militia, "the neighbors complained and said that they could not and will not pay it." The villagers decided that they wanted to seek a remedy from the landgrave, and the head of the village went along.

The testimony of the head of the village of Königswald clarified the process of creating the supplication still more:

> The village head Wolhaupt says that when everyone in Königswald had to give 1 *albus* for expenses incurred in Ulfen, the *Gemeinde* told him that they did not want to pay the money because it was too much. Then the head of the village of Rockensüß sent him one or two messages and wanted to know if his neighbors were going to give the money. When he showed this to the *Gemeinde* in Königswald, they said to him that he should join the people in Rockensüß and help them in their complaint; otherwise they would not consider him to be a proper head of the village, nor the *Vormunder* either. Thereupon, one *Vormunder* and a man from Rockensüß, two *Vormunder* from Königswald, and two men from Hosbach went to Heyerode to get the supplication written.[44]

Here again, the testimony highlights the way in which the community, rather than the village head, was responsible for the supplication. As he noted, the villagers demanded that he act on their behalf, or else "they would not consider him to be a proper head of the village." This is a curious formulation of their expectations. It was far from obvious that the proper role of the village head was to act as an advocate for the village in negotiations with the central administration, since he was so deeply entwined in the practice of *Herrschaft*. If the villagers had wished to suggest only that no proper villager would tolerate such a great burden, they could have emphasized that it was his duty as a "neighbor" to join with Rockensüß. But they specifically emphasized that he act in his capacity as village head— at least, that is what he testified. They were using his office as a confirmation of the justice of their complaint, and they expected him to abide by their determination of what his office entailed.

No doubt, the head of the village of Königswald weighed his testimony carefully. He knew that he would be the focal point of any punitive response by the landgrave. The process of supplication was not a threat to the practice of *Herrschaft*, but it was dangerous to allow the head of the village too much freedom to act as an embodiment of the interests of the village. One of the duties of the village head was to report all official decrees and correspondence to the villagers. Ordinarily, this would be a safe extension of the landgrave's authority into the village. But if the village head believed that he was the representative of the interests of the village, he might reverse the relationship of authority and provide a focal point for resistance. The summoning of the villagers for announcements involved the use of symbols central to the village's identity, such as the church bell and the linden tree. Thus, although the summoning of the villagers contained a hint of domination from the outside, the way in which the village head communicated the message might play a role in how the villagers responded to it. An extreme example of how the village head's attitude could shape a response can be seen in an incident in the village of Oberhona. The village head there instigated resistance to the directives of the landgrave's officials. He consulted with five of his fellow villagers, and together they rang the bell to convene the *Gemeinde* and "asked them whether they should obey the order or not."[45] This was deemed a serious breach of duty, and the six perpetrators were assessed substantial fines. What distinguished the Königswald case from that of Oberhona was that the head of Oberhona had taken the initiative and had explicitly rejected a promulgated directive; the head of Königswald claimed to be responding to the demands of his constituency and did not openly question the legitimacy of a directive.

None of the other heads of villages indicated that they had taken the initiative for making the complaint, but the commission and Gude may have good reason for suspecting that the village heads' presentation of the message had shaped the response of the villagers. A mixture of deference to authority and ability to manipulate the sphere of the village head's activities can be seen in the response of the largest village, Ulfen. The head of Ulfen disassociated himself from the process of drafting the complaint. There should have been no question about Ulfen being involved in any rebelliousness, since, as he testified, "he had held negotiations with the village (*Dorfschaft*) concerning the expenses, and the *Vormunder* had begun collecting them."[46] This line of response was reminiscent of the strong legitimating language of the heads of the villages of Dens and Weissenborn. Particularly noteworthy is the choice of the term "negotiate" to describe his interaction with the village; it underscores his administrative role. But Ulfen was far from being unimplicated in the supplication, and the village head's deference was ambiguous. The inhabitants of the village had begun to resist the collection when they received a message from Rockensüß asking whether they wished to join in supplicating. The village head and *Vormunder* from Rockensüß claimed that their original supplication had received a favorable response from the landgrave. The testimony of the village head of Ulfen suggests that Rockensüß's claim was enough to sway the debate in the village to outright support of the supplication. Ulfen thereupon sent its *Vormunder* to Rockensüß "on behalf of the *Gemeinde*," and the village decided to join the complaint with Rockensüß and to add an additional complaint of its own.

The difference between the testimony from Rockensüß and Königswald and that from the other villages of *Amt* Sontra was not due to superior communitarian consciousness in those two villages. A striking feature of all the testimony concerning the supplication explored thus far is that there is no indication of any dissenting factions within the villages. The village head in Königswald played off this notion of internal unanimity to justify his actions in the process of supplication. The head of the village of Berneburg, however, testified as if he were just a conduit of information, but his role in disseminating the information was crucial, and the results of his intervention did not reflect unanimity:

> The village head says he was not there at the beginning when the supplication . . . was discussed, but when it was finished, a message was sent to him from Rockensüß and he was asked if he wanted his Gemeine to join the complaint, which had already been presented to the landgrave. He reported this to the Gemeine, and almost everyone voted that they should join; however some paid their share of the war costs, which the village head had in his possession for delivery.[47]

This laconic summary of what must have been a tumultuous meeting of the village assembly effectively masks the way in which the village head may have contributed to the discussion. Perhaps he was on the side of those who paid their share, since he was in possession of their payments. If this is the case, then his actions can indeed be considered noncommunitarian. But the image of the communitarian political position of the head of the village of Rockensüß is also quickly dispelled by the resistance he experienced from his fellow villagers in 1628. Matthias Ruppel and Georg Germerod were both fined that year for refusing to follow the village head's commands that they perform labor services on the Landgrave's estate at Cornberg. Germerod accused the village head of being "a liar" to his face, which was not a minor jest. Zacharias Deuberich argued equally vehemently that the village head's auxiliary officers "are collecting the contribution like rogues."[48] We cannot assume that the prominence of Rockensüß and Königswald in the supplication process was due to superior communal harmony in the villages.

Nor can we assume that the circumspection of the village head of Dens was due to lack of communitarian commitment. There are many indications that the village heads in Dens and Berneburg took part in actions that challenged the unbridled exercise of Herrschaft. They were not as immune to the idea of the village head being the advocate of his community as their testimony about the supplication might suggest. If the village head called villagers to perform labor services, he could also organize resistance to labor services in a way that challenged the legitimacy of specific burdens.[49] By 1621, the villages of Amt Sontra had been passively resisting a wide range of burdens, centered on labor services in Cornberg, for more than a decade. Scarcely a year went by without some village being fined for obstreperous behavior. Unfortunately, the list of fines for 1621 is missing, so we cannot know what punishable actions were taken by the villages that year; in 1622, however, a very large fine was levied on "all the villages of Amt Sontra" for failing to produce logs for the saltworks.[50] It is noteworthy that this fine was imposed on all the villages of the Amt, thereby lending credence to the supplication on behalf of "all subjects" the previous year. The administration suspected that the failure to produce wood was no mere oversight but rather passive resistance, the product of collusion among all villagers centered around the village heads.[51]

Often, as with the case of the missing wood, fines were assessed on "the village,"[52] but the level of accountability for the village head and auxiliary officers varied from year to year. Sometimes they were singled out for separate punishment. In 1620, the head of the village of Königswald and the auxiliary officers were fined "because they acted irresponsibly in delivering wood to Cornberg."[53] This might be viewed as an isolated incident of negligence in the village head's official duties, but it is suggestive that the act of negligence concerned the delivery of wood, which was to become a more general problem two years later. There are other instances in which the punishment was directed at the village head because he was acting in concert with his fellow villagers. For example, in 1617, the village head and *Vormunder* in Rockensüß were singled out for fines because "they *and the village* were indolent in the labor services at Cornberg."[54] The head of the village of Ulfen and the auxiliary officers were also held responsible for fines "on behalf of their neighbors" in 1618.[55]

There is no pattern to the fines imposed on villages as a whole or on village heads; nor it is always clear when fines were imposed because of mere irresponsibility in the performance of a task and when they were the result of passive resistance of the village as a whole under the leadership of the village head. The source of resistance within the village could often be masked. This is one reason that it was dangerous to allow the village head to play an active role as the representative of the community. In 1616, the year before the village head of Rockensüß was fined for his failure to bring his fellow villagers to labor services, eight of the twelve villages in the *Amt*, including Dens, were fined for failing to assist with the landgrave's hunt.[56] There was, therefore, a mixture of isolated and coordinated resistance to specific manifestations of *Herrschaft*, such as labor service and the hunt, throughout the 1610s and 1620s in *Amt* Sontra. One can gain a good sense of how frustrating it must have been for the central administration to thwart these attempts to avoid labor services: A fine was imposed on the village of Dens "because they were called to mow at Cornberg and took five days of beautiful weather to do what they should have accomplished in just five hours."[57]

The supplication against *Amtschultheiss* Gude takes on a different character when viewed in the context of this long series of fines. Christoffel Gude and Heinrich Rodingus were the agents of the landgrave directly responsible for running the Cornberg estate and organizing the hunt. There is no evidence that the villagers ever relied on "legitimate" means, such as supplications, to resist labor services. They apparently relied on passive resistance to exhaust the coercive resources of the officials. Village heads provided

a focus for coordinating action across village boundaries. It seems plausible
that the decision not to participate in the hunt was arrived at in much the
same manner as the agreement between Rockensüß and Königswald to make
the supplication in 1621. The village heads communicated with one another, trying to discover the sentiment in neighboring villages. It seems
unlikely that Gude and Rodingus would have forgotten these encounters
when the villagers made this new supplication.

It is equally hard to imagine that the villagers themselves had forgotten
their long-standing resistance to the landgrave's impositions and suddenly
viewed him as an impartial judge. The juxtaposition of labor strikes and
formal supplications shows the range of strategies that villages could adopt
for achieving political ends. Different situations called forth different responses,
which emerged from the fact that neither community nor Herrschaft were
fixed ideas but were processes that involved constant testing and redefinition.

The church and the bell together formed the most powerful symbol of
village unity within the geographic boundary. The village activities associated with bell and church were those that involved the entire community,
such as attending religious services and participating in the village assembly.
Participation in the village as a neighbor could be done informally but might
also involve a communal gathering of some sort. The space where this communal activity took place was the church or the Anger and linden tree.[58]
There is no indication of how frequently the members of the village met.
Weekly or biweekly church services were probably the most regular occa-
sion for the gathering of the whole village, though there is no evidence
that church attendance was regular for most villagers. Formal proclamations
under the authority of the ringing of the bell were probably rare. The bell
was more likely to be used to summon people to discuss village matters, but
for many tasks, such as organizing the work in the fields, the bell may not
have been rung. Villagers may have gathered naturally in the course of
their workweek. There were certainly other occasions, however, when the
villagers came together as a body in a way that helped define the village.

One way in which villagers joined together to assert their local identity
was in periodic celebrations within the boundaries of the village. It was
rare for the village to sponsor communal celebrations on its own initiative.
There was, however, a regular villagewide celebration that seems to have
occurred throughout the Werra region and points to the connections between pride in the public symbols of the village and the desire for communal celebration: Kirmes.[59] Kirmes originated well before the Reformation as
a celebration of the village's founding date or the feast day of the saint for
whom the church was named. Although the central administration formally
disapproved of the Catholic undertones of the celebration and the fact that
it provided an opportunity for disorder and profligacy, Kirmes had become
too much a part of communal life to be effectively rooted out. There is no

complete contemporary description of *Kirmes* in the villages of the Werra region, so it is not clear what happened besides a lot of drinking and carousing. What we do know is that the celebrations were generally large and included outsiders as well as village inhabitants. For the insiders, *Kirmes* was an opportunity to show off to their neighbors; for the outsiders, it was an opportunity to get out of their own villages and take part in something distinctive. The resulting celebrations could get out of hand, so the administration stepped in to suppress any signs that *Kirmes* might be a more fundamental threat to the social order. *Kirmes* seems to have been as close to carnival as the Protestant Werra region came—and there was no Lent to follow it—but it does not appear to have had the social inversions and jokes against authority that characterized communal celebrations elsewhere.[60] Instead, it provided an opportunity to participate in games and competitions and to indulge in the stereotypical German vice of drinking.

Drink was the primary solvent of proper order. When Valtin Nolcke got drunk at the *Kirmes* in Breittau, he accused the pastor of the village of being a "priest" (i.e., a Papist). When he was called to testify about this accusation before the *Amtmann*, he did not deny it, but he jumped up and down and shouted rather than submitting to the officer's authority. As a result, he was fined 10 fl and placed in prison for eight days—by far the stiffest penalty meted out by the court that year.[61] The court considered his offense severe because it called into question the authority of the landgrave's officials. In contrast, the penalty of Hans Gude of Munchhospach was less severe. He set up a shooting stand in his house during *Kirmes* and started shooting during the night.[62] Gude posed less of a threat to the authority of the officials than to public safety, but the administration still stepped in to ensure that a local celebration did not develop into a challenge that the administration could not rebuff.

The activities of *Kirmes* suggest the unsurprising conclusion that villagers liked fun and games. Since the arrival of *Kirmes* was known in advance, it presumably called for at least some local preparation. Spontaneous communal celebrations outside of such "traditional" ones were inhibited by regulations from the central administration. Villagers had to get the approval of local officials before they could put on a dance or allow musicians in the village. The restrictions did not stop villagers from trying to enjoy themselves and giving their own meanings to the public space of the village. For example, eight villagers from Dens were fined for beginning a dance and removing the pastor's wood from the village *Anger*.[63] The dancers might have removed the pastor's wood to make more room to dance or as an act of rebellion against an authority who disapproved of dancing. It is, at any rate, interesting that the villagers laid claim to the public space of the *Anger* as the legitimate site of their revelry, which they believed justified the removal of the wood.

Most public celebrations had to take place within an approved framework.

When public spaces such as the *Anger* or church were used, even activities associated with specific households ended up being public occasions for most of the village. Celebrations of weddings and baptisms sometimes broke down into drunken brawls or shouting matches. In 1614, two separate weddings in *Amt* Sontra were marked by tumult. Claus Binge's son in Weissenborn was found guilty of provoking an altercation at one wedding, and Ciliax Wittich was fined for refusing to name the people who injured him at another one.[64] Villagewide celebrations contributed to village identity, but they did not necessarily produce amity or neighborly feeling.

The discussion of *Kirmes* and other local celebrations returns us to the observation that villages were identified in relation to one another, not just on their own. Each peasant had a home village where he resided and held most of his lands. An individual's integration into an *Amt* and into a village fixed that person's position in relation to all other villagers in other *Ämter*. The village, therefore, gave villagers an identity in the rest of Hessian society. Whenever villagers were noted outside their own villages, they would be identified by their home villages.[65] Even those who moved from the village still relied on the home village identity. It was common practice for the village head to certify on behalf of the *Gemeinde* that a villager was of good character and would make a welcome neighbor elsewhere. Few of these "passports" survived, but the ones that did attest to the piety and sobriety of the persons carrying them.[66]

The villagers' economic activity took place within the confines of the village, and they had access to whatever benefits the village could supply. The laws left villagers subject to the authority of the heads of the home village. Neighbors were seen both as individuals who lived in close proximity and as *Nachbarn* who participated in the same corporate body. Whether this made people any more sympathetic to causes of the village that did not directly affect them is open to dispute. Almost any village activity, however, would affect a villager eventually. This gave the villagers a stake in how the village participated in the larger political structures of the Hessian territorial state, even if their active participation was channeled by others in the institution of the *Gemeinde*.

Cooperation to protect the village from outside impositions and coercion to enforce solidarity within the village were the hallmarks of neighbors, but not everyone associated with the village was properly a neighbor. Those who were not technically neighbors, or those who were not perceived as such, were outsiders, even if they resided in the village. Although the village controlled the use of the land within its boundaries, it did not directly control ownership. Occasionally, land within the boundaries of one village belonged to the inhabitants of another village. Nonvillagers owned such land because of inheritance or marriage, though steps were often taken to ensure that these actions did not lead to land coming into the hands of outsiders.[67] The *Amt* account books note several individuals from surrounding villages who owned land within the boundaries of many villages. The holders of such property were duly noted as outsiders (*Ausmärker*) in the official records.[68] The residents of the village also viewed them as outsiders, not simply because *Ausmärker* did not participate in the perquisites of the village, but also because outsiders were not subject to the same collective burdens of taxation and other revenues assessed by the village. In addition, outsiders were already identified with other villages, which could be viewed as a conflict of interest. The holdings of outsiders were not large, but villagers jealously guarded the integrity of their village.

Officials of the landgrave formed another group of outsiders, though it was rare for them to reside in villages, since the *Amt* was usually based on a town.[69] The pastor was a more ambiguous outsider. His education and his responsibilities and loyalties made him seem like an outsider, but he participated in many internal matters as a neighbor and strove to maintain his legal status as such. The pastor lived in the parish house and controlled land for his own use as a traditional perquisite of his office. This necessarily involved him in the cycles of sowing and harvesting that affected village life. Consequently, the pastor technically had rights as a member of the village. A list of church privileges in the parish of Niederhona noted that the pastor had access to firewood, communal shepherd, beer brewing, and gardens "just like any other *Nachbar*."[70] The status of *Nachbar* was conferred by owing land and a house in the village but the pastor owned the land and house through his office—from a force outside the village—rather than from his own purchase or kin affiliation. One reason that the pastor's access to communal property was written into official records was to keep villagers from denying him access as an outsider. The method of selecting the pastor tended to bring outsiders who were known primarily by reputation into the village. Even those who grew up in the countryside would have been affected by a period of study in a town, since a gymnasium or university education was commonplace even for rural pastors.[71] Pastors were, therefore, a constant presence like the neighbors, and their primary identity came from the villages they served, but they were not full participants in the formation of collective identity because of their primary loyalty to an elite outside the village.

Villagers were limited to full participation in only one village, but not all inhabitants of the village were full participants. The most serious exclusions from full participation in the village were for reasons of social status or religion.[72] Full villagers were expected to follow the local religion. Those who did not might be branded outsiders and forced to leave. Full villagers were also expected to pursue an honorable occupation and to possess some land at some stage in their lives. There is no evidence of how many people were excluded from full participation in the village because they were dishonorable or merely poor and isolated; they were simply excluded from consideration in all matters. For the villagers, there were neighbors, and then there were outsiders. Even though some outsiders resided in the village, full villagers considered their presence to be an outside imposition, much like the presence of the landgrave's administration.

One group that illustrates outsider status within the village was the Jews.[73] Jews posed special problems in determining neighbor status because they were a substantial minority in some villages. Imperial and Hessian laws and customs limited the number of places where Jews could settle, so although most villages were not divided internally by the religious and cultural differences between resident Jews and Gentiles, some were. In the Werra region, the village of Abterode was a major center of Jewish settlement. Some Jews lived in the villages of Altenburschla, Rambach, and Aue as well. The settlement of Jews was constrained by the antipathy and suspicion with which Christian residents viewed the Jewish culture and religion. The territorial administration took advantage of this situation by demanding "protection money" (Schutzgeld) from the Jewish community in return for the right to settle in designated areas under the supervision of the landgrave's officials.[74] Jews were, therefore, residents in the village under special status from the landgrave himself.

The special status of Jews excluded their full integration into the local community. Their access to land was severely restricted, and they were kept from enjoying the perquisites of village membership, such as brewing rights.[75] Jews were not restricted to specific parts of the village, but many clustered together in poorer houses in the peripheral parts of the village. They formed a separate community within the boundaries of the village and had a separate communal organization patterned on their religious leadership, which underscored their separation from the Gemeinde. The institutional separation of the Jewish and Christian communities was reinforced by the different lifestyles of the two cultures. Christians were wont to complain about Jewish violations of the Sunday Sabbath as an act of unfair competition.[76] Christian pressure on the Jewish community was common but ritualized. As one of the conditions of protection from the landgrave, the Jews were obligated to attend a Christian sermon and prayer each year under the supervision of the Amtmann in Eschwege.[77] The reports of the superintendent indicate that some Jews managed to avoid the sermons and that none were moved to adopt the Christian faith because of their exposure to them. The purpose of these sessions seems to have been as much to make the Jews more conscious of their isolation as to try to convert them to Christianity. In fact, it is unlikely that the Christian community would have been willing to accept members of the Jewish community as full villagers even if they had decided to convert.

Throughout the seventeenth century, the separation of the two religious and cultural groups was maintained. For this reason, Jews seldom appear in the official records. Jews were occasionally the victims of insults or assaults, but these were not distinguishable from the insults and assaults that the other villagers inflicted on one another. Only rarely were the particular cultural characteristics of Jews singled out for attack. The Jews Calman and Moses of Abterode complained that the villagers threatened to drive them out of the village and forbade them to use maids on Saturday.[78] Other Jews of Abterode do not appear to have been threatened in this case. Direct attacks on Jews only rarely came to the attention of higher officials but may well have been common. Despite paying protection money, Jews had few advocates who would protect them against the collective prejudices of the villages.

Abterode is the only village where individual Jews appear regularly in the lists of householders. By 1754, over 30 percent of the households there were Jewish.[79] The percentage must have been significantly smaller in the seventeenth century, however. The introduction of official records for business transactions and debts in the mid-seventeenth century gave many Jews at least one legal document in which their interests were recorded.[80] Since Jews could not rely on the sanctions of the village community to secure their interests—indeed, could expect that the village community would work against their interests—they relied on the expanding interest of the state in overseeing local economic practice. Of the numerous cases of credit recorded in a "Credit Protocol" in Abterode starting in 1642, more than 20 percent of the recorded cases involved Jews.[81] In contrast, Jews are almost entirely absent from the *Amt* account books and local supplications.

For the most part, Jews made few claims on the local community, and the villagers responded in kind. Jewish interests were not considered when the village wrote a complaint to the landgrave, but outward conflict between the Jewish and Christian communities was rare enough to indicate that the two groups had reached reasonable equilibrium in their relations. The Christian community had written the Jews out of their definition of the village. This is not to say that Jews were not important to the economic life of the village, but they did not attain insider status.

Other religious or cultural groups had only a marginal impact on the villages of the Werra. Catholicism had more or less disappeared from the region, with the exception of an occasional dramatic conversion, which was quickly followed by a change of residence to the territory of the Archbishop of Mainz in Treffurt.[82] Lutherans were a more difficult lot to account for. Some practicing Lutherans must have lived in the reformed villages of the Werra, but it is difficult to discover how many there were and what impact they had on the community. They could not attend services in their villages and had to either walk to Saxon territory or attend services at a chapel of an unconverted noble, of which there were still several in the 1630s. Many Lutherans may have been tolerated by their reformed neighbors and accepted as full members of the community. It is unlikely that the Lutherans were ostracized from their community, especially if they were discreet about their practice and conformed to village standards in other matters. We do not know who the Lutherans were in any village. The pastor of Reichensachsen, at least, dismissed the Lutherans as outsiders. "The Lutherans," he wrote, "are off by themselves."[83]

Outsiders, wherever they resided, contributed to the definition of the village by the fact of their exclusion. The cohesion of the village was the cohesion of neighbors. Neighbors did not always get along with one another in their social activities, but they were committed to sustaining their own positions in the village as they understood them. The neighbor was synonymous with the villager; the outsider was antithetical to both. Villagers defined their village by those they belonged with and in reaction to the demands put on them by the central administration. They adopted positive symbols of their collective experience as landmarks of their village while demanding that members of the village conform to the established norms. People who did not share those symbols of membership were excluded and subjected to censure, even if they were residents in the village. The process of defining what a village was went hand in hand with defining how villagers ought to behave. This made the village something more than just a cog in the administrative apparatus of the landgrave. It made it the product of how its residents lived with one another, perceived one another, and reacted to the outside world.

The way in which the community came together to enforce its will on individuals points to an additional problem that must be considered in defining the village. Villagers were not interchangeable parts within the village. Their interactions were shaped by the individual personalities of villagers and other institutions that channeled or gave vent to their aspirations and ability to participate. The personalities of individual villagers in the sixteenth and seventeenth centuries are virtually impossible to reconstruct, but the institutions that shaped participation in the village can be explored. Thus, our next angle of vision looks at two different ways in which the voices of individual villagers were channeled: the opportunities represented by kinship and family and the opportunities represented by wealth and social alliance.

Notes

1. For recent treatments of this problem, see Pieter Spierenburg, *The Broken Spell: A Cultural and Anthropological History of Preindustrial Europe* (New Brunswick, NJ 1991), and Norbert Schindler, *Widerspenstige Leute: Studien zur Volkskultur in der frühen Neuzeit* (Frankfurt am Main, 1992).
2. David Sabean, *Landbesitz und Gesellschaft am Vorabend des Bauernkrieges: Eine Studie der Sozialen Verhältnisse im südlichen Oberschwaben in den Jahren vor 1525* (Stuttgart, 1972), and, more generally, Heide Wunder, *Die Bäuerliche Gemeinde in Deutschland* (Göttingen, 1986).

3. In other parts of Germany, the ensemble of buildings was often separated from the fields by a fence or ditch. This does not seem to have been true of the villages of the Werra. A fenced-in core of buildings certainly would have contributed to a firmer recognition of the physical layout of the village, but the sharp differentiation between the populated core of the village and its fields served some of that same purpose. On fences and ditches, compare Karl-Sigismund Kramer, *Grundriß einer rechtlichen Volkskunde* (Göttingen, 1974), 26. On the distinctive legal characteristics of the inner core of the village, see Karl Siegfried Bader, *Das Mittelalterliche Dorf als Friedens- und Rechtsbereich* (Weimar, 1957), 52–118.

4. For village forms in Hesse, see the important work of Martin Born, especially, "Siedlungsgang und Siedlungsformen in Hessen," in Martin Born, *Siedlungsgenese und Kulturlandschaftsentwicklung in Mitteleuropa* (Wiesbaden, 1980), 214–302, and *Studien zur Spätmittelalterlichen und Neuzeitlichen Siedlungsentwicklung im Nordhessen* (Marburg, 1970).

5. Born, "Siedlungsgang," 256. Compare also the map at the end of his article, Alan Mayhew, *Rural Settlement and Farming in Germany* (New York, 1973).

6. The ways in which access to public buildings was limited are usually spelled out in the "preliminary descriptions" of the cadastres. See Hessian State Archives, Marburg (StAM) Kat Grandenborn B2, for example.

7. StAM 318 Niederhone 1655.

8. See Pfarrarchiv Wichmannshausen, church accounts, which list every contributor to the reconstruction of the pews and where the members of the parish had assigned seats. In Niederhona, the church had seats for 122 women in 1655, but the pews for men had not yet been built. See StAM 318 Niederhona.

9. See Jürgen Kuczynski, *Geschichte der Alltag des Deutschen Volkes*, vol. 1 (Cologne, 1980). Compare also Kramer, *Grundriß*, 22. For lindens in the Werra region, see Alfred Höck, "Dorflinden, Kirchhofslinden, Gerichtslinden in Niederhessen," *Kassel 'Landkreis': Jahrbuch Landkreis Kassel*, 1978: 76–80.

10. Kuczynski, *Geschichte der Alltag*, 274–82.

11. Ilse Gromes, ed., *Bußen aus den Amtsrechnungen des Amtes Sontra 1590–1648* (Sontra, 1977), 22.

12. For this reason, jurisdictional disputes often hinged on whether the crime had occurred on the "open road" (*freie Landstraße*) or not.

13. The physical boundaries of the village were marked in the Kataster "Vorbeschreibungen." See StAM Kat. Rockensüß B2. There are helpful observations on the social function of boundaries in John Brinckerhoff Jackson, *Discovering the Vernacular Landscape* (New Haven, 1984), 5–21.

14. Eberhard von Künssberg, *Rechtsbrauch und Kinderspiel* (Heidelberg, 1952). See also Kramer, *Grundriß*. A good evocation of how villagers acted to define boundaries can be found in Hermann Heidrich, "Grenzübergänge. Das Haus und die Volkskultur in der frühen Neuzeit," in Richard van Dülmen, ed., *Kultur der einfachen Leute* (Munich, 1983), 17–41.

15. See the punishments mentioned in Gromes, *Bußen aus den Amtsrechnungen*, 21.

16. Ibid., 48.

17. Ibid., 79, 49.

18. Ernst Henn, *Flurnamen als Geschichtsquelle. Die Flurnamen der Gemarkung Sontra* (Marburg, 1977), and *Flurnamen und Triftwege. Alte Wirtschaftswege im Ulfetal* (Marburg, 1980).

19. Henn, *Flurnamen und Triftwege*, 117.

20. See ibid. 119, for a map of Grandenborn and the locations of the different fields. The three fields are identified both by the form of exploitation and by their relation to the buildings and geographical features of the village in Henn's

map. They go by the names "kornfelt genant das reortfeldt" ("ryefield called the deer area field"), "lentzfeldt genant im nederfeldt" ("springfield called in the lower field"), and "prochtfeldt genant in der auhe" ("fallow field called in the meadow").

21. StAM 17e Rittmannshausen 6.
22. Walter Kürschner, "Aus dem Kirchenbuch von Reichensachsen (und Langenhain) von 1639–1653," *Archiv für Hessische Geschichte und Altertumskunde* NF 9 (1913): 52.
23. StAM 318 Niederhona.
24. Ibid. reports on the costs of a new bell cast in 1591.
25. Bernhard Hermann Roth, ed., *750-Jahre Hoheneiche 1233–1983* (Hoheneiche, 1983).
26. Festausschuß zur Vorbereitung der 900-Jahr-Feier Meißner, ed., *900-Jahre Meißner-Abterode 1076–1976* (Meißner-Abterode, 1976), 67.
27. Compare the *Brauordnung* for Blankenbach in StAM S 494.
28. Herbert Reyer, *Die Dorfgemeinde im Nördlichen Hessen* (Marburg, 1983), 25–29.
29. StAM 17e Boyneburg 6.
30. Dekanatsarchiv Eschwege, Tagebuch, 21 1 39.
31. StAM 318 Niederhone.
32. Ibid.
33. Gromes, *Bußen aus den Amtsrechnungen*, 24.
34. Compare the observations by Lyndal Roper, "'Common Man,' 'Common Women,' and the 'Common Good': Gender and Meaning in the German Reformation Commune," *Social History* 12 (1987): 1–22.
35. See StAM S 494.
36. The rights of *Gemeinde* members to the products of the forest were discussed in the "Extract der Tannenbergischen Gerichtsprotocols sub Dato Nentershausen den 27.6.1661," in StAM 17d v. Baumbach, 8th packet.
37. StAM Kat. Rockensüß B12.
38. StAM S 494.
39. Gromes, *Bußen aus den Amtsrechnungen*, 18.
40. Ibid., 8.
41. StAM 17d v. Baumbach, 8th packet, 12 8 1661. The testimony in the case of Engelhard Wittich indicates that the *ganze Gemeine* was assembled members of the community, because the community dissolved as everyone started to go home.
42. Gromes, *Bußen aus den Amtsrechnungen*, 9.
43. StAM 17e Rittmannshausen 6.
44. Ibid.
45. StAM Rechnungen II Eschwege 10, 1670.
46. StAM 17/I 1173.
47. Ibid. The testimony is somewhat ambiguous about whether the payments had already been collected before the meeting or were handed in later as a protest against the decision of the rest of the village. The latter case, of course, would suggest even more dramatic cleavages in the stance of the villagers.
48. Gromes, *Bußen aus den Amtsrechnungen*, 62.
49. Sabean, *Power in the Blood*, 26, argues for a wider-ranging definition of resistance, which encompasses "anger with corrupt village magistrates" as well as outward rebellion. Peasant resistance has become a topic of special interest among German historians. Small-scale resistance of this sort must have been endemic in Germany, but it has received comparatively little attention. On the possibilities of resistance in the peasant community, see Winfried Schulze, *Bäuerliche Widerstand und feudale Herrschaft in den frühen Neuzeit* (Stuttgart-Bad Canstatt, 1980);

Peter Blickle, *Deutsche Untertanen, Ein Widerspruch* (Munich, 1981); also David Martin Luebke, "Factions and Communities in Early Modern Central Europe," *Central European History* 25 (1992): 281–302; Robert von Friedeburg, "Village Strife and the Rhetoric of Communalism: Peasants and Parsons, Lords and Jews in Hesse, Central Germany, 1646–1672," *The Seventeenth Century* 7 (1992): 201–26; and Robert von Friedeburg, "Landgemeinde, adlige Herrschaft und frühmoderner Staat in Hessen-Kassel nach dem Dreissigjährigen Krieg; Merzhausen 1646–1672," *Hessisches Jahrbuch für Landesgeschichte* 41 (1991): 153–76.

50. Gromes, *Bußen aus den Amtsrechnungen*, 59.

51. For much of what we have been describing here, there are interesting parallels in another Hessian region where villagers were in conflict with a major territorial noble. See the presentation by Georg Schmidt, "Agrarkonflikte im Riedeselschen Gericht Moos im 17. Jahrhundert," *Archiv für Hessische Geschichte und Altertumskunde* NF 37 (1979): 215–328.

52. Unfortunately, the landgrave's administration was interested only in the overall sum, not in how it was apportioned, so we do not know how these fines were assessed within the village.

53. Gromes, *Bußen aus den Amtsrechnungen*, 56.

54. Ibid., 51, my emphasis.

55. Ibid., 53.

56. Ibid., 47–49.

57. Ibid., 57.

58. Reyer, *Die Dorfgemeinde*, 30–34.

59. I have not been able to locate a general history of *Kirmes* for early modern Germany. There is some information in R. Beitel, ed., *Wörterbuch der Deutschen Volkskunde* (Stuttgart, 1974). For a recent exploration of the persistence of local religious customs against official attempts to change religious practice see Marc Forster, *The Counter-Reformation in the Villages: Religion and Reform in the Bishopric of Speyer, 1560–1720* (Ithaca, NY 1992).

60. The historiography of popular celebrations emphasizes their potential for subverting the social order by placing the lower orders of society on top, albeit only temporarily. These inversions could simply reaffirm the value systems of the lower orders for their own benefit, or they could serve as a base from which to attack the values of the higher orders. See, for example, Natalie Zemon Davis, "The Reasons of Misrule," in Natalie Z. Davis, *Society and Culture in Early Modern France* (Stanford, 1975), 97–123, and Yves-Marie Bercé, *Fête et Révolte: Des Mentalités Populaires du XVIe au XVIIIe Siècle* (Paris, 1976). I should emphasize that my conclusions about the lack of revolutionary potential in *Kirmes* or other communal celebrations refer strictly to the villages of the Werra region during the seventeenth century and are based more on the lack of positive evidence than a definitive exposition at the local level.

61. Gromes, *Bußen aus den Amtsrechnungen*, 64.

62. Ibid., 64.

63. Ibid., 18.

64. Ibid., 43, 42.

65. This is the case in the listings of *Büssen*, in which members of one community perpetrate crimes in other villages. The perpetrators are always identified by name and by the village with which they were affiliated.

66. StAM 17e Rockensüß 1, 1606.

67. See Chapter 3.

68. StAM Rech II Eschwege 13.

69. The case of the disputed boundary stone in Rittmannshausen described above

is an example of how difficult it was for officials to fit in with the villagers as neighbors.

70. StAM 318, Niederhona.
71. Kopialbuch Klasse Sontra mentions that the pastor in Rockensüß had studied in Hersfeld, Hamburg, Denmark, and Marburg.
72. Compare Rudolf Wissel, *Das Alte Handwerks Recht und Gewohnheiten*, vol. 1 (Berlin, 1971), 148, on how people who were Jews, Turks, heathens, or Gypsies were outside the law and thus dishonorable.
73. For a discussion of the legal restrictions on Jewish settlement in Hesse, see Karl E. Demandt, *Bevölkerungs und Sozialgeschichte des Jüdischen Gemeinde Niedenstein, 1653–1866* (Wiesbaden, 1980), 24–38. A new sourcebook gives an excellent overview of the ways in which Jews were regulated by the Hessian state before the Thirty Years' War and the consequences of that regulation at the local level: Uta Löwenstein, ed., *Quellen zur Geschichte der Juden im Hessischen Staatsarchiv Marburg 1267–1600* 3 vols. (Wiesbaden, 1989).
74. StAM Rech II Eschwege 10 and Rech II Wanfried 8.
75. Only in Abterode did Jews gain any control over land for themselves. Elsewhere, they acted as middlemen but could not hold property.
76. This appears to have been a very infrequent violation, however. Only once between 1590 and 1648 were Jews fined for violating the Christian Sabbath in Amt Sontra. See Gromes, *Bußen aus den Amtsrechnungen*, 83.
77. Wilm Sippel, ed., *Forschungsberichte der Stiftung Sippel*, vol. 8 (Göttingen, 1981), 89.
78. Ibid., 207. It is striking that this is the only reference to Jews in the superintendent's work diary until 1647. I take this as a sign that some equilibrium had been reached between the Jewish and Christian communities of the Werra, though undoubtedly it worked strongly to the disadvantage of the Jews. Moses and Calman's reliance on maids for the Sabbath suggests that they were as apt to shape religious practice to their own needs as were the Christians of the region, regardless of doctrinal strictures.
79. StAM Kat Abterode B12.
80. A *Währschaftsprotokol* was begun in Abterode in 1642. StAM Prot II Abterode 4. Although entries involving Gentiles outnumber those involving Jews, the number of Jews that made use of the book is striking in comparison to the near absence of any Jews in the *Amt* account books and other documents.
81. Ibid.
82. The case of the pastor in Abterode, Moritz Gudenus, is instructive, though his conversion must have been different because he belonged to a family that was close to the landgrave's. Gudenus later became the Catholic *Amtmann* in Treffurt. Compare StAM 4c Hessen-Rheinfels/Rotenburg 830.
83. Ki Reichensachsen 1638–1657.

Part II

The Constituent Parts

3

Households, Families, Lineages

According to the Village Book, the village was made up of householders (*Hausgesessene*). The administration was aware that it was impossible to rule effectively if one assumed that the village was always an indivisible unit. The idea of the household provided a means of defining the constituent part of the village that was the most important for rule. At the same time, however, households were created by villagers who had their own associations to the house. The house was a site of both production and consumption, where individuals lived and worked together to produce food for all members. It was also the site of a biological family—a lineage—which was recognized in the *Amt* account books under the name of the head of the family.[1] In many cases, the economic household and the lineage were identical, but not always. Thus, any discussion of the formal qualities of households leads to a consideration of how households were linked to other systems for fixing the location of individuals.

In this chapter, the discussion ranges from how one's position in the household affected participation in the public life of the village to how the calculations of the individual in kinship relations affected participation in the household. The central features to be considered are the house itself, the offices of the household, kinship and marriage, and strategies of inheritance. In the next chapter, these structures are overlaid on the other forms of interaction between individuals in the village to see how household production and consumption intersected with village production and consumption.

The links between the idea of householdership and seigneurial authority were strong. Householdership affected the landgrave's income, since each lot with a house on it paid dues, much as each parcel of productive land did. The payment that most explicitly linked householdership with seigneurial authority was the payment of a "hearth chicken" as part of the tenure for the house. Though the payment was token, it was carefully enumerated in the *Amt* accounts. The landgrave was quick to add to the list of householders whenever a new house was built but was slower to give up dues whenever an old house disappeared.[2] Since access to village privileges such as the use of communal grazing lands did not directly affect the income of the

72

landgrave as seigneurial lord, the central administration left its regulation to the village community. The house served as a location for fixing relationships just as the village did, so the institution of the household was both parallel to and in competition with the village.[3]

From the point of view of the administration, the household was effectively described by knowing the name of the head of household. The head of household became a de facto agent of *Herrschaft* through this assumption, with many of the same ambiguities associated with the office of village head in its relation to those whom the office ostensibly represented.[4] The burden of two strands of *Herrschaft*—organizing and collecting seigneurial revenues and enforcing discipline—could be placed on the head of household. Households formed the building blocks of the village. They were a means of linking the concerns of the administration with the order of life within the village. Both the household and kinship were part of the social fabric of the village. Any interpretation of the village must, therefore, understand how the ideas of households, families, and kinship worked together to focus individual action within the village.[5]

The Hessian central administration did not pry into the internal organization of the household in the sixteenth and seventeenth centuries, but there were normative pressures from the elite that influenced household forms. Parish registers illuminate a wide range of demographic and social structural issues of early modern European history, but for many years, the investigation of German demographic sources lagged behind French and English research. Recently, German historians have taken to exploring the potential of demographic history to explain broader social issues, in particular the "mentalities" of early modern family life.[6] In some respects, analysis of the relationship between the ideology of the family and its actual historical forms is particularly promising in the German context because of the lingering images that have not been discarded—the "whole house" (*ganze Haus*) and the pater familias (*Hausvater*). Both concepts loom large over our understanding of preindustrial German society, especially rural society.

Among the primary sources for demographic research are "registers of souls," which give a snapshot view of the composition of the household.[7] Registers of souls were not, in their original conception, designed to be a demographic source. They were concerned with the "spiritual" structure of the parish and, as such, reflected the point at which the spiritual and administrative concerns of the parish pastor intersected with his conception of demographic order. In the latter stages of the Thirty Years' War, pastor Lorenz Ludolph of the village of Reichensachsen in Hesse-Kassel undertook to create a register of souls of his village, which he included in his parish register.[8] There are, unfortunately, no comparable records for any village in the region prior to the war, so we cannot say with assurance that Ludolph's way of registering souls was shared by others before the war. Ludolph's approach gives us the earliest available glimpse of all the inhabitants of a single village of the Werra region in one conception.

Ludolph's register, or "account," as he called it, is interesting in a number of ways. First, unlike contemporary registers of souls in Austria, Ludolph continued his list for more than one year. There is, therefore, the opportunity to chart changes in the location of souls from one year to the next. Even more important, however, is that Ludolph's account was put together at his own discretion. There was no outside insistence that an account of souls was necessary, which no doubt explains why there are few comparable models from adjoining villages. Ludolph was exceedingly concerned about the spiritual welfare of his parish in the desultory waning years of the Thirty Years' War and seems to have conceived of the account as a better means of keeping track of his flock. He saw it as a better use of his time than the more mundane tasks of collecting church revenues, which he dismissed in the small prelude to his account of souls.[9] The account was, therefore, the product of intense interest on the part of its creator rather than part of the routine of his office that he could produce without reflecting on it.

How does one put together an account of souls? Ludolph may have known models from other regions, but he seems to have been guided by a general sense of how other nonspiritual accounts were conducted. Even though his primary concern was with souls, his approach to organizing his list betrayed more than just his sense of the spiritual community of his parishioners. Ludolph's understanding of how his parishioners fit within the village was colored by his view of the social organization. The best way for him to identify all the souls within the parish was to organize them according to household.[10] This is clear from the structure of the list; servants, children, lodgers, and inmates are all organized according to the household to which they belonged.

There are two distinct uses to which Ludolph's list can be put. First, it is a straightforward presentation of household composition. It tells us the numbers of children, servants, lodgers, and others that made up the households of Reichsensachsen and enables us to chart their changing composition over a two-year period and again after a lapse of five years. Second, we can filter this household composition through the framework that Ludolph provides and thus arrive at a clearer understanding of how Ludolph himself understood the structure of the household. What does Ludolph do when confronted with an anomalous household form? Can he make it conform to his prearranged framework?

The account of souls begins in 1646. It is divided into three columns. The first of these columns is for the head of the household—often, but not exclusively, male. Immediately next to that column is the column for the wife of the head of the household. Next to that column is the column for children, servants, lodgers, and anyone else affiliated with the household. A characteristic entry reads like this: Augustin Widitz / Catharin / Orthil,

TABLE 3.1

Distribution of Household Size in Reichensachsen, 1646–1652

YEAR	NUMBER OF MEMBERS							
	1	2	3	4	5	6	7	8+
1646	10	20	20	22	17	13	3	3
1647	7	25	22	24	16	10	7	3
1652	20	35	22	27	19	15	6	5

Source: StAM Ki Reichensachsen 1639–1653.

Johann Oswald, Elisabeth.[11] In the first year, the list began with 108 households living in the village on January 4. At the end of the year, Ludolph added eight households that had returned "from exile," two others that "moved here," and four people who "married in." A total of 451 souls were included in these lists. By 1647, Ludolph abandoned separate listings of the families that had returned, moved to the village, and married in, but he continued to add them as a group to his account at the end of the year. In 1647, he listed 114 households with a total of 478 souls. Ludolph's accounts were then disrupted for several years, but he made one last account in 1652, when he identified 149 households containing 573 souls.

Many of the features of the households in Ludolph's account of souls would be familiar to demographic historians. In general, Ludolph's entries conform fairly well to the pattern for "West/Central of Middle Europe" outlined by Peter Laslett.[12] Small nuclear families predominated. In 1646, the average household had 3.8 members. If those households that consisted of a single person or a married couple with no dependents were excluded, a household averaged 4.5 members. Thus, the average household was not large, even by the standards of nuclear households identified in other parts of Europe. There were few dependents, and by far the most of those were children.[13] There were only thirty-two households that included anyone other than a husband, wife, and children. Nor were there many large households with large concentrations of servants that might skew the average (see Table 3.1). Only twelve households had servants, and only six had more than six members of any sort. The largest single household was that of a local nobleman, Curt Leopold von Boyneburg, which included a sister, four children, five female servants, three male servants, and the shepherd Jacob Zinckgreve and his wife and two children. There were thirty households in Reichensachsen in 1646 with a single person or a married couple with no dependents. Some of these were the remnants of old households where the parents no longer had authority over their now independent children, and others were newly formed households. The latter would eventually have dependents but were still in an early stage of development. Of the thirty households without dependents in 1646, nine had acquired dependents by 1652.

It seems unlikely that children remained dependent on the head of household after they were old enough to set up households of their own. None of the entries in Ludolph's list shows spouses of sons or daughters as dependent on a household head. It was also rare for older parents to become dependent on their children as members of their children's households. Only thirteen households listed by Ludolph in 1646 contained relatives of the husband or wife besides their children. Three mothers-in-law were identified in households, and one household consisted of a single man, Jost Murhard, with his sister and parents listed as dependents. In 1652, six years after this initial survey, Murhard's household was virtually the same—except that his mother had died and a new maid was added. This suggests that Murhard's household was not a phase in the development of a stem family but rather an anomalous configuration that persisted through time. Most instances of coresident kin involved brothers or sisters of either the husband or wife of the household. The virtual absence of parents as dependents indicates that it was unusual for heads of household to relinquish their claim to that status even after their children had formed households of their own. The exceptions are useful, however, because they indicate that Ludolph was prepared to identify parents as dependents when that was appropriate. Thus there were few cases in which dependent parents resided with their children.

The development of the Hubenthal household between 1646 and 1647 illustrates how household formation changed as members went through their life courses. Christoffel and Martha Hubenthal had three sons and were acting as the guardians of the daughter of N. Schleiffer in 1646. Their eldest son Balzer married one Gedrud Vaupell, who had been serving as a maid for Hans and Barbara Methe that year. The same year that Balzer married, Christoffel Hubenthal died. In the next year's account of souls, Ludolph revised his list to account for the changes in the households. Christoffel Hubenthal's household continued to exist, but Balzer was no longer listed as a dependent and Martha was identified as a widow. The Methe household now consisted of just Hans and his wife. Balzer Hubenthal and his wife Gedrud appeared as the heads of a new household with no dependents. The rest of Christoffel Hubenthal's household was also transformed, since his son Lorenz also died and their ward Else was sent to nearby Mitteroda to a different household. (It is interesting that Ludolph is so meticulous in noting her disappearance from Hubenthal's household and that she is identified by name in the second list, while she was identified only as N. Schleiffer's daughter in the first.) By 1652, Christoffel Hubenthal's widow Martha was a household by herself; Balzer and Gedrud continued to develop their household separately, though they were still without children. Hans and Barbara Methe both disappeared from the records in the interim.

It is only because Ludolph made a new account of souls in different years that we can chart any changes in household composition. The size and composition of the household were subject to constant flux because of the short life expectancy of children and the danger of sudden death from disease. Between 1646 and 1647, sixty-six households underwent some change in their membership. Despite the changes in the individuals making up the households, the average size remained fairly constant. The conjugal family was the preferred household form in the Werra region, but Ludolph's format for presenting households hid one of the most noteworthy facts that influenced familial relations. It is well known that the demographic regime of preindustrial Europe led to frequent remarriage, with the creation of multiple links of stepparent, stepchildren, and stepsiblings within the conjugal family. It is impossible to tell from Ludolph's account in which households these relationships occurred. The model of the ideal household is strong enough to cover up this source of potential tension.

Ludolph's presentation of the households in his account of souls conformed to an idealized image of household structure comparable to that espoused by the *Hausvaterliteratur* and other normative works of the era. The literature of the *Hausvater* was designed to illustrate the way in which the head of the household ought to exercise economic and police authority in order to increase the well-being of all members of the household.[14] The image of the *Hausvater* owed much to similar thinking about the responsibilities of the territorial ruler to his territory. The household, like the village, was both an economic and an administrative unit in which the head was held accountable for his lands and goods by the landgrave's administration. In exchange, the administration did little to meddle in the internal makeup of the household but did contribute to the support of the idea of the *Hausvater* in order to buttress the authority of the head.

I have already suggested that the position of the head of the household within the household was buttressed by his or her status in relation to the administrative hierarchy. The household as a whole came to be embodied by the head, who was responsible for running it. The identities of individual inhabitants of the household were determined by their position in this structure. The tripartite structure of the list described above is derived from the characteristics of the household described in the *Hausvater* literature. Ludolph recognized three distinct offices in the household—head, wife of head, and everyone else. These three categories already illuminate one of Ludolph's fundamental assumptions about the structure of the household: Households ought to be headed by married men. Male heads of households were the only individuals with complete and unequivocal individual identities. The identities of all other members of the household were mediated by the identity of the head. In a different context from the account of souls, Ludolph distinguished between the "men" ("*Manschaft* [*sic*]") of the village who carried the burden of maintaining the economic well-being of the village and the "wife and kids" (*Weib und Kind*) who suffered when this support was undermined.[15] *Mannschaft* in this case was equivalent to the group of full participants in the village that made up the *Nachbarschaft*.

Ludolph's use of the term is one of the most direct expressions of the masculinity of public life in the village. As we shall see below, this gender definition of the head of household led to complications in the way Ludolph constructed his list.

The direct manifestation of this ideal of the autonomous male head of household was the order in which households were placed in Ludolph's list. Ludolph chose a loose alphabetical order based on the *first* name of the head of household. There are only two exceptions to this rule: the pastor himself and the schoolmaster, who turn up under P and S, respectively, for their occupations. Even the noble families were listed by the first names of male heads. Curt Leopold von Boyneburg appears between Curt Schickberg and Caspar Wagner; Philip Burkhard von Boyneburg appears between the pastor and Quirin Schmidt's widow.[16] Thus, the first entry in the list was Augustin Widitz, (not Widitz, Augustin) followed by Andreas Beck and Anton Lingemann. The souls of Catharin, Widitz's wife, and three children were identified through the soul of Augustin Widitz. The individualism of the heads of households and the subordination of the rest of the household were reinforced by this practice.

Ludolph's choice of first names also decoupled the individual identity of the household head from kin identity. It was unusual for administrative lists to be constructed on the basis of first names of inhabitants. Most secular administrative documents were arranged by geographical location of the house. A modern administrator might find it more practical and informative to arrange names according to family names rather than first names. It might have been easier for Ludolph to recognize people by their first names than it would have been for outside administrators, because he was in constant contact with all the inhabitants of the village. A more likely reason for his arrangement, though, is that Ludolph considered households more important than family lines. The autonomy of the household may thus be seen as the paramount principle of the structure of souls in Ludolph's village.

The absorption of the identity of individual members of the household into the identity of the male head took place on a number of levels. When a widow married a male head of another household, her identity merged with that of her new household. When Lucas Zwick's wife Margaretha died in 1646, he quickly married Orthil, the widow of Hans Busch of Weissenborn. Ludolph's account for 1647 duly noted the change in Zwick's household— the name Orthil appeared in the wife column in place of Margaretha. Orthil's identity became a part of Lucas's. If one glanced at the account of souls instead of reading it carefully, one might not even notice that Lucas's household had changed at all. In contrast, the position of widows in the account changed dramatically when they remarried. Orthil, Johann Wagner's widow, was listed in the account of souls for 1646 and 1647. In 1651 she married Curt Isenhut, and she and her son became absorbed into Isenhut's household. Her separate household entry disappeared. Ludolph himself seemed less concerned about the individuality of the wives; his later accounts of souls use their first names less frequently and instead refer to wives simply by the term *uxor*. Orthil Isenhut is among those listed as *uxor*, so if we did not have the evidence of her marriage in 1651, her identity would have been masked permanently.

Ludolph's tendency to submerge the identity of household members under the identity of the head of the household was consistent with the assumptions about a householder's authority and responsibilities in the "public" realm. Only rarely would the full name of someone who was not the head of a household turn up in official records, because the head was responsible for the actions of all the members. The orientation of all individual identities around the head of household can be seen in the lists of fines for petty and serious offenses in the district account books. In 1646, Christoff Homan of Rockensüß had to pay a fine "because his wife uttered sacrilegious words."[17] The fine assumed that the wife was subject to the discipline of the household, so the householder himself was ultimately responsible for the offense, and there was no need to name the wife more specifically. Offenses against members of the household were also described in relation to the head of household, rather than the individual members of the household affected. For example, Caspar Gliemerodt's wife in the village of Hasell was fined for insulting and fighting with Martin Gliemerodt's wife,[18] but neither wife's name was mentioned. Wives were not the only household members whose crimes were associated with the head of household. In the same village in 1642, Claus Germerod was fined "because his son cut down some of Hans Jacob's rye."[19] Once again, the identity of the son, whose name was not given, merged with that of the household, reinforcing the identification of the individual as an adjunct of the household.

Sometimes the head of the household was not obligated to pay a fine for a member of his household, but he would still be associated with the perpetrator by name because of the nature of his office. The case of Caspar Gliemerodt's wife mentioned above is interesting because she is singled out for the fine instead of her husband, yet her subordination within the household is clear because her name is not mentioned—she is just a wife. It was more common for the burden of payment to be assessed on members of the household who had some independent source of income. In Rockensüß in 1622, a fine was imposed on "Hans Ruppel's servant because he whacked Jacob Germerodt's boy (*Jungen*) with a whip so that he bled."[20] In this instance, responsibility for paying the fine seems to have devolved on the servant rather than on the head of the household, but even in this case both the perpetrator and the victim are identified by their relation to a head of household. It is possible that the court identified Hans Ruppel to point out that he had failed in part of his duties as a householder by allowing his unnamed servant to be so unruly.

Although the idealized vision of household organization saw each

TABLE 3.2

Identity of Household Heads in Reichensachsen by Gender and Marital
Status

HOUSEHOLD HEAD	1646	1652
Married male	76	106
Single male	6	6
Widowed female	19	26
Female, not identified as widow	7	11
Total	108	149

Source: StAM Ki Reichensachsen 1639–1654.

household headed by a married man, only 65 percent of all households in
Reichensachsen in 1646 consisted of married couples with or without children (Table 3.2). Bachelorhood was rarer than spinsterhood for heads of
households, so it is somewhat ironic that Ludolph equated the *Mannschaft*
with the productive sphere of the village. Only six households in Ludolph's
list for 1646 were headed by unmarried men; two of these had sisters or
servants as dependents, but none listed dependent children. Twenty-seven
households were headed by widows or other single women. It was socially
improper for a man capable of conceiving children to run a household without
a wife. It was also improper for a household to be headed by an unmarried
woman, but social, economic, and demographic factors made unmarried female heads of households more common than unmarried male heads.

Female heads of households presented conceptual problems for Ludolph's
ideal vision of household organization. The idea that a household must be
headed by a male was strong enough that Ludolph frequently referred to a
household by the first name of the deceased male head rather than by the
first name of the widow, who now must have acted as the head. Martha,
the widow of Christoffel Beck, appears in Ludolph's list as Christoffel Beck's
relicta Martha, between Caspar Kulmar and Christoffel Hubenthal.[21] Twenty-
three widows are identified in this manner in Ludolph's account, but eleven
other women (five with dependents) appear in the account on the same
principle as male heads. Catherin Messerschmidt appears in the list under
the letter C, between Curt Scheffer and Curt Beck. There is no indication
why Ludolph recognized some women as self-standing heads of households
who appear under their own first names and treated others as successors to
male heads of households. He probably had no conscious system. Of course,
some female heads of households were never-married women with no dependents who were not subject to some other household. The suggestion that
all the female heads with dependent children might be unwed mothers is belied
by Ludolph's claims to have baptized only one illegitimate child in his career.

The continued reliance on the deceased husband's name to identify the household is also prevalent in other records. For example, Baltzer Mench's widow was fined for hitting Baltzer Raben's stepdaughter. Even though the case involved two women—one of whom was not a blood relative of the head and the other of whom was now independent—the male identities were considered crucial to explaining the actors in the incident. There was no mention of how long ago Mench had died or what his widow's status was aside from being widowed. The household continued to have an identity even after the death of the head, but that identity was considered to be an extension of the will of the original male head rather than based on the new female head. The persistence of the name of a male head in a household that was actually headed by a woman was in part an effort to deny that the continuity of the household had been broken by the death of the man.

The primacy of the male identity of the household makes it difficult to assess the identity of subordinate members of the household. One explanation for Ludolph's and the administration's difficulties in sharply delineating individual identities is that those identities were shaped by the variety of roles one was expected to fill during one's life.[22] The reciprocal interplay of local perceptions and the formal statements of the *Hausvater* literature defined those roles as maintaining internal order and organizing work. Household roles were offices that contributed to the economic success of the whole.

Assumptions about proper household organization were also assumptions about the role of gender within the village. The attitude of villagers toward the wife in a household was tempered by the attitude toward the place of her household in the village. The husband may have been the *Hausgesessene* upon whom the official administrative responsibilities devolved, but the wife was the *Hausfrau* who saw to the day-to-day problems of organizing the house.[23] Indeed, *Hausfrau* was a common term for the female half of the couple, rivaled only by the term *Weib* in frequency of usage. It was a term that captured both the public attachment of the wife to her husband through marriage and her economic role as an integral part of the household. The term *Hausmutter*, which was the complement of *Hausvater* in the advice literature of the eighteenth century, was virtually unknown in the Werra region in the seventeenth century. For a woman, the primary tie was to the house, represented by the husband, rather than to the progeny. The role of wife was more important than the role of mother. In a sense, the *Haus* was not complete without a *Frau* who had responsibility for administering part of the whole.[24] Her position was adjunct to that of the head. It was sufficiently distinct to merit a separate column in Ludolph's account of souls, but not so different that she needed to be treated differently from other dependents in the records of the secular administration. Although the individuality of the wife was of little consequence to an observer like Ludolph, her contributions to the household were significant. Like her husband, the wife had an office that she performed within the household that distinguished her from the other dependents of the household in people's minds.

It is almost impossible to tell how accurately this view of the complementary roles of husband and wife reflected the reality of most households in the village. The information we have on relations within the household is too scanty to determine how effectively this formal organization was translated into practical authority for each person. Patriarchy and partnership, often invoked as opposing models of household organization, were probably objects of negotiation between husband and wife as part of the process of connecting the household to the village as a whole.[25] As in the case of subjects dealing with their lords, however, the acceptable instruments of coercion were all in the hands of the husband. Household discipline was husband's discipline, and beatings were an instrument for enforcing the husband's position. Successful integration into the village required that the husband not resort to beatings indiscriminately, but there was no formal recourse for a wife who was unjustly afflicted.[26] Social pressure could also prompt husbands to be severe in maintaining discipline within the household. It is hard to imagine that Christoff Homan's wife escaped without a beating for uttering the sacrilege described above. Villagers themselves enforced conformity to basic social rules from which one deviated only at peril. Male authority was often the social form that these rituals reinforced. One need only refer to the humiliations suffered by men who allowed their wives to beat them to find confirmation of this.[27] The central administration also had an interest in promoting male authority in the household. If the husband was unable to fulfill his office as disciplinarian, the elite was prepared to lend its weight to ensure that authority was not inverted. When Elias Henning of Reichensachsen began to openly flout his parents and insult and beat them, his father appealed to the von Boyneburg's administrator for help.[28] The von Boyneburg explicitly recognized that they had to punish Elias Henning as a warning to all other "no-good" sons who flouted parental order.

The structure of the household made wives social and economic actors who contributed to the position of the household within the village.[29] The conceptual separation of the head of household and wife suggests that most economic activity by the head of household took place in the fields, while the economic activity of the wife was located in and around the house proper. In practice, however, activities involving the house proper and the fields were blurred. Although men were fined more often than women for the nebulous crime of "field damages," women were occasionally held responsible for some damage to crops. In Ulfen, Barbara Grünwaldt; Margrethe, wife of Ciliax Knauff; and Georg Scheffer were all fined 10 albus "because [they] did damage in the fields to [their] neighbor."[30] The equal treatment of all three individuals is interesting because they represented three different roles in the household organization. Barbara Grünwaldt was a female head of household who was apparently never married. In another source she appears as a *Hausgesessene* of a house previously inhabited by Balzer Bodenstein but does not appear to have been related to him.[31] Margrethe is identified as the spouse of Ciliax Knauff and attached to his household. Her social position was that of an adjunct to a male head of household. Georg Scheffer seems to have been a head of household himself. All three were accused of the same crime, which indicates that the activity that led to the field damage—presumably careless or malicious handling of a plow or harvest animals—was one in which individuals with different positions within the household participated.

There were economic offenses that were characteristic primarily of heads of households and others that were the province of servants and children. Wives appear as offenders in both of these spheres, but they appear more frequently in conjunction with dependents than they do with heads of households. Men were more often found guilty of crimes that involved plowing and reaping in the fields, while women turned up more frequently in activities such as gleaning.[32] The wife's participation in some spheres of economic activity was limited by the preeminence of the male head of household in the most fundamental economic task of the household: the growing of grain in the fields. To this extent she was a dependent like all the other members of the household.

The third category in Ludolph's account of souls lumped together all other dependents of the household. The fact that children and servants were treated comparably by Ludolph indicates how the economic organization of the household touched on the familial relations within the household. In fact, the majority of households were made up of a biological family of a husband and wife and their children. The children were dependents and laborers. Only a few households also included servants or maids, who performed the tasks that children were expected to perform. Servants were identified as such by Ludolph, and the children were listed before the servants, yet the fact of their common dependence on the head of household and their similar economic tasks put them in a similar economic position within the household. In other words, the kin connections were subsumed under the economic category of the household. From Ludolph's perspective, responsibility for the soul of an individual, even that of a servant, fell to the head of the household rather than to the parents.

The contributions of the different dependents varied with their abilities and with the expectations of the head.[33] Both male and female children were involved in numerous activities in the fields and in the home. Many instances of fines for field damages are attributed to children. For example, Ciliax Knauff's daughter in Ulfen was fined 10 albus for field damage in 1597.[34] This indicates not only that children worked in the household but also that there was little gender-based division of labor for children. Nor were the children of more prominent households in the village spared from work in the household. The son of the pastor in Rockensüß was fined 20 albus in 1590 for allowing the pastor's animals to cause damage.[35] Most children in the village, like the pastor's son, spent much of their time looking after the animals.

The economic activity of servants was similarly identified in the lists of fines. Servants did not appear by their first names but were simply acknowledged as the servant of a head of household.[36] Their activities were also primarily directed toward caring for the animals. If servants participated in the heavier work of plowing or harvesting in the fields, it is not apparent from the lists of fines. Only heads of households were punished for plowing too close to another person's plot of land or similar offenses involving labor in the fields. It is likely that both servants and children did, in fact, work in the fields periodically, but the sort of work they did there was not likely to put them in a position to hurt the crops or fields of others.

There was a final group that Ludolph considered to be dependents of a head of household but had a less clear status in the administrative records. Ludolph associated both the relatives of the head of household or his wife and those people who inhabited the house as lodgers (*Miedlinge*) with the other dependents of the household.[37] Lodgers were identified by both first and last names, but they were listed under the first name of the owner of the house in which they resided. They probably did not participate in the economic activity of the household in the fields or in the home, though they must have made payment of some sort for the right to reside in the house.

For some lodgers, residence in a household was a temporary condition before finding a house of their own. Else, the daughter of Valtin and Anna Schintz, resided in her parents' house in 1646 with her children. She was identified as Henrich Wagner's wife, but he did not appear in the account. Presumably, he was a soldier who was away from the village. In 1652, Else was identified as a widow and resided in her own household with her children; Valtin and Anna Schintz formed a separate household with no dependents. Since Else was ostensibly tied to Henrich Wagner while she resided in her parents' household, her status was that of a coresident family—like a renter—rather than that of an integral part of the family.[38] At the same time that Else was listed in Valtin Schnitz's household, Ludolph listed another lodger, Trumpf Martha, in the same household. Unlike Else, Trumpf Martha was a poor woman who was able to remain in the village only by residing with other stable households. Her stay at the Schintz household was brief. In 1647, she was in the household of Michael Appel.[39] Trumpf Martha may have moved because she was no longer welcome in the Schintz household or because Michael Appel suddenly wished to have her stay with him, or her move may have represented a shift in the collective burden of looking after her. Although she may have contributed some skill to the household, she may also have been a charity case—more of a drain on the household than an economic asset.

For all the individuals in a given household, the household represented an economic unit of production based on the occupation of a house. It was also an administrative unit of control and education in which dependents were guided and disciplined by the head of household, who also determined the economic tasks to be performed. It is a recurring problem for historians to assess whether ordinary people accepted the prescriptive assumptions about their lives. There is no gloss by the villagers of Reichensachsen on Ludolph's categories, and the descriptions of fights are filtered through the assumptions of those writing them. The pervasiveness of the official household form is one sign that it may have had adherents among ordinary people as well as among educated observers. Individual initiative was not encouraged even among male heads of household, so the subordination of the identities of wives and family members was part of a hierarchical social system in which everyone, including the men, fulfilled a defined social role. The key to the exercise of one's social role, which influenced one's individual identity, was conformity.

To this point, our focus on the household and the legal and productive roles of its members has been determined primarily by how pastor Ludolph constructed his account of souls. Ludolph's account is rich in implications for the rural world, and the household was indeed a central institution of the village, but it was not the only way in which individuals were connected to one another in the village. All individuals in the village were caught up in two systems at the same time—the system of the household and a system of kinship. An individual's position in one system may or may not have been easily reconciled with his or her position in the other. Ties of kinship involved more than simple biological relatedness; they had social and economic consequences for the village as a whole, and especially for the individual members within a household. They created both obligations and opportunities for individuals that shaped their social roles.

From the moment of birth—even before—a villager was caught up in a network of kinship. Both villagers and the secular and ecclesiastical administrations had systems for classifying blood relatives. Some official documents referred to people by their kin affiliation in addition to or instead of their household affiliation. We have already seen how boys and girls were identified as sons or daughters of a head of household. These same documents mentioned other degrees of relatedness as well. Brothers and sisters, even brothers-in-law and stepmothers, were identified as such, frequently without giving their name but only their kin relationship.[40] The identity of individuals was partially determined by their blood relations to others in and out of the village.

Connections of relatives outside the household are harder to follow than ties to the immediate family. Some kin relationships are never mentioned in the official documents, though villagers must have been aware that those degrees of relatedness existed. Conspicuous in their absence from official documents of the Werra region are words for grandfather, uncle, aunt, and even mother.[41] In part, this is because the male head of household was the point of reference for all members of the household, so the most visible cross-generational relationship was of the son or daughter to the father. Villagers must have been aware, for instance, that when a fine was levied on a householder's brother, that brother was also the uncle of the householder's children, but the term uncle was unnecessary to make that connection. David Sabean has been able to trace deep-rooted connections between kin in economic interaction, but the primary evidence that he presents for viewing kinship as an organizing principle of that interaction is the prevalence of cases, not any formal expression of the actors' awareness of the degree of kinship.[42] The absence of formal expression of degrees of kinship does not mean that Sabean is wrong, of course, but it makes it harder to figure out how kinship worked when the records of all transactions are incomplete.

In contrast to the paucity of references to immediate biological kin other than the parent-child relationship and siblings, kinship ties that linked separate lineages appeared fairly frequently in the official records. The act of marriage brought about a dramatic change in the kin ties of the bride and groom and their families. The terms brother-in-law and son-in-law are at least as common as terms describing blood relations such as uncle or cousin. This attests to the importance of the new ties of kinship and the predominance of the male lineage for all members of the family, including the children. Householders sometimes relied on brothers-in-law to help children learn a trade. The minister of Grossenburschla traveled all the way to Soest in Westphalia in order to place his son in the care of his brother-in-law.[43] The attachment to conjugal relatives was not so dramatic among ordinary villagers, but there were still opportunities for such relatives to lend one another a hand. Even land could be shared by both sides of a family tied by marriage.

Until a child became old enough to marry, the kin network of the parents dominated the social ties of the child. It was rare for children to work as servants in another household. In most instances, a child grew up with his or her brothers and sisters or stepbrothers and stepsisters. Much of the aid and support a child received while growing up was based on blood relationships. The consciousness of kinship did not reach the point that lineages became involved in vendettas, but kin sometimes worked together in opposition to other groups of villagers.

Relatives also quarreled and fought among themselves. There were sources of conflict among siblings inherent in the organization of the family and household. In 1610, there were two separate cases involving fights between relatives in Amt Sontra. Martin Jacob of Berneburg was reported to have fought with his brother, and Valtin Kaufman was fined for trying to hit his sister and nearly hitting his father instead.[44] Domestic violence was only a small share of the overall violence reported, however. There were seventeen other fights that did not involve relatives in *Amt* Sontra in 1610, and the two instances of domestic fighting were more than usual. In many years there were none, which is notable in view of the propensity for violence in the village. Those fights that occurred were most frequently between siblings of indeterminate age, but perhaps adolescents.[45] Young children might be exonerated for their crimes because of their "lack of understanding," but brothers and sisters lived together in the household until adulthood, and growing up together must have led to strains. One should not take this situation as evidence that there was no affection between family members, however. Examples of familial affection are harder to come by than examples of tension because official documents recorded potential disruptions of village life rather than factors that might have contributed to stability. The house was the locus of both affection and competition, and the particular household structure and individual personalities brought one side or the other to public view.

The transition from dependency in a household to self-sufficiency in one's own household was a major step in an individual's life. Marriage created another level of kin relationships, so the choice of a marriage partner affected not only the individuals getting married but also their families and, ultimately, the web of social relations in the village. The process of selecting a mate was a delicate and serious one.[46] An engagement had nearly the same force as the marriage vows themselves. In order to guarantee that an engagement was kept, the act of engagement was done in the presence of witnesses. When Martha Glantz of Völckershausen was engaged to Kleinhans Dietzel of Altenburschla, the agreement was made between Martha's father Joachim and Dietzel. "The father promised him his daughter in the presence of his cousin Adam Ritze, whereupon daughter and mother gave their hand."[47] The circumstances surrounding the engagement of Orthie Kangiesser and Henrich Holderbuel were even more formal. Henrich's brother-in-law sought her out for Henrich, and the engagement took place three years before formal vows were scheduled, on Annunciation Day. It took place in the presence of Simon Huebethal, Lips Hartwig, and Henrich's brothers Jacob and Conrad Holderbuel.[48]

The contrast in approaches between the two engagements indicates that there was no single method for arranging or confirming marriage agreements. Different members of the family could serve as liaisons or witnesses. It is likely, however, that parents—especially fathers—had a disproportionate influence on marriage choices. In the first example, Joachim Glantz arranged a marriage for his daughter Martha, and she appeared to have no say in the choice. The arrangement hit a temporary snag, however, when Martha heard that two of Kleinhans's horses had died and she attempted to get out of the engagement.[49] She was concerned about the deaths as an omen and realized that the loss of two horses meant a serious economic strain for the household. There is much that remains hidden in the way that the case was brought before the superintendent. Martha's refusal to accept the engagement may have been rebellion against her father, but her father may also have encouraged Martha's refusal in order to justify his backing out of the agreement. Martha and Kleinhans were eventually reconciled, but it is obvious that Martha had to be convinced that the marriage would be successful in order to be won over. In the case of Orthie and Henrich, the motive force behind the engagement was Henrich himself, with the assistance of his brother-in-law. But although Henrich took the initiative in finding himself a bride rather than waiting for someone's father to choose him as a potential son-in-law, he did not attempt to arrange a marriage without the direct participation of other family members. His marriage mattered to the entire family.

There were various means of confirming an offer of marriage. It was customary for the man to give his potential bride a ring, sometimes accompanied by another token such as a hat or a handkerchief, as a symbol of the promise. The woman then gave the man a handkerchief as a sign of her acceptance. Many villagers took these symbols to signify a formal engagement.[50] The danger of these symbols was that they could be used to circumvent the careful screening process used by parents. Our discussion of household organization suggests that a first marriage enabled both husband and wife to escape dependent status and achieve an independent household identity, which was very appealing. Secret marriages were sometimes agreed to in order to accelerate that independence, even though the value of an independent identity was precarious if one or both of the lineages involved disapproved of the match. The lack of witnesses, however, meant that one party could renege on the agreement. Many of the cases brought before the superintendent involved ambiguous secret marriages. Not surprisingly, it was often a pregnant woman who claimed that an offer of marriage had been made, and she was likely to be disappointed in the superintendent's verdict unless she had credible witnesses. There were also cases of a man trying to hold a woman to a previous agreement when she had changed her mind and decided to marry another. For example, Johannes Beck of Niederhona was so convinced that he had an agreement to marry Barbara Scheffer, the daughter of the village head, that he began the process of getting a dispensation for the fact that they were related in the third degree. He must have been shocked by Barbara's refusal shortly thereafter. She admitted that she had pretended to be married to Johannes in order to fend off advances from soldiers, but she denied that an engagement had taken place and emphasized it with the observation that she would rather die than marry Johannes Beck and that everyone in the village knew that he was a fool.[51]

Public announcement of an engagement was a form of insurance for both partners, since it frequently took a long time for the wedding to be completed. Secret engagements sometimes became public when a family member or neighbor posed a direct question to one of the parties, who admitted that there was an engagement. Because an engagement to marry was assumed to be binding, some villagers behaved as if they were already married once the announcement was made. They took advantage of the assumption that a promise was the same as the vows to engage in sexual activity before the wedding was performed. This was not interpreted as an excuse for sexual license, however. The sexual fidelity of both partners was essential. The case of Henrich Holderbuel and Orthie Kangiesser mentioned above is a good illustration of the sexual assumptions that accompanied the wedding preliminaries. It also indicates why the formal process of engagement was so precise. Henrich wished to abrogate his engagement to Orthie on the grounds that she had been in the village when soldiers were there and was no longer a virgin. Orthie insisted that although she had suffered physical abuse from the soldiers, nothing had happened to her that "had not happened to the married women of the village as well."[52] The superintendent in Eschwege, Johannes Hütterodt, insisted that Henrich had to go through with the marriage. As long as he could not prove that Orthie had had sexual relations with the soldiers, he had no grounds for calling off the wedding. Fifteen days after Hütterodt judged the case, the schoolmaster in Schwebda reported that Henrich and Orthie had reconciled and would marry.[53]

There are no comparable examples of a woman trying to break off a wedding engagement because of the alleged sexual infidelity of the man, so one may speak with some justice of a sexual double standard. There were, however, strong sanctions against male sexual activity out of wedlock. Harboring a "common prostitute," whether she actually charged money for sexual relations or was merely a notoriously promiscuous woman, was a punishable offense. If premarital sexual activity between a future husband and wife resulted in pregnancy, the church still considered it to be a punishable offense. Given the propensity of official documents to identify crimes by the male head of household, it is not surprising that the husbands were held accountable for paying the fines for pregnancies that resulted in births less than nine months after the wedding. The fines, although not as substantial as those for pregnancies out of wedlock, were as high as those for most crimes of violence in the region.

Family disapproval was not the only constraint on choosing a marriage partner. According to church doctrine, blood relatives in the third degree (i.e., related through great-grandparents) were considered too closely related to marry.[54] This forced villagers to have clear images of their kin networks. If two people who were closely related wished to marry, they asked the pastor if he would marry them, the pastor referred the issue to the superintendent if there was any doubt about their consanguinity. It was possible for those related in the third degree to attain a dispensation with only a modicum of bureaucratic intervention, though at a substantial cost. This was not, however, an issue that the local pastor was allowed to decide for himself. Instead, the problem had to be passed through the regular channels of the ecclesiastical hierarchy. Some villagers erred on the side of caution when confronted by this route. Stephan Keyser of Rambach at first offered marriage to a widow, then withdrew it when he decided that he was not allowed to marry his son's wife's sister and extended a proposal to someone else.[55] Only after the pastor brought the case to the attention of the superintendent and he ruled in favor of the marriage with the widow was Keyser prepared to relent. Other pastors were less careful. Hütterodt expressed annoyance when two related individuals were married in his diocese before he had issued a decision in their case.[56] Though he asserted that this should not have been allowed, there is little evidence that he took any additional steps to punish either the pastor or the married couple, aside from demanding the dispensation fee.

The appeals to superintendent Hütterodt are especially interesting because of the degree to which the genealogies of the applicants are spelled out. If villagers wished to avoid substantial punishment for marrying someone too closely related, they had to be aware of all their relatives through three generations. The evidence suggests that they succeeded in doing this with little difficulty. The extent to which these different strands were followed is best illustrated in the request of Georg Fischbach of Weissenborn that his son be allowed to marry the widow of Hans Schütze.[57] Two separate genealogies were drawn up to determine how closely Wendelin Fischbach was related to Anna Schütze. From this, Hütterodt determined that Wendelin was related to Anna in the fourth degree directly and in the third degree through marriage, which led Hütterodt to suspend judgment.

The bond of marriage was considered so strong that it was treated the same as blood ties in calculating the degree of relatedness. The stumbling block for Wendelin Fischbach was that he had a great-grandfather in common with his prospective bride's former husband. This was not a blood tie but a sacramental tie, though a dubious one at that, since Protestant doctrine had supposedly ended the sacramental nature of marriage. Similarly, Georg Windauss of Rieda was barred from marrying Gela, Martin Feige's widow, of Reichensachsen because she shared a grandparent with Georg's former wife.[58] The number of cases in which prospective partners asked for dispensation suggests that villagers were less troubled by incest in the third degree than the church was. In a small village, it was difficult to find a suitable mate who was not related in some way. But the case of Georg Windauss—whose prospective mate lived in a fairly distant village—indicates that the ingrown character of the village was not the only reason for relatives trying to marry one another. The contribution of the bride to the prosperity of the household was a primary consideration in making the match.

It was possible for individuals who were related in the third degree to marry if the couple was willing to ask for dispensation from the consistory and pay a substantial penalty for permission. Hütterodt's judgment in Georg

Windauss's case was that "this [marriage] can not be allowed. In case he pleads for dispensation from the government, he will have to reckon with a penalty of 20 or 30 Gulden; so he should forget it."[59] Some people were willing to pay that price. The minister in Breittau reported that Benedict Iba and Anna Francke, who were related in the second degree, wished to get married and "received dispensation from the consistory by paying 50 Reichstaler."[60] Whatever resistance the church offered to this sort of match, it was not comparable to the forces within the Iba family to maintain contact between the two branches. As in the cases of Windauss and Fischbach, Anna Francke, the object of Iba's affection, was not a blood relative but was related to him through her previous marriage to Peter Francke, which suggests that family property was a major consideration in the union. The Protestant ecclesiastical hierarchy tacitly accepted a double standard of those who could afford dispensation and those who could not, which resulted in a compromise with the interests of the village elite in maintaining their social standing.

A major consideration in selecting a marriage partner was what the prospective partner's family could contribute to the new household and to one's own lineage. A marriage was the merging of some of the resources of two distinct groups of kin. The economic situation of the parents of the married couple would eventually affect the livelihood of the couple and, by extension, the lineage of the parents. Our discussion of household organization indicated that village economic organization and familial association were inextricably linked.[61] The point at which these ideas connected most forcefully was when one's public status changed. The smith Herman Osan of Berneburg discovered one way in which the finances of his in-laws impinged on his own lineage. He complained to superintendent Hütterodt because his father-in-law contracted a debt of 50 fl, which became Osan's responsibility on his father-in-law's death.[62] In the meantime, Osan's wife had died as well. Osan reasoned that he should be relieved of this burden of debt because his wife had died without producing any potential heirs. As far as he was concerned, the fact that his family's alliance with the Bornscheuer family had not produced anyone to carry on the lineage meant that the Bornscheuer line had failed to live up to its part of the marriage bargain. This absolved him of responsibility to that lineage. Osan's sense of reciprocal responsibility may have been self-serving, but villagers were aware that kinship, including kinship based on the sacraments, entailed a series of reciprocal responsibilities and that households had to be organized on the basis of those responsibilities.

The case of Herman Osan also points to the other aspect of kin relationships that figured prominently in the economic organization of the village. One reason that villagers paid so much attention to the various ties of kinship was that all households had both property and legal obligations that were passed through kin networks, and these would be redistributed on the dissolution of the household. When a householder died, both his debts and his property had to be passed on. The claims of all kin had to be weighed. Inheritance was the centerpiece of this system of reciprocal obligations.[63] For some in the village, inheritance represented an opportunity; for others, it was a burden. In Osan's case, his connection had brought him none of the things that he desired, so he turned to the superintendent to try to escape the burdens that his kin network imposed. Hütterodt inquired about the other heirs to Gangolf Bornscheuer to see who else might have been held responsible for his debts, but Osan was not exempted.[64] The way in which a household disposed of its possessions thus had far-reaching consequences for many individuals within the village.

Householders could not arbitrarily dispose of their resources but were constrained by the customs of the village and the expectations of those who surrounded them. Inheritance strategies were subject to the conventions of the other villagers, since there was little way to ensure adherence to a particular strategy after one's death. As a result, almost all villagers disposed of their property in the manner characteristic of the region in which they lived. The primary question in inheritance was whether the property was to be divided up among some or all of the potential heirs or given in one parcel to a single heir. By the seventeenth century, the customs of inheritance for different parts of Germany had been established for some time. Partible inheritance was the custom in some areas, and impartibility was customary elsewhere. The boundaries separating one region of inheritance customs from another were fairly distinct, but they did not necessarily follow the political boundaries. The area of the Werra River had been under the political control of Hesse since the twelfth century, yet rather than adopting the characteristic primogeniture of most of Hesse-Kassel, the Werra valley was influenced by the Thuringian custom of partible inheritance.[65] Villagers in this eastern part of Hesse had persisted in their traditional practice despite repeated ordinances from the landgrave prohibiting the breaking up of *Hufen*.[66] There is no evidence that local officials interfered with the local customs, though they complained of the difficulty of collecting rents from the broken-up land. One minister wrote, "things are so torn apart, that one cannot bring it together, because in most individual instances $\frac{1}{2}$, $\frac{1}{4}$, $\frac{1}{6}$, $\frac{1}{8}$, yes $\frac{1}{16}$ part of a *Metzen* is collected."[67] There was no compelling economic or social reason for villagers there to practice partible inheritance while their compatriots a few miles deeper into Hessian territory had a single heir. Yet the manifest interest of the central administration in keeping peasant estates together did not compel the villagers of the Werra to change their ways and adopt the practices of their neighbors.

Although partible inheritance was more likely to lead to disintegration of holdings into smaller and smaller units than impartible inheritance, the pace and extent of disintegration were by no means uniform. There are instances in which a single bit of land was broken up into equal pieces among several people. The traces of this can be seen in the *Amt* account books. Sometimes a piece of land was listed in the accounts as the joint property of several villagers. For instance, three-quarters *Hufen* of land was identified as belonging to Heintz Braun, Kleinhans Schelhase, and Hans Guldeman in the account book for Cornberg in 1607.[68] These three individuals may have been related to one another despite the differences in their names, but the later distribution of the property suggests that they were only distantly related, if at all. By 1631, the land had been broken up into nine smaller parcels and distributed among twelve different people with ten different surnames.[69] This distribution of the original piece of land indicates the tendency of a single parcel to disintegrate to such an extent that the original unity of the holding is preserved only in the designations in the official documents. A change in surnames, as in the case described above, does not necessarily indicate that a family lineage was not being perpetuated through land transfers, however. A piece of land that Henn Ruppel inherited from his father before 1607 became the property of Hans Stebel from 1618 to 1629. In 1630, the account books listed the property in the hands of Jacob Ruppel, Philip Muller, and Christoffel Hohman, with the remark in the margin that the property was "inherited from the father and father-in-law."[70]

The different configurations of individuals who had legitimate claims to the inheritance of a piece of property made record keeping difficult. Not all *Rentmeister* were as fastidious as those of Cornberg in noting the source of the right of inheritance or the names of all those who actually inherited the property. Sometimes the owners of property in a village were listed simply as "heirs" (*Erben*) or "associates" (*Consorten*) of a previous owner, without giving either their numbers or their first or last names. In one case in which the owners were specified, ten different individuals were listed. In Rockensüß, Germerod's *Erben* included two people named Germerod, two named Stebel, and one each named Rehman, Jacob, Stange, Gernhart, Ruppel, and Tilleman.[71] Two of those owners were listed as having heirs of their own, who were the actual holders of the property. Thus, among Germerod's heirs were Claus Gernhart's *Erben*. These "second-level" heirs were not mentioned by name or number in the account, however. The trail of legitimate heirs was quickly lost in the maze of names and associations that were mentioned in the official records, particularly the accounts. Some of these changes were simple inheritances, but in many cases the officials abandoned all attempts to keep track of the actual landholders—allowing the names in the account book to remain unchanged for decades.[72]

Even if legitimate heirs were given equal parts of the property as their portions of the inheritance, this did not mean that the land was always broken up into ever smaller units. Instead, some heirs sold their shares of the inheritance to the other heirs in order to keep the property together.

The administration had no convenient means of recording whether the heirs held on to their shares of the inheritance except in the property lists of the account books, which were sometimes unchanged for years. But the administration oversaw the land market by demanding a fee, called *Lehngeld*, on all property sold. Through this, it was able to monitor the process by which ownership of the land passed from one generation to the next, though only imprecisely. Between 1610 and 1620, there were fourteen sales of land involving villagers from Rockensüß who paid *Lehngeld* to the *Vogtei* Cornberg.[73] Eleven of these sales were between relatives. Four entries explicitly stated that the sale involved the purchase of the whole of an estate that had originally been broken up among a number of heirs, including the purchaser. The largest of the purchases listed in the account book indicates how this inheritance strategy worked: "Martin Germerod of Rockensüß bought from the siblings of his wife, their father's estate, including the house and out-buildings for 600 fl, from which his wife inherited 200 fl, there remains 400 fl."[74] Presumably, each of the three heirs to the estate, valued at 600 fl, had received an equal share. It is noteworthy in this case that the land passed down through the daughter; this demonstrates that the principle of partible inheritance extended to female heirs, making it possible for the son-in-law, as head of a household, to benefit from the inheritance. It is likely that all the heirs to this property were female; otherwise, one of Martin's wife's brothers probably would have tried to keep the property in his hands. This process of buying out portions of an inheritance maintained the insularity of the village—insiders bought up those portions of an inheritance in the hands of outsiders. For instance, in 1609, Hans Ruppel der Alte bought half a *Viertel* of land in the fields of Rockensüß from the heirs of his brother-in-law, Henn Moller of Friemen, for 140 fl.[75] Household strategies were linked closely to the organization of the village in which the household resided. The land did not end up in the hands of an outsider and would not do so as long as there was a legitimate heir to the property within the village.

For the process of buying out portions of the inheritance to work, there had to be some cooperation among members of the kin network. Given the potential for disputes among kin that we have seen, it is not surprising that the issues of inheritance were not always resolved peaceably. Friedrich Rudloff's heirs in Ulfen were fined 30 fl "because they went against the official command to negotiate and chased the stepmother from the house before they had reached an agreement with her."[76] The fine was substantial because Rudloff's property was valuable, but disputes could be equally bitter when there was little to distribute or even debts that had to be apportioned.

Even when the wishes of the deceased were unambiguously expressed, the claims of potential heirs could hold up the execution of the will. Orban Mengel willed a sum of money to the church in Niddawitzhausen, which was reaffirmed by his wife on her deathbed. But Friederich Thiele was a legitimate heir, and he disputed the donation.[77] He contended that the donation reduced his rightful share of the inheritance. Thiele's actions prompted the minister in Niddawitzhausen to complain to the superintendent, but Thiele succeeded in delaying the execution of the will. Disputes of this sort exacerbated tensions within the lineage. They were occasionally fought in the courts for years.

Reconciling the various factions within a family in a situation involving a disputed inheritance was difficult. Inheritances were disputed because members of a family believed that their economic standing was threatened or that a social convention was being violated. An open land market might have eased those tensions, but family resources were not likely to be used to purchase land to provide independence for dependent household members unless it brought some economic gain to the household as well. The economic role of the household shaped and focused the interests of the individuals who resided in it. The pressure to conform could lead to individual resistance or resentment. The extent to which members of the household could tolerate the suppression of their individual identities within the household depended on how they perceived their chances of eventually attaining independence. For women, full independent identity was possible only at the cost of social marginality. Women could, however, aim to become the wives of heads of households, which conferred a higher status than did mere dependence. For the sons or daughters of heads of households, the practice of partible inheritance offered them the prospect of acquiring the necessary wealth to establish households of their own. But even then, the connection to a lineage limited options through community restraints. Familial disputes affected the village by influencing how households and lineages interacted. Households and lineages were building blocks of the village, but they took on additional meaning because they were tied to tangible property within the village. Problems with inheritances and marriages were just two of the ways in which this connection surfaced in the village.

The previous chapter ended with the observation that villagers were not interchangeable parts of a unified whole called the village. Although the administrative structure of the territory relied on the assumption that the village was a corporate body with a single voice, there were, in fact, disparate groups in the village that shaped its voice through their interaction. Our discussion of household structure, marriage strategies, and inheritance strategies points to one of the ways in which the disparate voices were channeled. Household and kinship were two of the lenses through which villagers viewed their participation in the village. The social composition of the village shaped the definition of the village because day-to-day life involved contact between people who were identified by their positions in households and kin networks. But not all kin networks or households participated equally in the village. Differences in social position led to different expectations and sometimes to conflicts between groups of villagers.

This affected the social roles that household and kinship created. One house-holder need not be just like his neighbor. Some had more and some had less opportunity to arrange favorable marriages or leave large inheritances to their kin. The economy of the village was not the same thing as the economy of the household. Before the village could present a united profile to the outside world, these potential sources of instability had to be over-come or suppressed. This points to yet another lens through which villagers perceived their role in the village—a lens of work, wealth, and day-to-day interaction outside the framework of the household. We must turn our view away from households and lineages for their own sake and toward the com-peting interests within the village in which considerations of household and kinship were important, but not the sole motivation.

Notes

1. The historical and anthropological literature on the family and the household is immense. A recent statement of the importance of the household as a unit of analysis is Robert Netting, Richard Wilk, and Eric Arnould, eds., *House-holds: Comparative and Historical Studies of the Domestic Group* (Berkeley, 1984). Basic historical accounts are Peter Laslett, *Household and Family in Past Time: Comparative Studies in the Size and Structure of the Domestic Group Over the Last Three Centuries in England, France, Serbia, Japan and Colonial North America with Further Materials from Western Europe* (Cambridge, 1972); Jean-Louis Flandrin, *Families in Former Times: Kinship, Household and Sexuality*, trans. Richard Southern (Cambridge, 1979), and Michael Anderson, *Approaches to the History of the Western Family, 1500–1914* (London, 1980). For Germany in particular, see Michael Mitterauer and Reinhard Sieder, *The European Family: From Patriar-chy to Partnership* (Chicago, 1982), and Dieter Schwab, "Familie," in Otto Brunner et al., eds., *Geschichtliche Grundbegriffe*, vol. 2 (Stuttgart, 1972), 253–302.

2. This is especially clear in the entry for hearth chickens in the village of Rockensüß. Hessian State Archives, Marburg (StAM) Rech II Sontra 3.

3. The relationship between house and household is explored briefly in Ingeborg Weber-Kellermann, *Die Deutsche Familie* (Frankfurt, 1974), 91–96. See also Michael Mitterauer, *Grundtypen alteuropäischer Sozialformen* (Stuttgart-Bad Cannstatt, 1979).

4. This point anticipates some of the arguments of the rest of the chapter. I take the notion of head of household as office in part from Hermann Rebel's im-portant study, *Peasant Classes: The Bureaucratization of Property and Family Relations under Early Habsburg Absolutism, 1511–1636* (Princeton, 1983). Rebel's analy-sis suggests that householdership was not an "office" until it was "bureaucratized" through the deliberate manipulation of *emphyteusis*, the right to use seigneu-rial land with the provision that the user not cause the lands to deteriorate in any way. This suggestion about the prebureaucratic household before the six-teenth century is not well developed by Rebel, however. See also the careful presentation of Thomas Robisheaux, *Rural Society and the Search for Order in Early Modern Germany* (Cambridge, 1989).

5. One of the best recent attempts to do this is Arthur Imhof, *Die Verlorene*

Welten: Alltagsbewältigung durch unsere Vorfahren und Weshalb wir uns heute so schwer damit tun (Munich, 1984).

6. Imhof, *Die Verlorene Welten*, and Arthur Imhof, ed., *Historische Demographie als Sozialgeschichte*, 2 vols. (Darmstadt, 1975). Imhof and Michael Mitterauer are the leading scholars of demographic and family history in the German-speaking world. See, in general, Mitterauer and Sieder's *The European Family*. Another work that connects family history to the history of mentalities is Pieter Spierenburg, *The Broken Spell: A Cultural and Anthropological History of Preindustrial Europe* (New Brunswick, 1991).

7. For the uses of "Books of Souls," see Michael Mitterauer, "Vorindustriellen Familienformen Zur Funktionsentlastung des 'ganzen Hauses' im 17. und 18. Jahrhundert," in Mitterauer, *Grundtypen alteuropäischer Sozialformen*, 35–97, and Peter Schmidtbauer, "The Changing Household: Austrian Household Structure from the Seventeenth to the Early Twentieth Century," in Richard Wall, ed., in collaboration with Jean Robin and Peter Laslett, *Family Forms in Historic Europe* (Cambridge, 1983), 347–78.

8. StAM Ki Reichensachsen, 1639–1653.

9. Walter Kürschner, "Aus dem Kirchenbuch von Reichensachsen (und Langenhain) von 1639–1653," *Archiv für Hessische Geschichte und Altertumskunde* NF 9 (1913): 54–55.

10. I adopt here the terminology of Peter Laslett and the Cambridge Group for the History of Population and Social Structure in *Household and Family in Past Time*. However, I usually refer to "households" as something more akin to what they call "housefuls."

11. StAM Ki Reichensachsen, 1639–1654.

12. Peter Laslett, "Family and Household as Work Group and Kin Group: Areas of Traditional Europe Compared," in Wall, *Family Forms in Historic Europe*, 526–27. Historical investigation of family forms has effectively debunked the idea that rural preindustrial families were large and always included an extended family under one roof. See Mitterauer and Sieder, *The European Family*, 24–44. The "steam family," which included several generations under one roof, was present in some areas, usually those with impartible inheritance. See Lutz Berkner, "Peasant Household Organization and Demographic Change in Lower Saxony (1689–1766)," in Ronald Demos Lee, ed., *Population Patterns in the Past* (New York, 1977), 53–70.

13. Mitterauer and Sieder claim that 7 to 15 percent of the population worked and lived as servants in the households of others. The figure for the Werra region appears to have been much smaller than that.

14. The classic statement on this form of household organization is Otto Brunner, "Das 'ganze Haus' und das alteuropaische Ökonomik," in Otto Brunner, *Neue Wege der Sozialgeschichte*, 2nd ed. (Göttingen, 1968), 103–27. See also Mitterauer, "Vorindustriellen Familienformen"; and Gotthardt Frühsorge, "Die Begründung der 'väterlichen Gesellschaft' in der europäischen oeconomia christiana. Zur Rolle des Vaters in der 'Hausväterliteratur' des 16. bis 18. Jahrhunderts in Deutschland," in Hubertus Tellenbach, ed., *Das Vaterbild im Abendland*, vol. 1 (Stuttgart, 1978), 110–23. Frühsorge cautions that *Hausvater* was understood as a legal rather than a sociological category by seventeenth-century writers.

15. Ki Reichensachsen.

16. Ibid., 1646.

17. Ilse Gromes, ed., *Bußen aus den Amtsrechnungen des Amtes Sontra 1590–1648* (Sontra; 1977), 83.

18. Ibid., 82.

19. Ibid., 77.

20. Ibid., 58.

21. StAM Ki Reichensachsen 1638–1654.

22. I rely here on the interesting attempt by Hermann Rebel to see beyond the "individual" to the social roles that made up the person. Rebel, *Peasant Classes*, 50–53. For the construction of "whole persons" from a somewhat different perspective, see David Sabean, *Power in the Blood: Popular Culture and Village Discourse in Early Modern Germany* (Cambridge, 1984), 30–36.

23. For the use of the term *Hausfrau*, see Gromes, *Bußen aus den Amtsrechnungen*, 83. On the prevalence of the term *Hausmutter* in the historiography, see Peter Petschauer, "From *Hausmutter* to *Hausfrau*: Ideals and Realities in Late Eighteenth Century Germany," *Eighteenth Century Life* 1982: 72–82.

24. The centrality of women to the work process of the house in the countryside has become the object of increasing scholarly attention. See Christina Vanja, "Frauen im Dorf. Ihre Stellung unter besonderer Berücksichtigung Landgräflich-Hessischer Quellen des späten Mittelalters," *Zeitschrift für Agrargeschichte und Agrarsoziologie* 34 (1986): 147–59; and Heide Wunder, "Frauen in der Gesellschaft Mitteleuropas im späten Mittelalter und in der Frühen Neuzeit (15. bis 18. Jahrhundert)," in Helfried Valentinitsch, ed., *Hexen und Zauberer—Ein Europäisches Phänomen in der Steiermark* (Graz, 1987), 123–54.

25. An excellent presentation of the negotiations over male and female roles in the household can be found in David Sabean, *Property, Production, and Family in Neckarhausen, 1700–1870* (Cambridge, 1991). A more general survey of the issues is Heide Wunder, *"Er ist die Sonn,' sie ist der Mond": Frauen in der Frühen Neuzeit* (Munich, 1992).

26. I have found no evidence of a husband brought to trial for beating his wife too severely, nor any tales such as Natalie Davis describes of wives resorting to accidental violence in order to defend themselves from the onslaught of enraged husbands. Natalie Zemon Davis, *Fiction in the Archives: Pardon Tales and Their Tellers in Sixteenth Century France* (Stanford, 1987). There is, however, an excellent example of stoic resolve by a wife afflicted by a husband who is a complete failure as a householder in StAM M1 Landau 720. This source is not from the Werra region, however.

27. The motif of the "bad wife" who beat her husband was well established in the literature of the period. Claudia Ulbrich, "Unartige Weiber. Präsenz und Renitenz von Frauen im frühneuzeitlichen Deutschland," in Richard van Dülmen, ed., *Arbeit, Frömmigkeit und Eigensinn* (Frankfurt, 1990), 12–42. For the use of charivari to enforce conformity to gender roles—but with the twist that women were the active agents for enforcement—see Christina Vanja, "Verkehrte Welt: Das Weibergericht zu Breitenbach," *Journal für Geschichte* 5 (1986): 22–26.

28. StAM 17e Reichensachsen 10.

29. For a recent reevaluation of this, with special emphasis on the kinds of materials available for Hesse, see Christina Vanja, "Frauenarbeit in Dörfern des 15. Jahrhunderts–Möglichkeiten zur Auswertung von Rechnungen und Zinsbüchern," in *Instituto Internazionale di Storia Economica "F. Datini": La Donna Nell-Economia Secc. XIII–XVIII* (Prato, 1990), 391–96.

30. Gromes, *Bußen aus den Amtsrechnungen*, 62. Note that Margrethe is identified by her first name, which is an exception to the usual rule of omitting the first names of wives of heads of households. The term *Nachbarin* to describe the victim may have been a loose rendition of the plural of neighbor, but it was more likely a reference to a woman who participated in the life of the village as a member of the community of householders.

31. StAM Rech II Sontra 4, 1623.

32. See Gromes, *Bußen aus den Amtsrechnungen*, 46, for a case involving women; ibid., 67, for one involving men.
33. On children and work within the family in Germany, see Sheilagh Ogilvie, "Coming of Age in a Corporate Society: Capitalism, Pietism and Family Authority in Rural Württemberg, 1590–1740," *Continuity and Change* 1 (1986): 279–331, especially pp. 291–96.
34. Gromes, *Bußen aus den Amtsrechnungen*, 6.
35. Ibid., 2.
36. Ibid., 58.
37. Ki Reichensachsen.
38. Ibid.; compare 1646 and 1652.
39. Ibid.
40. Compare StAM Rech II, passim. David Sabean has pointed to the prominence of brothers-in-law in the social calculations of Württemberg peasants. David Sabean, "Bees in an Empty Hive: Brothers-in-law in a Württemberg Village around 1800," in Hans Medick and David Warren Sabean, eds., *Interest and Emotion: Essays on the Study of Family and Kinship* (Cambridge, 1984), 171–86.
41. See Rech II, passim.
42. Sabean, *Property*, 371–415.
43. Wilm Sippel, ed., *Forschungsberichte der Stiftung Sippel*, vol. 5 (Göttingen, 1981), 51.
44. Gromes, *Bußen aus den Amtsrechnungen*, 32, 33.
45. This raises the question of whether there was a notion of adolescence in village society of the seventeenth century. Robert Muchembled demonstrated that young men were the primary culprits in crimes of violence in the villages of Artois. See Robert Muchembled, *La Violence au Village (XVe–XVII Siècle)* (Turnhout, 1989), 41–42. On stress among young adults, see Michael MacDonald, *Mystical Bedlam: Madness, Anxiety and Healing in Seventeenth Century England* (Cambridge, 1981), 72–112.
46. Thomas Robisheaux, *Rural Society and the Search for Order in Early Modern Germany* (Cambridge, 1989), has argued that the church administration consistently backed parents trying to thwart the wedding plans of unsuitable couples as part of a strategy of protecting the patrimony of large farmers. Social criteria do not seem to have played as large a role in the discussions before the superintendent in Eschwege, though they almost certainly lurked in the background. The parents of the party trying to adhere to the purported promise of marriage were involved more frequently than those of the party trying to escape the obligation. It appears that sexual reputation within the village was as great a consideration for bringing the case as social mobility.
47. Sippel, *Stiftung Sippel*, 5:39.
48. Ibid., 19.
49. Ibid., 39.
50. See Sippel, *Stiftung Sippel*, 8:82.
51. Ibid., 102–4. Johannes made one more attempt to win Barbara over several months later. See ibid., 123.
52. Sippel, *Stiftung Sippel*, 5:18–19.
53. Ibid., 20.
54. Ibid.
55. Ibid., 165.
56. Ibid., 25.
57. Ibid., 176.
58. Ibid., 30.

59. Ibid., 30.
60. Ibid., 21.
61. For a good elucidation of the ways in which property influenced kin interac-
    tion, see David Sabean, "Kinship and Property in Rural Western Europe be-
    fore 1800," in Jack Goody, Joan Thirsk, and E. P. Thompson, eds., *Family and
    Inheritance: Rural Society in Western Europe 1200–1800* (Cambridge, 1976), 96–
    111. Giovanni Levi, *Inheriting Power: The Story of an Exorcist* (Chicago, 1988),
    provides a very nuanced analysis of how kinship and power were intertwined.
62. Sippel, *Stiftung Sippel*, 5:96.
63. E. P. Thompson, "The Grid of Inheritance: A Comment," in Jack Goody, Joan
    Thirsk, and E. P. Thompson, eds., *Family and Inheritance: Rural Society in Western
    Europe 1200–1800* (Cambridge, 1976), 328–60, nicely lays out the ways in
    which inheritance of the use right in land entailed the inheritance of a whole
    set of functions and roles associated with rural society.
64. Sippel, *Stiftung Sippel*, 5:96.
65. This is a surprisingly neglected aspect of local history of the Werra region. A
    map of the distribution of inheritance customs in West Germany is in Alan
    Mayhew, *Rural Settlement and Farming in Germany* (New York, 1973), 185. See
    also Max Sering, ed., *Die Vererbung des ländlichen Grundbesitzes in der Nachkriegszeit*
    (Munich, 1930). The process by which this practice was preserved would make
    an important study but is, unfortunately, beyond the scope of this work.
66. *Hufen* were units of land that were theoretically capable of supporting a large
    household. *Sammlung fürstlich- hessische Landesordnungen*, vol. 1, contains sev-
    eral such ordinances, beginning in the reign of Landgrave Philipp.
67. StAM 318. A *Metzen* was a measure of volume equivalent to about ten liters.
68. StAM Rech II Cornberg 4, 1607.
69. Ibid., 1631.
70. Ibid., 1630.
71. Ibid.
72. Compare StAM Rech II Sontra 10, 1650–1670.
73. StAM Rech II Cornberg 4.
74. Ibid., 1613.
75. Ibid., 1609.
76. Gromes, *Bußen aus den Amtsrechnungen*, 7.
77. Sippel, *Stiftung Sippel*, 5:39.

4

Wealth, Ties, Tension

In 1668, Balsser Kochrich carved—or had carved—above the door to his house the following inscription: "The Lord's blessings will make you rich without effort if you remain steadfast and industrious in your station in life and do what you are told." Inscriptions were not rare in the Werra region, but most simply referred to the builder of the house and perhaps cited a passage of Scripture. Kochrich's more individual statement of beliefs draws together several of the qualities of sociability within the village that have already been discussed. The previous chapter noted the centrality of the house as the location of production and consumption and as the site of family or kin relationships. The house was also part of the ensemble of buildings that created the village's profile. One can, therefore, interpret Kochrich's message as both an admonition to the members of the household and a contribution to the public definition of sociability. The quote reaffirms that villagers should steadfastly conform to the norms of the community and work industriously. The reference to the Lord's blessings points to the fact that the moral umbrella of the church had worked its way into general village consciousness and served as a principle of internal order. The most striking feature of the inscription for the issues yet to be explored is its reference to "station in life" (*Stand*). It is far from clear what villagers believed their station in life to be. The inscription gives no clue whether there was a single station in life for all the villagers or several different stations based on one's position in the village economy. But it reminds us that villagers were conscious of their social world and its economic basis.

The social world of the village was shaped by both the material circumstances of the village economy and the perceptions and relations that emerged out of that economy. The riches that Kochrich's inscription promised had to come from an agricultural base. Seigneurial and state administration, communal organization of work in the fields, and calculations of household and kinship all depended on its development. The nature of the agricultural economy is not adequately described by the traditional opposition between self-sufficient production and consumption based on the house, and market-oriented production based on the individual, which are often conceived as stages in the process of the development of modern capitalism. Both market forces and self-exploitation characterized the village economy.[1] Our analysis must therefore begin with the global criteria of economic development and how they were connected to local circumstances. Both European and local economic activity shaped social relations within the village. Once the basic social groups have been identified, we will be able to see how other forms of interaction took place within the village and build a more complete picture of the everyday world.

We have already shown that *Amt* administration was in part seigneurial administration, which rested on extracting revenues from rural cultivators. The demands of *Grundherrschaft* compelled some integration into the market but rested on the notion of householdership of the "whole house." Conversely, fostering market integration was a means of overcoming some of the limitations of the inheritance practices enforced by village custom. The rural economy was comparatively unwieldy and inflexible because the interests of *Grundherr*, village, and household had to be brought into some kind of balance, usually—but not always—at the cost of innovation. The economic base of the *Ämter* of the Werra region, codified in the Treysa Assessment, is one indicator of seigneurial assumptions about revenue.[2] The figures on which the assessments were based are lost, but taxes were based primarily on the value of land, house, and animals, modified by a deduction for the amount paid in seigneurial dues and a nominal assessment for any trade practiced by the head of household. We can assume that the values in the Treysa Assessment are an estimate of fixed property in the villages of the *Ämter* with only minor modifications for other kinds of income. In the landgrave's lands in *Amt* Sontra, that value came out to an average of 123 Reichsthaler (Rthlr) per householder, or about 5,600 Rthlr per village. These figures are almost certainly too small to represent the genuine market value of the fixed property. Even small and rickety houses sold for as much as 40 fl, and substantial ones cost more than 100 fl; large tracts of land in the fields often cost several hundred fl. (A fl was worth slightly less than a Rthlr. The former was valued at either 26 or 27 *albus*, and the latter at 32 *albus*.) Thus, the Treysa Assessment was more useful for comparing values between *Ämter* than for achieving a complete picture within an *Amt*. Nevertheless, it represented the amount of value located in an *Amt* that the administration could reasonably rely on for its own fiscal demands. It gave a window onto the scale of economic activity that could be expected from the village.

In addition to its interest in the fixed property of the *Amt*, the central administration was concerned with how much revenue the lands of the *Amt* could produce on a regular basis for the seigneurial jurisdiction. To find that out, the administration had another means of assessing the economic activity of villagers: the district account books. Most seigneurial income was derived from *Grundherrschaft* and its attendant privileges, but a lord could not arbitrarily raise those payments because they were set by custom. Any increase in seigneurial revenue had to come from more skillful exploitation of demesne lands or increased economic activity by villagers, which funneled money into privileges reserved to the landgrave.

A brief survey of the accounting procedures used to measure *Amt* revenues provides a good sense of how the landgrave and his agents could locate economic improvement. The account books of the landgrave divided district income in cash and in kind into three general categories: regular, additional, and irregular. Regular income was useless as a guide to the economic circumstances of villages, and additional income had an ambiguous relation to economic circumstances; irregular income provided the best indicator of economic prosperity.

Regular income was derived from fixed rents, so it never varied from year to year. It was deemed so regular that not one *Heller* of it was ever reported as uncollected, whether it was collected or not.[3] The uniformity in handwriting indicates that the sections for regular income were sometimes written years in advance of the year of submission. Deficiencies in collecting were thus masked by the accounting procedure. The reason for this apparent fiscal incongruity was that the *Amtmann* or *Rentmeister* was personally responsible for making up any deficits.[4]

The category of additional income was difficult to use as a barometer of local prosperity because fiscal agents performed numerous manipulations in order to keep the accounts balanced. Ordinarily, expenditures were expected to equal income exactly, though this balance was occasionally achieved by shipping a surplus to the *Räte* in Kassel rather than by spending it in the *Amt*. It was common practice to carry over the difference between income collected and expenditures as a *Receß*, or remainder. Sometimes this remainder was money for which the *Amtmann* could find no immediate use, because he was allowed to spend money only on authorized projects, but often it was income that had not been collected and so could not be spent. In either case, the remainder was carried over to the next year's account as additional income whether it had been collected or not. The category of additional income thereby conflated uncollected income with income collected but not spent. As remainders mounted, the amount of additional income grew dramatically. Therefore, one might expect the category to be a useful guide to economic troubles: The larger the additional income, the greater the difficulty in collecting revenues. Unfortunately, additional income included yet another element that was clearly a sign of good agricultural production: income generated from the sale of grain and poultry. This category reflected the produce of the personal demesne of the landgrave, and to the extent that demesne production was high, the figure for additional income grew as well.

The category of irregular income was less subject to the oddities of accounting procedures and more dependent on the production of villagers rather than of the landgrave's own demesne. Irregular income was derived from all the perquisites of administration that were subject to yearly variation. These included some fairly constant figures, such as *Dienstgeld* for labor services converted into money payments, as well as many entries that varied greatly from year to year, such as *Lehngeld* collected on the sale of peasant property and *Triftgeld* for the number of sheep grazing on the landgrave's lands. For most entries, the amount collected rose or fell depending on the vigor of the local economy. Fines for crimes—another source of irregular income—seem to have been an exception to this rule, but even these varied according to the ability of the populace to pay.

The nature of *Amt* income meant that it was in the landgrave's interest that the rural economy be vigorous. He did not, of course, intervene directly in the productive process in the village, but he did try to keep an overview of the direction of local production so that he would know how much revenue to expect in the future.

The landgrave's concerns about local prosperity dovetail with those of historians of the rural economy. There were undercurrents of change and expansion throughout the late sixteenth and early seventeenth centuries that must be explored in order to understand the economic circumstances of the villages of the Werra. It is now well established that Europe as a whole experienced two great inflations during the sixteenth century: of prices and of population.[5] These two inflations were related to each other to some extent, though historians have not worked out all the ramifications of their connection. An assessment of their impact in Germany—and, by extension, in the Werra region—has been clouded by the looming presence of the Thirty Years' War, which made it harder to assess the natural trend of development. Inflation is growth, but it is not necessarily good growth. There is no consensus about whether the effects of the price revolution and demographic expansion produced continued expansion or decline in Germany in the late sixteenth and early seventeenth centuries.[6]

The issue was debated by two of the ablest German economic historians in the 1950s without definitive resolution. Friedrich Lütge argued that the German economy continued to grow up to the early years of the Thirty Years' War. Some sectors of the economy were indeed in decline, but the key sector of agriculture experienced little difficulty, and manufacturing continued to soak up rural laborers. Wilhelm Abel, in an essentially Malthusian analysis reminiscent of the Annales school of the 1960s, portrayed a Germany that has reached a population peak and production crisis. The price inflation of the sixteenth century came to an abrupt end at the beginning of the seventeenth century, hitting bottom in 1605 to 1607 and resulting in a recession that lasted several years. Horrible as the war may have been, it was merely an acceleration of a process that was already under way and, thus, cannot be held responsible for Germany's later economic weakness.

The war, therefore, descended on a stagnant economy that was likely to collapse at the slightest strain.[7]

One difficulty in resolving the dispute is arriving at acceptable global criteria for determining growth or decline. We will see that, at the local level, the general trend was for growth up to the outbreak of the war. Population continued to expand and revenues increased, though the degree of increase was mitigated somewhat by the rate of inflation. Overall, there was no reason to expect imminent economic collapse in the Werra region in the first two decades of the seventeenth century.

The economic situation of the Werra region can be viewed from the perspective of seigneurial revenues and demographic development. These are obviously not complete perspectives, but they give some sense of the general trends that mattered for village internal structure. The landgrave kept his own assessment of the prosperity of the Ämter in the form of a list of "assessments" of the surplus to be expected of the districts from year to year in the period 1570 to 1610 (see Graphs 4.1 and 4.2). These yearly assessments show that the prosperity of the region and of the landgraviate as a whole went in cycles. The assessments of the three largest Ämter of the Werra region were at their lowest between 1580 and 1585. From about 1590 onward, the assessments show general inprovement up to 1610, the final year of the seventeenth-century depression identified by Abel. If we begin with the five-year average of each Amt at its lowest point during those years and compare that with the five-year average at its high point between 1606 and 1610, the assessments increased almost 50 percent in Amt Sontra and more than 60 percent in Amt Eschwege/Bilstein and Amt Wanfried.[8] The trend after 1590 was consistently upward. The rate of increase was about equal to the rate of inflation over the same period, so seigneurial revenues showed neither startling growth nor imminent crisis. There was no sign that revenues could not continue to keep pace with inflation after 1610.

Because the assessments were completed after a long upward trend, they produced a high "official" estimate of how much each district could be expected to produce. Nevertheless, the surplus created was only a tiny fraction of the total wealth of the districts. Eschwege and Sontra were expected to produce 1,700 and 500 fl respectively, which was about 0.5 percent of the assessed taxable property value of town and Amt in the Treysa Assessment; town and Amt Wanfried showed a surplus of 200 fl, which produced a paltry yield of 0.17 percent of its assessed value. Assessments of yield in the Amt were discontinued for the years immediately prior to the war, but the district account books suggest that the trend identified there continued up to 1618. Between 1607 and the start of the war, total revenues in the accounts of Amt Sontra hovered around 2,300 fl. Both total income and irregular income peaked in 1618.

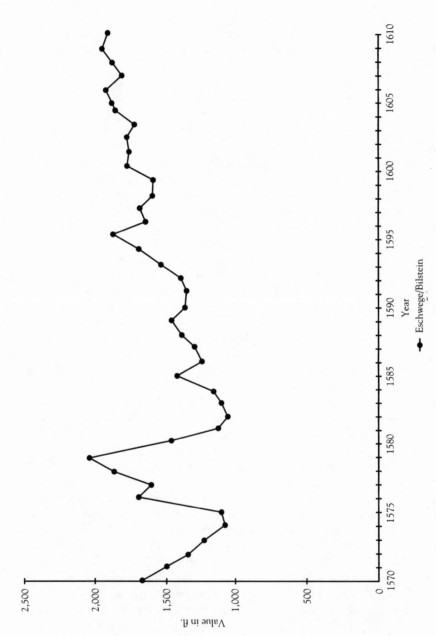

GRAPH 4.1   ASSESSED VALUE IN AMT ESCHWEGE/BILSTEIN, 1570–1610

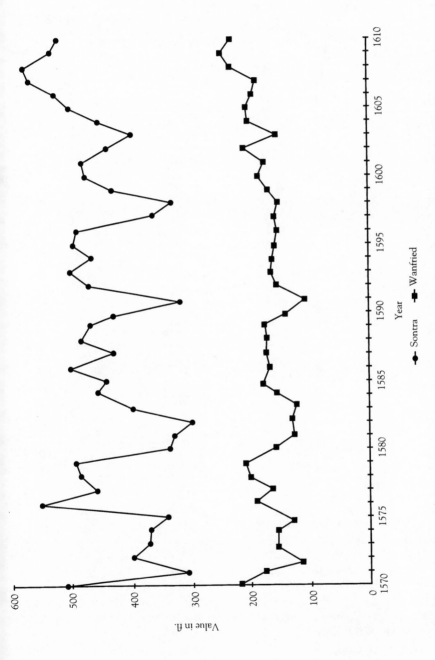

GRAPH 4.2 ASSESSED VALUE IN AMT SONTRA AND AMT WANFRIED, 1570–1610

TABLE 4.1

Deaths, Births, and Marriages in Grandenborn, 1587–1618

YEAR	BURIALS	BAPTISMS	MARRIAGES
1587	7	9	3
1588	8	11	9
1589	19	11	0
1590	0	19	1
1591	11	11	2
1592	6	12	6
1593	9	17	2
1594	9	8	4
1595	6	17	5
1596	7	11	4
1597	19	3	2
1598	89	0	2
1599	6	15	4
1600	7	28	1
1601	8	15	3
1602	6	23	7
1603	7	13	3
1604	11	23	2
1605	8	21	5
1606	5	12	6
1607	23	18	3
1608	8	20	4
1609	9	20	6
1610	5	19	1
1611	7	14	1
1612	7	14	5
1613	4	nd	1[a]
1614	13	17	nd
1615	10	8	nd
1616	14	21	nd
1617	8	14	nd
1618	2	14	nd

Source: Pfarrarchiv Renda, Ki Grandenborn.
[a]nd = no data.

Information on the direction of population development of the Werra region in the late sixteenth and seventeenth centuries is harder to come by than for the development of revenues, but there are several signs that the population was generally on the increase up to 1618. The village of Grandenborn is the only one in the Werra region for which there is sub-stantial demographic information for the prewar period (Table 4.1).[9] Its parish register provides a picture of a series of demographic events that characterized the village's population in the late sixteenth century. The list of burials and baptisms commences in 1587 and continues until 1647. The records include children and infants as well as adults.[10] The information in the parish register indicates that Grandenborn followed a demographic pattern that was characteristic of most of Western Europe in the early modern period. The result of that pattern was that the population of the village grew consistently from 1587 to 1620.

The first demographic event that strikes one in the parish register is the great increase in mortality in 1598, caused by a European plague epidemic. That epidemic was the second in two decades in the Werra region, but there are no surviving records for the earlier outbreak. Grandenborn was struck by the plague epidemic in conjunction with widespread famine, which left many traces in the historical literature of demography.[11] The plague of 1598 can be taken as an example of how a traditional mortality crisis affected the life of the village. Both the severity of the crisis and the long-term impact of the plague were in keeping with the "crisis of the old type" described by Meuvret and Goubert, among others.[12] Grandenborn suffered eighty-nine deaths in the plague, which was dramatically above the average of about nine per year for the previous ten years. This was followed by a rapid recovery: The number of deaths in subsequent years dropped, and the number of baptisms rose. In the ten years after 1598, there were ninety-nine more births than burials, more than enough to replace the eighty-nine people lost in 1598, though, of course, not in the same age configuration. If we assume for heuristic purposes that there was no migration in or out of the village, there were ten more inhabitants in Grandenborn in 1608 than there had been ten years earlier, despite the devastating effects of the plague. The surplus of births over deaths continued through 1618, indicating a continual population increase. In the ten years prior to 1598, Grandenborn averaged twelve baptisms a year; in the ten years afterward, it averaged more than eighteen. Prior to the war, then, Grandenborn was caught in the cycle of crisis and renewal that characterized much of the European countryside before the eighteenth century.

We do not know how severely other villages of the Werra were affected by the epidemic of 1598, but it is likely that many suffered as severely as Grandenborn. Despite the epidemic, there was no dramatic decline in the number of householders anywhere in the Werra region. In *Amt* Sontra, the number of hearth chickens given for each house in the villages remained reasonably stable in the thirty-five years leading up to the war, indicating that the number of householders neither expanded nor declined. The numbers varied from village to village. Königswald had the same number of householders paying hearth chickens in 1618 as it had in 1583. During that same time, Ulfen shrank from 114 to 107 households, and Rockensüß grew from sixty three to sixty seven households.[13] The villages of *Gericht* Boyneburg reported an average gain in the number of householders between 1583 and

1623 of 14.2 percent. There is reason to approach that report with caution, however, because it was produced during the war to describe war damage. There may have been a propensity to exaggerate the size of the village in 1623 so as to accentuate the extent of decline at the time of the report in 1639, but none of the figures seem out of line with the figures for 1583 and the general information on German demography of the late sixteenth century. The view of the village economy that the landgrave had through his administrative documents pointed to growth and prosperity, and he confidently built his policies around the assumption of continued prosperity.

The figures from the *Amt* account books and the landgrave's assessments give a good general impression of the productivity of the region but tell us little about the internal economic practice of the village. How did agricultural production look when viewed from within the village? We have already noted how the formal organization of work on the basis of the household and the centrality of the inheritance of property helped shape economic relations. Both of these were influenced by the fact that the primary economic activity of the village was agriculture. Almost every villager was involved in agriculture in some way, though few were exclusively cultivators. Agricultural activity took place in the fields and gardens that surrounded the village. The land of almost all villagers was of three types, which together characterized the Western European model of rural production: arable, meadow, and garden.[14] Rainer Beck presented an outstanding portrait of the interrelationships between grain production, animal husbandry, and supplementary gardens in the village of Unterfinning in Bavaria.[15] These interrelationships created a distinct village ecology associated with peasant production, Villagers kept animals for fertilizer for three-field crop rotation, which necessitated meadowland that could be used for pasture. The ecological balance of arable land and meadow in the village was firmly established and relatively inflexible. An individual villager could not change his or her mode of cultivation or husbandry without encountering these ecological limits or, more likely, the concerted opposition of fellow villagers. In Beck's presentation, "village economy" acted as an intermediary between "market economy" and "household economy" in defining economic rationality.

The patterns Beck discerned for Bavaria hold for the villages of the Werra as well, though the Werra produced rye and wheat rather than spelt and so had greater potential to participate in the European grain market. Some of the grain produced in the region may have been marketed in Eschwege or Münden, but the main crop was rye rather than the more profitable wheat, and much of it was probably consumed locally.[16] Beck's model of the ecological constraints on production explains the communal character of work in the fields. Working together at harvest and planting was not a product of neighborly love but a necessary component of the rhythm of the seasons and the resources of the village. There was, after all, an optimum time to plant and to harvest, but there were only so many people available to do the work. Three-course crop rotation was enforced by the village because it was the most efficient means of working with the available labor and supplies to produce a good yield. The institution of the *Gemeinde* formalized the system. The village decided collectively when to plant and when to harvest; then the process of negotiating over how to proceed could begin. There is every reason to believe that the negotiations resulted in an informal system of bartered labor that does not appear in any formal records. Those villagers who had the most to barter with—a plow, cart, draft animals, or cash, for example—would be able to recruit others to complete their work first, but then they would help the others.

If all the villagers had possessed exactly the same resources, the communal regulation of the work process at peak seasons would have been less pressing. But, of course, there was differentiation within the village that led to differences in status and access to resources. Since the primary basis of wealth in the village was agriculture, ownership of land was a significant measure of status. It was a measure that villagers could see every day as they labored in the fields. The boundaries of the villages were clearly marked, so the total amount of land available to the villagers was limited. Villagers perceived the fields surrounding the village as one of its distinguishing features, so those villagers who controlled large holdings were distinguished from those who had modest holdings.

Patterns of landholding in the villages of the Werra were complex. A villager's landholdings consisted of small bits of land in open fields.[17] The quality of the land varied from village to village and also within a village, but information on the quality of specific bits of land is no longer available. In earlier centuries, land had been organized in *Hufen*, which were units that were theoretically capable of supporting a large household. One is tempted to assume that the quality of old *Hufen* land was superior to that of later clearings, but the landholdings of villagers often included lands of varying types, not just *Hufen* land. There were two main results of the complicated household dynamics caused by inheritance strategies, individual aggrandizement, and population pressures: *Hufen* land was divided up into smaller pieces, thereby losing its character as the land of the elite, and villagers diversified their landholdings within the village, thereby complicating the structure of *Grundherrschaft* over individuals.

The breakdown of *Hufen* land is a sign that families did not treat specific pieces of property as the site of the lineage, as in a noble estate. In the example cited in the previous chapter, Martin Germerod bought out the other heirs to his wife's inheritance in order to maintain a large holding. But Germerod had no sentimental attachment to particular parcels of land; his objective was to augment his own holdings. Just three years before inheriting the estate of his wife, he had traded his original house for a larger one. When he received the property from his wife's relatives, he quickly broke it up and sold the house and outbuildings to Claus Ruppel that same year.[18] The continuation of the lineage rested on conferring a usable estate to the heirs, not on the preservation of an original holding identified as the site of the lineage. Holding rich land was advantageous, but household-ers participated in an active land market in which the value of each indi-vidual property was well known to all. It is probable that the circulation of large, intact properties was subject to different market forces than were smaller pieces, as was the case in Hohenlohe.[19] The inheritance strategies described in the previous chapter were designed to counteract the forces of the mar-ket in land as well as the disintegrative force of competing interests within the household. But they were only partially successful. For smaller proper-ties, the market for land was available, and villagers were willing to partici-pate in it actively.[20]

The population pressures of the late sixteenth century undoubtedly con-tributed to activity in the land market. Only one out of seventy pieces of property in Reichensachsen identified in the *Salbuch* for *Gericht* Germerode did not change owners between the creation of the book in 1590 and its revision in 1613.[21] Unfortunately, the *Salbuch* rarely reveals how the prop-erty changed hands, but much of it must have been sold. In many cases, the family names attached to the property changed. The rapid movement of pieces of property from one individual to another—indeed, the almost universal willingness to allow land to change hands—indicates that land was frequently treated as a commodity to be traded. The result was a crazy quilt of ownership, especially when population pressures made the transfer of property more prevalent. For one piece of property of 2 *Acker*, three successive owners (Jacob Schreiber, Hans Berwalt, and Lamprecht Treffurt) were listed, and a note in the margin indicates that one of those *Acker* was exchanged in 1610 for "another and better" piece of property.[22] The words "exchanged" and "traded" turned up occasionally in the *Salbuch* to indicate how property changed hands.

The best illustration of how complicated it became to maintain an over-view of who owned what piece of property is in an entry in the *Salbuch* for Germerode, which, although more complex than most, was entirely consistent in format with many other entries in the book on the devolution of property:

Michel Gorgus heirs [crossed out, replaced by] *modo* Reinhart Schmied [crossed out, replaced by] Hans Berwald 609, from house, outbuildings and 1 *Hufe* land of which Hans Wolfthals heirs have $\frac{1}{8}$ *Hufe*, the follow-ing people give for 1 *Malter* of oats: Hans Hell, Claus Schintz [crossed out, replaced by] Hans Weiner and Hans Berwald, Reinhard Schmied [crossed out, replaced by] Curt Beck and Curt Almerod, Augustin Gorgus [crossed out, replaced by] Hans Weiner and Magdalena Schmidt, Hans Weiner, Hans Beck, [added later: Curt Reße *pro* Reinhart Schmid and Hans Gorgus], Henrich Borghardt [crossed out, replaced by] gives Reinhard Schmidts Widow, Curt Hell [crossed out, replaced by] Curt Beck [added later: Hans Gorgus], [added later: Augustin Beck *pro* Gerd Schmids], [added later: Reinhard Schade *pro* Hans Beerwald 612].[23]

A total of twenty individuals with twelve different surnames were associated with this one piece of land in a twenty-year period. The extraordinary fluidity of landholding suggests why villagers labeled land within the boundaries of the village by geographical features and its place in three-field crop rotation rather than by the family names of its owners.

There were other props to the rural economy besides the ownership of land. The other important element of agricultural production was the keeping of animals. There are no lists of animals in the villages until 1639, when the effects of the Thirty Years' War were most dire, but there is ample evidence that there were cows, horses, oxen, pigs, and sheep, which were kept for their role in fertilizing as well as for meat, animal by-products, and muscle power. Almost every house must have had a few chickens and geese as well. There is no sign of dogs or cats in the sources, except for the landgrave's hunting dogs. Horses, oxen, and cattle were the three most essential contributors to the rural economy. Horses were the preferred draft animals, but some villagers used oxen instead. Cattle might also be used to pull a plow, but their primary contribution to the rural economy was manure that could be used to fertilize the fields. There is no evidence that cattle were raised as a primary source of food. Dairying and stock raising never became specialties in the Werra region.

The one animal that was probably raised for market rather than for its contribution to rural production was the sheep. It is also the one that can be found with the least difficulty before the war in the account books for *Amt* Sontra on a regular basis. The number of sheep in the *Amt* fluctuated from year to year but generally ranged between 6,000 and 9,000. Between 1564 and the start of the war, the largest number of sheep occurred in 1618, when there were 9,401; but as recently as 1611, the number of sheep had been only 5,951. No reasons are given for the fluctuations in the numbers, which may have been due to disease or sale for market. Payment of *Triftgeld* for the right to keep sheep on open pasture was the responsibility of individuals in the village rather than the village as a whole, so the decision to keep sheep involved complicated household strategies. Among the striking features of sheep owning in the villages of *Amt* Sontra is that many villagers stopped raising them after one or two years. Between 1606 and 1620, the number of villagers in Rockensüß who owned sheep ranged between six and eleven. Most owned about a hundred head. The largest single flock was 221 sheep owned by Hans Ruppel the Elder in 1612. Hans Ruppel was also the only villager in Rockensüß to own sheep every year from 1606 until 1617. Some villagers owned sheep in an irregular pattern, such as Matthias Eschenborner, who owned sheep in 1606, 1608, and 1610 but not in 1607 or 1609. There is no indication what Eschenborner did with his sheep in those years, though it is possible that ownership of flocks could shift from household to household based on internal economic interests.

Because land and animals were so central to the main activity of the village—agricultural production—they were important measures of social status. But they were not the only measure of status within the village. Any assessment of social distinctions within the village must consider the kinds of work that could confer status as well. The social rankings based on landholdings varied somewhat from village to village, depending on how diverse the economic activities in the village were. The nonagricultural economy of the villages of the Werra was not large, but it did contribute to the overall prosperity. In those villages that were almost entirely devoted to agricultural production for their income, differences in property size had an immediate impact on the productive capacity of households. In villages with a greater variety of economic activity, small landholdings did not necessarily mean an inferior economic position, since a villager could become wealthy from handicrafts, for example. Villagers with large landholdings in those economically diversified villages were not always dependent on agriculture for their wealth. Unfortunately, it is not clear how easily villagers differentiated between land and agricultural production as a source of wealth and as a sign of wealth.

One kind of work that conferred social distinction was that of the educated elite: the pastor and the occasional *Amt* official who resided in the village. They had a different status even though they often participated in agricultural production as well. The social standing of rural pastors could vary greatly even in as small an area as the Werra valley, depending on the quality of the parish under their tutelage. Those who ministered the largest and most prestigious parishes moved in the same social circles as the *Amtmänner*. The pastors in poorer parishes could labor their entire lives and barely get by on the lands allotted to them. The pastor in Thurnhospach pleaded to the landgrave to be transferred elsewhere, his position was so poorly paid that he could raise his children only to be shepherds.[24] It was not unusual for pastors and schoolmasters to slowly work their way up to more prestigious positions through judicious changes of venue within the general vicinity. Israel Göddicke, for example, began as a schoolmaster in Reichensachsen but eventually managed to become a pastor in nearby Lüderbach. Schoolmasters were more likely to be recruited from the villages they served. Even if they came from the outside, they were likely to be from less educated and less respectable backgrounds than the pastors and found it easier to integrate themselves into the village.

Other occupations within the village were more centrally connected to the village economy as a whole. Innkeepers and millers were two of the most prominent trades in the countryside and formed a distinct stratum within the village. They were almost always among the wealthiest villagers because of their trades. When the miller and innkeeper Hans Pipart of

Bischhausen died in 1615, his will divided his large estate among his four children. He bequeathed the mill, worth 1,500 fl, to one of his children and then divided up a 500-fl inn, a 400-fl house, and 2,400 fl of lands among the other three.[25] Lands valued at 2,400 fl must have been extensive, indicating that villagers who became wealthy from their trades expressed it in part through the ownership of large tracts of land. The owner of the main tavern in Abterode, Hans König, was one of the largest landholders in the village as well as one of the most prosperous tradesmen. Because the trades were so profitable, they were carefully regulated by the fiscal interests of the Herrschaft and the towns of the region. Ordinarily, there were only one or two millers or innkeepers in a village. Many villages had none. Both tradesmen paid special fees for the right to run their trades and were granted a local monopoly in exchange. Innkeepers brewed and distilled liquor for sale in their taverns; this put them in conflict with the towns, which sought to protect their exclusive right to export beer and brandy to the villages. Millers faced the constant suspicion of their neighbors, who feared that they were being cheated out of part of their produce during milling. But both innkeepers and millers were amply compensated for their worry.

There were other trades in the village that were just as central to the village economy but provided less income and did not allow for the accumulation of land. Some of those trades were regulated by the guilds of the neighboring town. At least one villager in Amt Sontra joined the linen weavers' guild almost every year from 1580 to 1618. The potters' and tailors' guilds were also actively represented in the Amt. Guild members could be found in every village, though most were concentrated in the largest villages close to Sontra: Ulfen, Breitau, and Rockensüß.[26] Other villagers pursued nonguild trades that were connected to the regional economy in a broader way. Some villages became centers of specialized labor while maintaining an agricultural core. The village of Abterode had a "free district" attached to it that was granted privileges in order to foster coal and copper mining in the area. There were few people in Abterode who were identified primarily as miners, but the existence of mines in the Werra region provided a source of income besides agricultural labor. The occupation that benefited most from mining in the Werra region was transportation. There were some teamsters in Abterode, but the primary concentration of transport workers was in the villages near the saltworks at Allendorf. An individual's trade was important and unusual enough to be used as an additional means of identification in official records. People such as Hans Gercke, teamster, established a role for themselves in the village through the exercise of their trade. Thus, the economy of the village was not exclusively devoted to agriculture. But so long as communal organization was centered on agricultural production, the success of individual artisans was necessarily constrained by the demands of the seasons for agricultural employment.

A constant characteristic of population growth under the old regime was that it increased the amount of rural poverty. The amount of land under cultivation could grow only so much, and then the tendency to subdivide into smaller and smaller units began. The effects of the population increase did not strike all villagers equally. In general, as the number of poor increased, the distinction between rich and poor sharpened as well. That pattern has been observed by Thomas Robisheaux in Hohenlohe, Hermann Rebel in Upper Austria, and Bernd Roeck in Augsburg.[27] A consequence of the increasing distance between rich and poor was that some members of the village used their superior position within the village community and village economy to gain additional benefits for themselves, to the detriment of those in a weaker position.

It is easy enough to assert that there were noticeable gradations of wealth and power in the late sixteenth century within the villages under investigation; it is less easy to demonstrate this concretely. When outside observers spoke of the peasantry, they usually spoke of an undifferentiated mass. The most common designation for inhabitants of the countryside was "common man" or the less gender-specific "poor people."[28] The term "peasant" (Bauer) was often used to speak generically of rural cultivators, though it sometimes had a more specific meaning as well. There was some awareness even among the elite of a distinction between "rich" peasants and "poor" peasants. This distinction is reflected in the literature of the period,[29] but the literature never specified what the difference was—except that one had more wealth than the other—nor how great that difference might be. The parable compiler Otho Melander related several tales of rich and poor peasants in which the rich peasant disdained the poor one.[30] Melander's parables are of interest because he came from Niederhona in the Werra region and used the villages of the region as the site of many of his tales, so the social distinction between rich and poor may have had at least some grounding in his own experiences. But although Melander came from the rural world, his work often lampooned the coarseness and ignorance of the common people. He was interested primarily in depicting the boorishness of the peasantry in order to make didactic points rather than understanding the internal composition of the village. The stereotyped rich peasant was an object of ridicule because he did not show Christian charity to his poorer neighbors. Melander's approach does not contribute to a nuanced understanding of social distinctions within the village, except to remind us that contemporaries recognized that the interests of more successful and less successful peasants could come into conflict.

Villagers themselves, in their correspondence with the central administration, rarely used a vocabulary that highlighted distinctions in social status within the village. As already noted, there were strategic reasons that some villagers wished to portray the village as a homogeneous mass in their correspondence with the landgrave. Villagers used the terms "common man" and "poor people" with much the same lack of differentiation as did the elite. For most villagers, the most potent social distinction was between those individuals who had access to the communal property of the village and those who did not. The status of *Nachbar* was a dividing line between two broad social groups within the village. The physical manifestation of that distinction was possession of a house of one's own, however small and dilapidated that house might be. This guaranteed access to the communal property of the village and ensured that one was somehow contributing to production in the village.

Nevertheless, it is clear that villagers also had means of distinguishing the social status of *Nachbarn*, beyond just describing some as "rich" and others as "poor." The most common terms of social distinction were *Hufenbauer*, *Kötner*, and *Brinksitzer* or some variation on these terms (such as *Hufner*, *Kossaten*, or *Beisassen*). Similar terms were used throughout Germany.[31] In principle, these terms referred to three distinct social groups in the village. The *Hufenbauer* owned the largest tracts of land, sometimes an entire *Hufe*; the *Kötner* owned less land but had some property; and the *Brinksitzer* really did sit on the brink of both the village and the margins of survival. In practice, usage was varied. In the village of Lüderbach, the village was divided into two groups: *Bauern* and *Hintersiedler*.[32] The former group was smaller than the latter and, based on the size of payments for their land, must have been the most prosperous members of the community. In Reichensachen, several villagers labeled themselves *Kötner* in a 1669 letter from "all poor von Eschwege subjects in Reichensachen" in which the supplicants wished to gain an exemption from payments because of their poverty.[33] They must have expected the term to serve as sufficient proof of their comparative impoverishment. In the village of Abterode, there was both *Hufen* land and *Kothofen*, but both sorts of land had been broken up so often by the seventeenth century that many villagers owned little parcels of each.[34] The social distinction implied by the terms may have had some significance in the Middle Ages, but by the seventeenth century the social meaning had been lost; both terms indicated just another block of land in the village's fields. Other villages did not mention *Kothofen* but did distinguish *Hufen* and other more marginal land that had been cleared later in the Middle Ages, called *Rodtacker*.[35] In those villages, ownership of *Hufen* land could go hand in hand with higher status, but this occurred because *Hufen* remained comparatively large tracts of land rather than because the term itself conferred social status. In an eighteenth-century analysis of *Hufen* land in the village of Rockensüß, ownership had become so fragmented that the lands were identified as "torn up" (*zerrissene*) properties.

When we turn from locating the general social designations of different groups within the village to discovering which villagers belonged to which groups, the picture becomes even more complicated. The varieties of *Herrschaft* in the villages make it difficult to determine just how much land and how much movable wealth a household held. The standard accounts of lands covered only those lands subject to a specific *Herrschaft*. These accounts show striking disparities in landholdings between villagers, but this does not guarantee that the small landholders of one account were in fact small landholders in others. Many villagers had a variety of different lands, and official accounts covered only one variety. In many cases, the parcels listed in one account included the greater part of the villager's holdings, but there were exceptions. Eighteenth-century records underscore just how much information is missing for the late sixteenth century because administrators relied on *Salbücher* instead of tax records. The cadastre of Reichensachen from 1754, for example, lists twenty-two different forms of land tenure from various landlords, only three of which appeared in the *Amt* accounts.[36] One villager had land in fourteen different tenures. There is no reason to think that seventeenth-century landholding patterns were any less complex. It is little consolation to historians that the administrators of the seventeenth century faced the same problems of sorting through the different forms of tenure. We cannot rectify the absence of cadastres by adding together different *Salbücher* and *Amt* accounts because too many have disappeared over the centuries.

The links between artisanal activity, agricultural property, convertible wealth, and social standing in the villages of the Werra region were also very complex. Some trades were practiced by *Kötner*, who had a low status; other trades may have enabled a household to join the ranks of the most prominent *Hufenbauer*. Villagers might have recognized these distinctions, but if they did, their recognition is hidden in the available documents. The existence of separate social categories such as *Kötner* and *Hufenbauer* could also mask a continuum from poverty to wealth. The best guide to the distribution of wealth within a village for the prewar era comes from the first years of the war in the village of Abterode.[37] Ninety-two households paid the contribution tax in Abterode in 1624. The contribution was a tax on the total wealth of the villager, so it included the expected return on a trade as well as the value of agricultural property, houses, and movable wealth. The burden was assessed at a flat percentage rate for all villagers, so the amount paid in contribution was directly proportional to the amount of wealth the villager possessed.

It is obvious from the distribution of payments by villagers within Abterode that there was great inequality of wealth (Graph 4.3).[38] The ten wealthiest villagers paid 40.6 percent of the village tax, and the twelve poorest villagers together paid just 1 percent. Because some names were common in the village, several people on the list are identified by nicknames, some of which were based on the trade the villager practiced. All the villagers identified by their trade belonged to the wealthy elite of the village. With the exception of the schoolmaster, who was just over the median wealth for the village, all were among the twelve wealthiest members of the village.

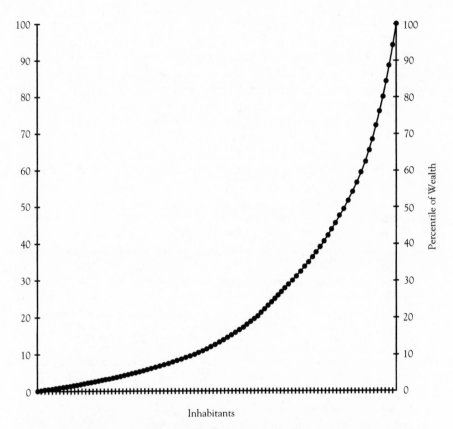

GRAPH 4.3   WEALTH DISTRIBUTION IN ABTERODE, 1624

In Abterode, the miller and innkeeper were the fourth and twelfth wealthiest householders, respectively, but also among the village elite were two teamsters and a blacksmith. The three jurors of the village were among the ten wealthiest villagers. Another striking feature of the distribution of wealth is that two widows were among the twenty wealthiest villagers, but this was an exception to the general situation of widows. There were sixteen female heads of households on the tax list, most of whom were concentrated among the poorest households in the village. Nine of the women were among the twenty-one poorest members of the village: those who paid 1 albus or less in tax.

The relationship between rich and poor in the village takes on another character if we compare the structure of wealth indicated by the contribution of 1624 with a list of landholding in the village from the *Amt* account book for 1630.[39] Eighty-nine householders were mentioned in the account book, with landholdings ranging from more than 1 *Hufe* of land to less than 1 *Acker*. Forty-five of the landholders mentioned were on the contribution register of 1624, and another thirteen have similar names but cannot be positively identified because they used different nicknames. What is most striking is that the upper half of wealth in the 1624 register is almost entirely represented in the 1630 list of landholdings, but the bottom half is only sparsely recorded. Wealth almost invariably was derived from or translated into land, and this contributed to a stable elite of villagers. At the same time, poverty and lack of land were self-perpetuating. It is not clear whether those taxpayers of 1624 who were absent from the 1630 list of land had disappeared from the village or simply never had land to record.

In economic terms, the most crucial boundary in the village was between those who had a good chance of supporting themselves from their own production and those who were in danger of falling into destitution. The lack of complete information makes it difficult to determine where the boundaries for wealthy and poor should be drawn, but there were certainly more poor than wealthy. It seems plausible that the differences between rich and poor led them to react differently within the structure of the village. The inequalities were heightened because the household was the unit that channeled an individual's participation in the economic activity of the village. Social inequality was bound up in the way the communal qualities of the village intersected with the inflexibility of the agricultural economy.

The existence of distinct social groups was not determined solely by objective criteria such as wealth or land, though these contributed to and can be used as indicators of social status in many cases. Such external signs of status were reinforced by the circle of individuals who supported one another in their social activities. To understand the internal dynamic of the village, one must explore how people lived and interacted on a day-to-day basis. Village sociability found expression in communal activities, but its most central feature was the creation of a social environment that is, unfortunately, hidden from the view of historians.[40] A true *Alltagsgeschichte* would have to account for what villagers discussed while working in the fields or around the house or even which villagers worked together, for these were truly the everyday tasks. No one thought to mention these things, however, except in unusual cases. Indeed, the available evidence from the Werra does not conclusively demonstrate many indisputable characteristics of work in the village, such as that villagers adhered rigorously to a three-field planting rotation organized and regulated by the *Gemeinde* as a whole.[41] Our understanding of how villagers interacted is, therefore, limited to formal statements of association that carried specific social roles, such as godparentage, or to breaches in the bounds of normal interaction that produced a response either in the *Gemeinde* or in the legal records. Although neither of these forms of interaction occurred every day in the village, they can help uncover some of the patterns of association that dominated everyday interaction.

The first of these—fictive kinship in the form of godparentage—forms a bridge between ties based on a strict desire to define the lineage and ordinary socializing within the village.[42] It was a formal link, like kinship and household, but it allowed for a wider range of social choices. Choosing a godparent was not a mere formality. The godparent was always mentioned prominently in the parish register next to the name of the father. The tie between the godparent and the child in the act of baptism was made explicit by giving the child the Christian name of his or her godparent.[43] Usually, there was only one godparent for each child, and the godparent was the same sex as the child being baptized. The main exception to the single-godparent rule occurred when the child was illegitimate. In such cases, as many as eight different villagers from different households would serve as godparents, perhaps to create a sense of collective responsibility for someone who was not "properly" connected to the community through a household.

Baptisms were important ceremonies and social occasions for which much of the village gathered. The appearance of the ritual coparent with the biological parents and the child established public ties between families that had nearly the same force as kinship itself. The godparent was expected to provide the child with both spiritual guidance and support in times of need. He or she was also expected to help pay for the baptism ceremony. The pastor in Grandenborn noted the importance of coparenthood because it was associated with one of the sacraments of the church.[44] A parable related by Otho Melander emphasized how important it was to act as a godparent.[45] In the parable, a rich peasant refuses to act as godparent for the child of a deserving poor villager because he wishes to avoid expense (a common enough treatment of rich peasants in the parable literature). The rich peasant is punished for his lack of charity when the prince hears of the case and comes personally to act as godfather to the poor peasant's child. The prince holds a big celebration in honor of the baptism, then presents the bill for the celebration to the rich peasant. The moral of the tale is stated explicitly at the end: It is a Christian duty to act as a godparent to any Christian child when asked.

Although the godparent's general responsibility to see to the Christian education of his or her godchild was certain, the specific actions the godparent took to fulfill that responsibility were less so. The relationship of godparent or godchild was rarely mentioned in the account books, and then only as another tag with which to identify an individual rather than in conjunction with some action taken while acting as godparent. Baptism is the only moment at which the relationship of godparent mattered to the ecclesiastical administration. Presumably, godparents contributed gifts or advice when the children reached confirmation. It is also likely that godparents maintained social contact with the parents of their godchildren and even spent time with the children. This is in keeping with the general descriptions of godparenting that exist, but it is not confirmed by specific instances in sources for the Werra valley. Indeed, one notable characteristic of the work diary of superintendent Hütterodt is the absence of any discussion of godparents.[46] This is in conspicuous contrast to the prominence of godparents in the parish registers.

Whatever the godparent may have contributed to the life of the child, he or she was a symbol of the ties between two families. A critical part of the tie that was confirmed in the sacrament of baptism was giving the godparent's name to the child. This had the pragmatic consequence that, as long as the child lived, the household could call on no other villager with that same first name to act as godparent to other children. Wealthy villagers began to circumvent this problem by using double first names, such as Johann Friedrich, but this did not become commonplace until the eighteenth century. This principle of naming suggests that the selection of a godparent involved careful consideration of several possibilities, since choosing one way might exclude future options.[47] The principle of naming also provided one of the few situations in which women, whose primary positions within the village were as the wives or daughters of heads of households, served as links between two households in a formal capacity on their personal authority.

One sign of the social function of godparentage is in its application to the elites and marginal members of the village. The most obvious social distinction within the village was between the pastor and officials on the one hand and the ordinary villagers on the other. This distinction was reinforced by the choice of godparents by village pastors. When the pastor of Reichensachsen had a daughter in 1640, he asked the daughter of the nobleman Philip Diede zum Fürstenstein to come from Eschwege to stand as godmother.[48] Pastor Ludolph consistently sought high-ranking people from outside the village as fictive kin. When he had a son in 1644, the pastor of Oetmannshausen stood as godfather.[49] A similar pattern existed in Abterode, where there was a greater concentration of officials. When the pastor Franciscus Engelhard had a daughter, the wife of the *Rentmeister* Johann Philipp Arnold stood as godmother. Minister Engelhard stayed with his own social group by acting in turn as godfather to the son of the *Amtmann* of Eschwege/Bilstein, Johann Werner Hattenbach, two years later.[50] Pastors in isolated villages would have had a more difficult time finding godparents of the proper social standing, but in Reichensachsen and Abterode there were few exceptions to the rule of sticking with high-ranking outsiders. Of the seven children born to the pastor of Reichensachsen, only one did not have either a pastor or a noble as godparent, and even that godparent was not a member of the village of Reichensachsen. The distinction drawn between pastors and members of their congregations is starkly evident in the selection of godparents, and the act of choosing reinforced the distinction.

Among ordinary inhabitants of the village, there may have been less need for a demarcation of social strata in the choice of godparents. Johannes

Kunemund was a butcher in Abterode with just over 1 *Acker* of land. Butchers could make a good living in a large village such as Abterode, so his landholdings do not necessarily indicate his true wealth. However, his small holdings limited the ways in which he could participate in the village. The godparents of Kunemund's four children were people he would have been acquainted with from his work. For his son, Kunemund chose Claus Gercke, a fellow butcher, as godfather. Presumably, this choice cemented ties within the community of butchers and may have guaranteed the boy a position as an apprentice when he grew older. The three godmothers were a more diverse group, but they also seem to have been selected on the basis of their social positions. One of the godmothers was the wife of the shepherd, Hans Hasselbach. This choice is curious, since shepherds were sometimes considered dishonorable, but a butcher was likely to have frequent business with a shepherd, and Kunemund may have wished to secure the tie.[51] The two other godmothers were the wife of the village head and the wife of Heinz Hieronymous, a man with no reported landholdings but for whose child Kunemund had stood as godfather four years earlier. The wife of the village head was another curious choice, for hers was a prominent household,— one that easily could have neglected a small landholder like Kunemund. The village head would have been familiar with all the members of the butcher's trade in the village, however, because he had to make sure that the butchers did not violate any of the landgrave's regulations. Kunemund may have been anxious to have such a prominent villager's wife as godmother to compensate for the low status of the shepherd's wife. One might also recall here the parable by Otho Melander about the rich villager who refused the request of the poor villager. Kunemund may have been trying to bring himself to the attention of the village elite. All these interpretations assume the primacy of the husband as head of household in shaping the ties of godparentage, but it is possible that networks of godparentage for female children rested on ties between the women involved rather than the men. In either case, interpersonal relations in the village were filtered through the structure of the household.

The strategy of reciprocal godparentage noted above in the case of Johannes Kunemund and Heinz Hieronymous was also followed by members of the same social strata. Hans Gercke and Johannes Schroeter each held a small to middling amount of land in the village. The two families forged close ties because Gercke's wife, Eulalia, stood as godmother for Schroeter's daughter in 1657.[52] Overall, however, Schroeter cultivated ties to larger landholders than did Gercke. Of the six godparents of Gercke's children, five had landholdings listed, ranging in size from 3 *Acker* 3 *Viertel* to 7 *Acker*. This put them in the same class of landholders as Gercke himself. Of the four godparents of Schroeter's children, Gercke was the only one who belonged to that group. Johannes Schroeter's other ties were to two other families named Schroeter, both of which were larger landholders than Johannes.

Johannes Schroeter may have been cementing ties with more successful branches of his own family. Schroeter was a common name in the village, however, so the similarity of names may have been coincidental.

Johannes Schroeter's and Hans Gercke's households were also active as godparents for other households. In both households, the wife was a god-parent more often than the head of household. This seems to be coincidental or particular to these women rather than a sign that women acted as god-parents more often than men. The sex of the godparent was determined by the sex of the child being baptized. Johannes Schroeter's wife, Anna, was a godmother four times, once in 1658 after she had been widowed. In con-trast, Johannes was a godfather only once. Similarly, Hans Gercke stood as godfather only once, but his wife, Eulalia, was a godmother twice: once for Johannes Schroeter's daughter and once for Hans Schroeter's daughter. Hans Schroeter's sons had acted as godparents for her children in 1641 and 1648.

The distinction between the act of choosing a godparent and being cho-sen as a godparent seems especially consequential when applied to wealthier villagers. Melander's parable of the rich and poor peasants suggests that poor people sought out wealthier villagers to act as godparents for their children.[53] There may have been other principles that guided villagers in the selection of godparents as well. Social pressure may have prompted vil-lagers to choose more or fewer close kin or inhabitants from outside the village. Most godparents were chosen from within the village, but there were one or two godparents chosen from outside the village every year. Unfortunately, villagers themselves never stated for posterity their criteria for choosing. Although relationships of fictive kinship were primarily bonds between individuals and between households and lineages, they also had consequences for the sense of the village. Baptisms were public occasions, and godparentage was understood to be a social duty determined by the values of neighborliness, even between strata within the village. In that sense, godparentage reinforced the existing order by reaffirming the idea of internal harmony through social pressure.

Other forms of social interaction were not as formalized as godparentage. Nonformal interaction is a nebulous topic because, unless it was deemed improper, there is little evidence of it. It is likely that informal associations engendered by age, common skills, or common opposition to others existed.[54] The evidence of ritual hazing of neighbors or other group activities is sparse, but such groups were a logical opportunity for young men to act in concert. There were also places and occasions where members of the village could meet and socialize, either at church or in the tavern over a drink. Lorenz Ludolph, the pastor of Reichensachsen, mentioned the term "friendship" once as a general characteristics of the village in the context of the Thirty Years' War, but he did not go on to explain what the characteristics of friendship were.[55] However elusive the notion might be, the mutual support of people as associates probably played a role in organizing social life.

But enmity was also a powerful force defining social relations.[56] It would be a mistake to assume that all social interaction in the village fostered village unity. We have already discussed how communal organization created a tension between individual goals and the direction of the community. Villagers did not always get along with one another as individuals either, and their quarrels sometimes bubbled to the surface and induced the officials responsible for public order to intervene in the life of the village. The lists of fines imposed on villagers for their transgressions are one of the richest sources for analyzing interpersonal relations in the village, in part because they indicate where villagers deviated from the accepted norms of behavior.

It is tempting to describe the incidents in the lists of fines as examples of social tension. Their sheer numbers demonstrate that violent altercations occurred regularly in the village. Fights were a component of the society in which villagers lived; this makes them a social phenomenon but does not mean that they are a product of social stratification. Thus, the term "social tensions" is used in the broad sense of frequent and sometimes violent disputes between villagers rather than in the specific sense of underlying conflict between strata or cliques. The notion of enmity as an organizing principle of interaction was related more closely to personal relations than social-structural relations.

Robert Muchembled's survey of violent crime in Picardy showed that most crimes took place in very specific circumstances.[57] They usually took place in the evening; they involved young men, many of whom were unmarried; and they usually took place while the participants were drinking in a tavern. This is a likely model for the crimes of the Werra region as well. But Muchembled's concern was primarily with capital crimes. What is notable about the criminality of the Werra region is that it was only rarely so violent that it led to capital cases. Small-scale violence was fairly common, but manslaughter or murder was rare. High fines and perhaps an aversion to deadly violence sufficed to keep altercations within certain bounds. The difference between the relative acceptance of petty violence and the utter rejection of dangerous violence can be seen in the stiff fines for the few incidences of the latter. Ordinarily, a fight in which one of the participants was made "blue and bloody" was punished with a fine of 1 to 3 fl.[58] Infliction of a crippling injury incurred a much higher fine. Hans Rubesam was fined 10 fl, the cost of a cow, for hitting Martin Kielholz so that his arm was crippled.[59] Heimbrot and Hans Bornscheuer were fined 30 fl for shattering the arm of the *Hofmann* of Hundelshausen, even though he provoked them.[60] Life-threatening attacks were treated as severely as crippling attacks. Caspar and Hans Stebell of Rockensüß were fined 20 fl because they stabbed Hans Schellhase "nearly dead."[61]

The court drew a distinction between genuinely dangerous violence and the petty violence of everyday interaction. Villagers themselves also seem to have been aware of the difference and only rarely allowed their anger to flare up dangerously. But even though villagers managed to control their violence to avoid deadly wounds, their fights were not mere rituals. Assaulters grabbed any object to use as a weapon. Knives, stones, beer mugs, axes, rakes, whips, pitchforks, and hoes were all mentioned as weapons used in fights in Amt Sontra. Many of these could have produced life-threatening injuries. The paucity of instances of crippling or deadly wounds may be attributable to the ability of assaulters to discern when to stop their attacks or to the intervention of other villagers who kept the assaults from getting out of hand. In either case, the result of a typical assault was a severe beating but not an injury that would threaten an individual's ability to provide for the household.

Most outbreaks of violence were random events. One villager provoked another in some way, and the provocation quickly escalated to a fight. Alcohol consumption often contributed to quick tempers. Sometimes, however, the pattern to the violence suggests that it was the product of something other than just a quick temper. The case of Blum Sontag in Königswald is illustrative. Sontag was a very unpopular man in his home village in 1607. There is nothing to indicate why he was so unpopular, but the increasing violence and the increasing fines paid for crimes against him show that he could be protected from assault only by the active intervention of the landgrave's courts. The incidents began in an ordinary manner: Martin Gliem was fined 1 fl 4 albus for beating Blum Sontag "blue and bloody."[62] This was a common offense, and the fine was a common penalty for it. At that point, the assault seemed like a random act of anger. Shortly thereafter, however, Hans Holzheuer was fined 3 fl "because of the insults and slanderous words he used about Blum Sontag." This fine was higher than the one for the beating, and it was becoming increasingly clear that Sontag was being attacked by several people. Later that year, Heimbrot Ulrich and Hans Seitz were fined 20 fl for beating Sontag and his wife and then running away, leaving them lying in the street. There are no further cases of assault on Blum Sontag after that. The stiff fine probably put an end to the physical intimidation of Sontag, but no doubt his life in the village continued to be uncomfortable. The last fine was so high to stop the escalating violance and because the injured people lying in the street could have died of exposure and untreated wounds. Whatever animus Martin Gliem and Hans Seitz shared against Sontag was not enough to keep them permanent allies. Ten years after the attacks on Sontag, Hans Seitz was fined 2 fl for hitting Martin Gliem, and Martin Gliem was fined 1 fl for fighting back.[63]

Fights were an obvious manifestation of tensions in the village, but equally obvious—and more indicative of the values of the villagers—were the insults they threw at one another. Most often, the fines did not specify what one villager said to another. The compilers of the lists did, however, use several different phrases to describe how insults were given. Most often, the insulter was described as having "rebuked" or "slandered" his victim. Sometimes more elaborate descriptions were used, such as when a villager approached another "with inappropriate (or uncouth or useless) words" and similar formulas.[64] The phrase that best captured the essence of what an insult meant was "attacked with defamatory (*ehrrührig*) words." Honor was at the core of all insults. The purpose of the fines was to protect the honorable reputation of the person being rebuked. Any statement about a person's reputation was treated as public testimony; when a slanderer called someone dishonorable, it was a direct attack on his or her public face. Attacks on a person's honor were treated as seriously as attacks on his or her body. Thus, in the town of Sontra, David Geilfus was fined 1 fl 4 albus for beating Hans Weissenborn, but Weissenborn was fined 3 fl "because he gave cause to the fight with the slanders he poured out, that Geilfus's father had not paid him properly."[65] The insult was severe enough that it merited a greater fine than the violence that followed.

The person making insults was aware of the public character of his or her accusation. At least for a moment, an adversary might be lowered in the esteem of others. Insults were an attack on honor, which placed the person attacked outside the bounds of village society. When fines did mention the specific insult used, the most frequent accusation against a man was that he was a "rogue" (*Schelm*). The insult carried with it connotations of uprootedness and thievery, perhaps even highway robbery. It could be redoubled by claiming that the man was a "born rogue" (*blut Schelm*) who could never have access to village society. When a woman was insulted, she was most often called a "whore" (*Hure*). This did not mean a prostitute in the sense of taking money, but it did connote a loose woman who slept with men out of wedlock. When the insult was directed at a married woman it struck at the core of her identity in the household.[66] The reputations of both men and women shaped ties within the village. An insult undermined the basis of those ties by calling a reputation into question. For this reason, insults were punished by the village in the landgrave's courts. The tensions that gave rise to the insult had to find a different outlet to be resolved by the community.

There is no simple explanation why some village tensions led to violence while others remained at the level of insults. Villagers recognized that there were limits to how both could be used. It is striking that village officials— especially the *Schultheiß*, but also the pastor and court officials—were among the most frequent victims of insults but were almost never physically abused. Their ambiguous position in relation to other villagers made them natural targets for accusations of dishonorability, but physical assault on an official brought a substantial fine. The absence of assaults on village officials suggests that physical and verbal attacks were controllable and were directed toward specific issues. In many instances, one villager went up to the house of another and "challenged" (*herausgefordert*) his neighbor. We cannot know how many of these altercations were premeditated and how many were spontaneous. The close living conditions and constant pressure for con-formity provided ample opportunity for irritations that could either flare up immediately or simmer for a while before leading to a fight. In both circumstances, however, the fight that resulted was the product of a tension within the village that recurred regularly between many different villagers.

We know that some villagers were wealthier than others and that some possessed more land and had greater access to positions of power than oth-ers. Yet social stratification influenced the structure of the village only insofar as villagers took notice of it in their actions with one another. The survey of the choice of godparents in the parish registers indicates that members of the same stratum tended to stick together in that social activ-ity, thus reinforcing the social distinctions of the strata. As the evidence for the largest landholders indicates, this was not a hard-and-fast rule but a propensity. Nor is there any reason that the different strata of the village should have been isolated from one another. The wealthier members of the village had means of maintaining their status other than by avoiding poorer members on a social level. In times of dearth, villagers would be quite aware of distinctions of wealth and security. The social environment of the vil-lage was futher complicated by endemic tensions and irritations that erupted in fights and insults. These tensions need not have been a result of the social distinctions, though some probably were. Recourse to violence and insults was more often the product of the constant close contact between individuals and the limited range of social activity. Life in the village in-volved a complex interplay of tensions and solidarities that were embedded in a formally ill-defined but widely understood system of strata formed by landholding and wealth.

Instability and fear were constants for villagers in seventeenth-century Germany. The "outside world" was threatening in so many ways, whether by the effects of climate or disease or the penetration of state authority into a delicately balanced social network.[67] The Werra region remained rela-tively impervious to the most obvious manifestations of those fears, such as witch crazes and pogroms, though there was no shortage of fear of the super-natural or of outsiders. The Werra also managed to escape the most disrup-tive elements of the apocalyptic horsemen: war, disease, famine, and death. There was, therefore, a certain continuity to the internal development of the villages of the Werra. The Netherlands and France had been ravaged by troops throughout the late sixteenth century, and even some parts of the Holy Roman Empire had been subject to small-scale military actions but in 1618, the villages of the Werra had not experienced warfare in the lifetimes of their inhabitants. That, of course, changed in the years after-ward. What were the consequences of this new phenomenon for the social, cultural, and political order? The following chapters pick up that theme and chart the war's transformational power.

Notes

1. Two interesting theoretical statements that emphasize the link between market and household economies, even as they present competing models of autonomy and risk avoidance, are Heide Wunder, "Finance in the 'Economy of Old Europe': The Example of Peasant Credit from the Late Middle Ages to the Thirty Years War," in Peter-Christian Witt, *Wealth and Taxation in Central Europe* (Leamington Spa, 1987), 19–47, especially 44; and William Roseberry, "Domestic Modes, Domesticated Models," *Journal of Historical Sociology* 1 (1988): 423–30. A forceful and effective statement of the inadequacy of the opposition of kin-oriented and market-oriented models of economic activity is David Sabean, *Property, Production, and Family in Neckarhausen, 1700–1870* (Cambridge, 1991).
2. See Table 1.1.
3. Hessian State Archives, Marburg (StAM) Rech II Sontra 3.
4. This led to tensions when an *Amtmann* or *Rentmeister* died with the accounts out of balance. The official's heirs were held responsible for the deficit, which could lead to lengthy wrangling over the inheritance. See, for example, StAM Rech II Eschwege 10.
5. Wilhelm Abel, *Agricultural Fluctuations in Europe from the Thirteenth to the Twentieth Centuries* (New York, 1980), 91–146.
6. There are many surveys of the economic effects of the war that discuss the issue of conditions before the war. The issues are delineated nicely by Theodore Rabb, "The Effects of the Thirty Years' War on the German Economy," *Journal of Modern History* 34 (1962): 40–51, but he does not arrive at a resolution of the issue. Almost any German dissertation on the subject begins with the historiography of this question. See especially Ingomar Bog, *Die Bäuerliche Wirtschaft im Zeitalter des Dreißigjährigen Krieges* (Coburg, 1952).
7. Compare Abel, *Agricultural Fluctuations*, 147–57, and Friedrich Lütge, "Die Wirtschaftliche Lage Deutschlands vor Ausbruch des Dreißigjährigen Krieges," in Friedrich Lütge, *Studien zur Sozial- und Wirtschaftsgeschichte* (Stuttgart, 1963) 336–95.
8. *Amt* Eschwege/Bilstein grew 63.9 percent, from an average of 1175.8 fl in 1581–1585 to 1927.8 fl in 1606–1610; *Amt* Sontra grew 49.1 percent, from 369.8 in 1580–1584 to 551.4 in 1606–1610; *Amt* Wanfried grew 61.3 percent from 138.6 in 1580–1584 to 229.6 in 1606–1610.
9. Pfarrarchiv Renda, Ki Grandenborn.
10. The village was small enough that it is plausible that no one would die in a given year. Prior to the war, there was one year with no burials. In 1618, just two people were buried.
11. Andrew Appleby, *Famine in Tudor and Stuart England* (Stanford, 1978), 109–54.
12. Jean Meuvret, "Les Crises de Subsistances et la Démographie de la France d'Ancien Regime," *Population* 1 (1946): 643–50; Pierre Goubert, "En Beauvaisis: Problémes démographiques du XVIIe siécle," in Pierre Goubert, *Clio Parmi les Hommes* (Paris, 1976), 141–59. Meuvret and Goubert understood the crisis to be a product of food shortages—thus the name "subsistence crisis." Other demographers and historians have attacked the Meuvret-Goubert model by insisting that an epidemic mortality crisis could take place without the presence of a "subsistence crisis," or at least without famine acting as a catalyst. The significance of Goubert's model and the range of criticisms are carefully presented in Arthur Imhof, *Einführung in die Historische Demographie* (Munich, 1977), 15–18, 46–49; and Jacques Dupâquire, *Pour la Démographie Historique* (Paris, 1984).

According to Imhof and Dupâquier, the issue revolves around how the crisis gets started rather than how the demographic system compensates for losses brought about by the crisis. Although this issue is not irrelevant to the discussion that follows, it distracts from what seems to be a lasting contribution of Goubert's model, which is the elucidation of a cycle of crisis and recovery that operates regardless of the ultimate cause of the mortality. The postcrisis recovery seems to be as much a part of the "crisis of the old type" as the fluctuations in grain production that ostensibly caused it.

13. StAM Rech II Sontra 3, 1618.

14. In general, see Wilhelm Abel, *Die Geschichte der Deutschen Landwirtschaft vom frühen Mittelalter bis zum 19. Jahrhundert*, 3d ed. (Stuttgart, 1978), and B. H. Slicher van Bath, *The Agrarian History of Western Europe, 500–1850* (London, 1963).

15. Rainer Beck, *Naturaler Ökonomie: Unterfinning: Bäuerliche Wirtschaft in einem Oberbayerischen Dorf* (Munich, 1986).

16. On the other hand, rye was more marketable than the spelt that was commonly grown in southern Germany. Compare Beck, *Naturaler Ökonomie*, and Thomas Robisheaux, *Rural Society and the Search for Order in Early Modern Germany* (Cambridge, 1989).

17. There is no basic work on open fields in Hesse. On open-field scattering of parcels, see Donald McCloskey, "English Open Fields as a Behavior towards Risk," in P. Uselding, ed., *Research in Economic History* (Greenwich, 1976), 124–70. There is evidence that scattering was caused not only by how peasants worked and inherited the land but also by how *Grundherrschaft* itself was splintered. See Martin Born, *Siedlungsgenese und Kulturlandschaftsentwicklung in Mitteleuropa* (Wiesbaden, 1980), and *Studien zur Spätmittelalterlichen und Neuzeitlichen Siedlungsentwicklung im Nordhessen* (Marburg, 1970).

18. StAM Rech II Sontra 3, 1610.

19. Robisheaux, *Rural Society*.

20. Robisheaux, *Rural Society*, 79–91, provides the best recent introduction to the land market. More generally, see Alan Macfarlane, *The Origins of English Individualism* (Oxford, 1978). Macfarlane notes the openness of the land market in England and takes it as evidence that England was not a "peasant society."

21. StAM S 240.

22. Ibid.

23. Ibid.

24. StAM 22a 8.27 Thurnhospach.

25. StAM 17e Bischhausen 59, 6/7/1615.

26. StAM Rech II Sontra 3.

27. Robisheaux, *Rural Society*; Hermann Rebel, *Peasant Classes: The Bureaucratization of Property and Family Relations under Early Hapsburg Absolutism, 1511–1636* (Princeton, 1983); Bernd Roeck, *Eine Stadt in Krieg und Frieden* (Göttingen, 1989).

28. The term "common man" has become a central category for the investigation of the reception of the Reformation due to the many works of Peter Blickle. Peter Blickle, *The Revolution of 1525* (Baltimore, 1982). An effective critique of the gendered quality of Blickle's analysis, with some interesting reflections on the multiple meanings of the root "common," is Lyndal Roper, "'Common Man,' 'Common Women,' and the 'Common Good': Gender and Meaning in the German Reformation Commune," *Social History* 12 (1987):1–22.

29. See Kurt Uhrig, "Der Bauer in der Publizistik der Reformation bis zum Ausgang des Bauernkrieges," *Archiv für Reformationsgeschichte* 33 (1936): 70–125; Hans Dieter Gebauer, *Grimmelshausens Bauerndarstellung: Literarische Sozialkritik und*

ihr Publikum (Marburg, 1977), 1–18; and especially Renate Haftlmeier-Seiffert, *Bauerndarstellung auf deutschen illustrierten Flugblättern des 17. Jahrhunderts* (Frankfurt am Main, 1991).

30. Otho Melander, *Joco-Seria Das ist / Schimpff und Ernst: Darinn nicht allein nützliche un denckwurdige / sondern auch anmutige und lustige Historien erzehlet und Beschrieben werden*, 2 parts in 1 vol. (Darmstadt, 1617).

31. See Alan Mayhew, *Rural Settlement and Farming in Germany* (New York, 1973).

32. StAM S 590.

33. StAM 17e Reichensachsen 18.

34. StAM Rech II Eschwege 10, Abterode. It is not immediately obvious what *Kothofen* are. According to Vilmar, the term *Hof* in the Werra region meant garden rather than courtyard; *Kot* was related to *Koden* or *Köter*—cottager. At first *Koden* referred to those who had no land at all, but it quickly came to designate those who had small tracts of land but not full Hufen. A. F. C. Vilmar, *Idiotikon von Kurhessen*, 2d ed. (Wiesbaden 1969), 214–15, 172.

35. StAM Rech II Sontra 3.

36. StAM Kat Reichensachsen B9.

37. StAM Rech II Abterode 1, 1624.

38. Compare Robisheaux, *Rural Society*, 68–91, on the inequality of wealth in the villages of Hohenlohe.

39. StAM Rech II Eschwege 8, 1630. It is, unfortunately, not certain that the list is actually from 1630. Some of the vagaries of the accounting procedure that make it difficult to pin down the precise year have already been discussed. The list is from the same general time period, as the overlap of names demonstrates.

40. On the idea of "sociability" in the early modern village, see Jean-Pierre Gutton, *La Sociabilité Villageoise dans L'Ancienne France* (Paris, 1976).

41. Beck, *Naturaler Ökonomie*, 64–74, demonstrates convincingly that cooperation at the level of the *Gemeinde* was essential for the ecological integrity of production in the fields. There is no reason to doubt that the same ecological logic applied to the villages of the Werra, but there is no concrete evidence that it did.

42. For an important statement on the relation of godparentage to kinship and property relations, see John Bossy, "Kinship, Community and Christianity in Western Europe from the Fourteenth to the Seventeenth Centuries," in Derek Baker, ed., *Sanctity and Secularity: The Church and the World* (Oxford, 1973), 129–43. See also Sidney Mintz and Eric Wolf, "An Analysis of Ritual Co-Parenthood (*Compazdrago*)," in Jack Potter, May Diaz, and George Foster, eds., *Peasant Society: A Reader* (Boston, 1967), 174–99, for an overview of the development of ritual coparenthood in Western society. Coparenthood is an apt name for the act of participating in the baptism of the child. In the parish registers, the godparent is called *compater* or *Gevatter*.

43. Pfarrarchiv Renda, Ki Grandenborn.

44. He gave an account of the origins of the practice in the margins of the parish register. See Ki Grandenborn 1587–1669. "Die Gevatterschaft ist aufkommen 140 Jahren nach Christi unser Herren geburt und ist der Coste gewessen ein Bischoff Higinus" ("Godparentage began 140 years after Christ's birth and the first officiating clergy was one bishop Higinus").

45. Melander, *Joco-Seria*, 155–56.

46. Wilm Sippel, ed., *Forschungsberichte der Stiftung Sippel*, vol. 5 (Göttingen, 1981), passim, refers to one individual as *Gevatter* but never investigates instances of conflict over godparentage.

47. It was rare, but not unheard of, for two living children in the same family to

have the same name, possibly due to marrying in rather than parental choice. It was quite common, however, for parents to give a child the same name as one of their deceased children.

48. StAM Ki Reichensachsen.
49. Ibid.
50. Ki Abterode.
51. Shepherding was almost universally recognized as a "dishonorable" trade. See, for example, Mack Walker, *German Home Towns: Community, State and General Estate, 1648–1871*(Ithaca, NY, 1971), 104, and Rudolf Wissel, *Das Alte Handwerks Recht und Gewohnheiten*, vol.1 (Berlin, 1971), 172–83.
52. Ki Abterode.
53. See Melander, *Joco-Seria*, 155–56.
54. Arthur Imhof, *Die Verlorene Welten: Alltagsbewältigung durch unsere Vorfahren und Weshalb wir uns heute so schwer damit tun* (Munich, 1984), 41–50, tries to recapture the network of friends that Johannes Hooss may have had while growing up in the small village of Leimbach.
55. StAM Ki Reichensachsen 1639–1654.
56. See, in particular, David Sabean, *Power in the Blood: Popular Culture and Village Discourse in Early Modern Germany* (Cambridge, 1984), 31–34.
57. Robert Muchembled, *La Violence au Village (XVe–XVII Siécle)* (Turnhout, 1989).
58. Ilse Gromes, ed., *Bußen aus den Amtsrechnungen des Amtes Sontra 1590–1648* (Sontra, 1977), 30.
59. Ibid.
60. Ibid., 26.
61. Ibid., 10.
62. Ibid., 25.
63. Ibid., 51.
64. Ibid., passim. The standard terms are *gescholten* (scolded), *geschmähet*, (slandered), or *injurirt* (damaged). The formula is sometimes *mit ungebührlichen Wörter angefahren* (approached with inappropriate words) or *mit ehrrührigen Wörter angegriffen* (attacked with defamatory words).
65. Ibid., 60.
66. For an elaboration on this idea, see Sabean, *Property*, 139–46.
67. For two perspectives on the notions of fear and insecurity in the lives of villagers, see Jürgen Kuczynski, *Geschichte des Alltags des Deutschen Volkes, Vol 1., 1600–1650* (Cologne, 1981), 124–45, in which one chapter concludes with the observation, "Angst, Angst und Angst"; and the more general survey by Jean Delumeau, *La Peur en Occident (XIV–XVIIIe siécles): Une cité assiégé* (Paris, 1978), 31–74.

Part III

External and Internal Crisis

5

War Comes to the Village

The Papists are not merely undertaking simple and common
marches, but rather persistent invasions and executions against
one and another Evangelical territory, whereby one cannot
fail to see that it leads to a religious war in Germany.
—Landgrave Moritz, January 1619[1]

The fate of the Werra region during the Thirty Years' War was determined
primarily by two things: Hesse-Kassel's strategic location in the center of
the Holy Roman Empire and Landgrave Moritz's firm adherence to the
Protestant cause.[2] The region was threatened with invasion in 1621 and
was invaded and occupied for the first time in 1623. Nearly every year
thereafter, the region was occupied by troops for some length of time, marched
through by troops headed to some other destination, or threatened with
invasion. The Werra region was, therefore, one of the first parts of Germany to feel the impact of the war and one of the most frequent victims of
its depredations for the rest of its course.

The general contours of the war have been described many times in both
broad surveys and specialized works, but those general contours hide as much
as they reveal about the experiences of small states such as Hesse-Kassel.
Traditionally, historians divide the war into "phases," which are named
according to the leading power of the Protestant coalition against the
Hapsburgs.[3] The first phase, from 1618 to 1621, is usually called the Bohemian phase, because the key Protestant force was the rebel nobility of Bohemia and their newly elected king, Friedrich V of the Palatinate, and most
of the fighting took place in Bohemia itself. That phase ended when the
Bohemian rebels were crushed at the Battle of White Mountain in 1620.

Sometimes the Bohemian phase is included as part of a larger Bohemian-
Palatine phase that lasted until 1625, since the immediate consequence of
the collapse of the Bohemian rebellion was that the war's center of gravity
shifted to the west of the empire, where Friedrich, the "Winter King," was
punished for his decision to accept the Bohemian crown. Alternatively, the
defeat of the Bohemians is said to inaugurate a new Dutch-Palatine phase

134

from 1621 to 1625. The expiration of the Twelve Years' Truce between Spain and the Netherlands and the declaration of the ban on Friedrich V brought together a new coalition, which fought with armies raised by Protestant adventurers such as Christian of Halberstadt, Georg Friedrich of Baden, and Ernst of Mansfeld. The emperor's allies, most notably Duke Maximilian of Bavaria and the Catholic League, continued their successes after White Mountain, as each of the Protestant forces was defeated in turn. The Palatinate was occupied by Catholic troops and turned over to Maximilian as partial repayment of his support of the emperor.

As the situation looked increasingly desperate for the Protestants, King Christian IV of Denmark intervened, beginning the Danish–Lower Saxon phase of the war, which lasted from 1626 to 1629. The war's center of gravity shifted to northern Germany, and the intensity of the struggle increased with the creation of a new army under the command of Albrecht von Wallenstein. The emperor's forces once again inflicted a series of defeats on the Protestant forces and forced Christian to withdraw from the war in the Peace of Lübeck. The emperor's victory seemed so complete that he issued the Edict of Restitution to cap the Catholic triumph. But he was unable to savor his triumph for long, because a new Protestant champion arrived on the scene: King Gustavus Adolphus of Sweden.

The Swedish phase, from 1630 to 1635, turned the tide of the war. A string of Swedish victories shifted the main theater of war from the Protestant north and center to the Catholic south. After Gustavus Adolphus's death in battle in 1632, the momentum of Swedish advance stalled, and the war drifted more and more into a general stalemate, with the center of gravity changing from year to year. When Swedish actions began to flag, Richelieu decided that France could no longer stand in the background. He brought French forces against the armies of the Hapsburgs in 1635, inaugurating the last, French, phase of the war. The French phase was the most desultory and in many respects the most destructive part of the war. Almost all parts of the empire continued to be plagued with marauding troops.

Although the framework of distinct phases has some logic, one of the features of this war that distinguished it from previous long, drawn-out conflicts was that competing armies remained in the field without break for all thirty years. Few villagers, therefore, would have thought to divide the war into phases. The continual presence of armies in the field meant that even the lulls between phases had military ramifications for small states such as Hesse-Kassel. Naturally, the failures and successes of the leading power in the Protestant coalition made a staunchly Protestant power like Hesse-Kassel more or less vulnerable to invasion, but the danger of invasion depended much more on how Moritz and his successors pursued their own policies.

Technically, Moritz remained neutral at the beginning of the Bohemian phase of the war. His professed neutrality was primarily a strategy to deny the emperor's forces marching routes through his territory. Armies were forbidden by imperial custom to march through the territories of noncombatants without permission. At first, all armies made a pretense of adhering to that custom. Moritz referred requests for a right to pass, along with his own observations on the pros and cons of allowing the passage, to his council for discussion.[4] Not surprisingly, Moritz rarely granted permission to Catholic armies. But the emperor and his allies found a means of circumventing Moritz's intransigence by appealing directly to the territorial nobility, who were willing to grant permission in exchange for promises that their property and privileges would be protected. That strategy was to become a constant feature of the war and was institutionalized in the granting of *salva guardia*.

No one was fooled by Moritz's profession of neutrality; it was clear which side he supported. Moritz had actively solicited international support for Protestant principalities against the Hapsburgs from the beginning of his reign. He was a major instigator of the Protestant Union, which was designed to provide the Protestants with a military force strong enough to resist the armies of the Catholic powers. His correspondence with the administrators of his territory and his Estates between 1600 and the start of the war is replete with warnings about the impending danger of war.[5] Unlike Johann Georg of Saxony or Ludwig of Hesse-Darmstadt, who also ruled Protestant territories, Moritz did not denounce the Bohemian rebels or support the emperor's efforts to suppress them. Behind the scenes, he lent diplomatic support to Friedrich V and supported Christian of Halberstadt, Ernst of Mansfeld, and Bernhard of Weimar in their efforts to raise independent Protestant armies.

Hesse-Kassel moved from secret to open resistance to the emperor after the *Reichshofrat* resolved the disputed succession of Hesse-Marburg against Moritz in 1623. The court ruled that Moritz's *Verbesserungspunkte* violated the terms of Landgrave Ludwig's testament of 1595, which called for the maintenance of orthodox Lutheranism in Hesse-Marburg, and ordered that the entire territory be given to Hesse-Darmstadt.[6] To compound the indignity for Moritz, the court ordered that Hesse-Kassel pay an indemnity to Hesse-Darmstadt for the time that it had improperly occupied the territory. The emperor was eager to enforce the decision of the *Reichshofrat* and support his ally Ludwig, so there was little reason for Moritz to remain behind the facade of neutrality. The dispute with Hesse-Darmstadt and its political consequences were to make Hesse-Kassel the most consistent opponent of the emperor for the rest of the war.

But Hesse-Kassel was ill equipped to defy the emperor and *Reichshofrat*. In the absence of a grand anti-Hapsburg coalition, Moritz had to rely on his own resources for defense. In 1600, Moritz had begun to restructure the military of the territory on the basis of locally recruited militias.[7] He embraced the theoretical works of Maurice of Nassau and used them to justify the rejection of mercenary forces and to assert the value of militias. He built an administrative framework for recruitment of officers and soldiers on the basis of four "quarters" of Hesse, each named for a river. That system allowed him to raise a force of 5,300 infantry and 1,390 cavalry by 1623.[8]

The militia was designed for defense of the territory as a whole rather than the region where it was recruited. Villages had no organized means of defense aside from the forces raised by the landgrave; they had to fend for themselves. Moritz seems to have assumed that territorial nobles would adopt a military role when danger came and act as local military enterprisers to defend their lands. At any rate, he kept lists of those noblemen who "kept themselves prepared militarily."[9] The lists were generally short. When the council received a report that the von Boyneburg family was beginning to stockpile weapons in 1622, the council members asked sarcastically "whether they are also making other war preparations, more as a joke than seriously.[10]

Neither the preparations of the nobility nor the militia availed the Werra region when confronted with a well-organized force. Both the nobility and militia were quickly pushed aside, and they retreated to the comparative security of walled towns. There were periodic attempts to revive the militia after its initial failure, but it never became an effective fighting force. The army that Hesse was able to field after 1627 relied much more on mercenary recruitment than local mustering. It was designed to be an instrument for political maneuvers rather than territorial defense. During some of the most brutal years of the war, the landgrave used the army to invade Westphalia, even while imperial troops invaded Hesse itself.

The failure of the militia was complete, but the reasons for that failure were disputed. Even militias had to be supplied and paid, and that cost money. Although Moritz had built up a "finance state" from the more efficient exploitation of his seigneurial revenues, he was still dependent on the territorial Estates for the large grants that were necessary to keep the Hessian army active. He could not keep the army in the field more than a few weeks without the cooperation of the Estates. But the most powerful group in the Estates, the nobility, had been unwilling to grant anything before the war, as the negotiations and resolutions of the Hessian diets held prior to 1620 show.[11] They continued to be unwilling to grant anything once the war began. The nobility of the Werra was even more obdurate in its opposition to Moritz's plans than was the nobility of other regions, perhaps in response to Moritz's introduction of the *Verbesserungspunkte* into the Werra against their will.[12] The result was that Moritz continued to pursue an ambitious external policy that was not supported by a unified internal administration. While Moritz pressed for more troops to defend Hesse against the Catholic threat, the nobility pressed Moritz to demobilize the troops that he had raised and negotiate with the Catholics, even as Spinola's troops were on the Hessian border.[13] Moritz's struggle with the Hessian Estates epitomized the sort of struggle that occurred in the internal politics of most

German principalities in the early modern period—between a ruler who wished to consolidate his central authority through a standing army and a nobility that wished to defend its privileges through control over taxation within the territory.[14] But his inability to move the Estates to support his policies weakened his already overreaching foreign policy.

The struggle between the landgrave and the Estates over the resources of the territory became a sidelight once it became apparent what military occupation meant. Logistics compelled troops on all sides of the Thirty Years' War to live off the territory that they occupied. In theory, the terms of this exploitation were regulated by a "provisions ordinance," which was designed to regularize payments and set limits on what was permissible by local commanders. It was a common procedure to billet troops in one district and to demand that the houses where they were billeted supply oil or candles, wood, and salt directly to the soldiers, along with the standard tax—the contribution—to the treasury of the occupying force.[15] The line between contributions, usually "granted" through the acceptance of a salva guardia, and extortion was very fluid. The contribution could be extracted by the troops directly and flowed to both the soldiers of the landgrave and his enemies. In order to fix the burden of the contribution through the salva guardia, an informal pattern quickly developed in which the different levels of the hierarchy within the army negotiated with corresponding levels of the administrative hierarchy within the territory. The commanders of the Catholic armies, Tilly and Wallenstein, negotiated directly with Landgrave Moritz or the Hessian Estates specifically, and commanders of individual companies negotiated with Amtmänner. Individual soldiers dealt with individual villagers. Communication at the highest level was concerned with establishing the general guidelines for occupation, especially the provisions that the local population was to provide for the troops and staff. The execution of those guidelines was left to the local commanders and the Amtmänner. This system of negotiation made it possible to get contributions from districts that were not under direct military occupation, while maintaining a veneer of legitimacy over the landgrave's own authority.

Villagers, of course, neither contributed to making Moritz's policy nor figured in his calculations of the potential costs of the policy. But they did serve as one of the main props of the war effort. In order to understand how the Thirty Years' War affected the villages of the Werra region, one must first examine how the war manifested itself at the local level. A first approach is a simple chronicle of the comings and goings of troops and the steps villagers took to respond to them. But we must also investigate how the fate of the locality was bound up with the attempts of Herrschaft to come to grips with the same forces against which the villagers were struggling. Such an investigation leads to a discussion of how villagers made sense of the experiences of the war and tried to shape them to their own needs in increasingly desperate circumstances. This chapter, therefore, traces three parallel narratives: Hesse-Kassel's maneuvering in the complicated political landscape of the war, the institutional response of the Werra region to military occupation and taxation, and the ways in which villagers described their own circumstances over the course of the war. By linking the various narratives of death and destruction produced in the Werra region during the war to the sequences of occupation and political disintegration within Hesse-Kassel as a whole, we can gain a more nuanced view of how villagers experienced the war from beginning to end. No effort is made here to quantify any of these effects; the material impact of the war is the subject of the next chapter.

The Bohemian phase of the Thirty Years' War left Hesse virtually untouched. The armies of Spinola threatened from the left bank of the Rhine, but they were too far away to agitate people living along the Werra. From 1618 to 1620, Hesse turned its attention not to repelling invading troops but to repelling recruiters for the Catholic armies, who threatened to take able-bodied Hessians into service against the interests of Hesse. The immediate response to the Catholic threat was to ban recruiting by foreigners on Hessian soil. Hessian officers were ordered to suppress diligently any secret recruiting and to confiscate the enlistment advances the soldiers received and send the money to Kessel.[16] One military activity in the Werra region was the construction of defense works around the town of Wanfried, commencing in 1619. This, however, was the only way that Hesse engaged the enemy in the earliest stage of the war.

After Tilly disposed of the Bohemian rebels at White Mountain, armies of both sides began to march in various parts of Germany. The Eichsfeld region, which bordered on the Werra, was a staging ground for armies of both sides because the structure of *Herrschaft* was very complicated. Both arch-Catholic Mainz and Protestant Saxony-Eisenach possessed seigneurial rights in the region. *Amt* Treffurt was the gateway from the Eichsfeld to Hessian territory, since it was divided among three lords: Hesse, Saxony, and Mainz. As it turned out, Protestant troops were the first to draw the Werra region into the larger conflict. In 1621, a small force under the command of Achatius von Dohna, marching in support of Friedrich V, was destroyed in a surprise attack at Gandern in the Eichsfeld by forces of the Duke of Braunschweig-Wolfenbüttel, who supported the emperor.[17] Moritz had not granted passage to Dohna's forces before the attack, in part because the commanders of the Wolfenbüttel forces, Rheden and Helversen, threatened to retaliate against Hesse if Dohna were allowed to leave the jurisdiction of the Lower Saxon Circle. Moritz did, however, allow them to retreat through the Werra region after their defeat. Rheden and Helversen retreated northward, since Dohna was no longer a threat.

It was difficult to translate Moritz's apprehensions about the emperor's plans into effective action at the local level. The approach of Dohna's troops produced a confused response, and subsequent requests were handled equally inexpertly. On 31 December 1621, the *Burgermeister* of Wanfried wrote to the landgrave, warning of the presence of more troops in the Eichsfeld.[18] These forces undoubtedly belonged to Duke Wilhelm of Saxony-Weimar, who had raised yet another force to defend Friedrich V, despite the objections of his cousin, the Elector Johann Georg.[19] Christoph Boppenhausen, the *Rentmeister* in Eschwege, reported that:

> Yesterday evening between 9 and 10 o'clock, the lieutenant in Wanfried informed me through two subjects of the *Amt* from Frieda, that the Duke of Saxony, who occupied the town and *Amt* of Treffurt along with two villages, Altenburschla and Heldra, last Sunday, now requests that he take quarters in Grebendorf, which is right by the town [Eschwege] and belongs to it—also in Oberhona and Niederhona in *Amt* Bilstein, and then to the village Albungen an der Werra, which belongs to the Diede. . . . But because no order or patent was shown to me, I have deferred the complete occupation. . . . But after our gracious lord's letter tells us what to do, the lieutenant, corporal and we the officials will obediently carry out your orders.[20]

Boppenhausen's note is interesting because it shows how relations between troops and local officials were regulated by an assumption that territorial prerogatives remained in place. The note betrayed no particular alarm or loss of control; it was an attempt to get official sanction to negotiate with the invaders so that he would not be accused of betraying the interests of the landgrave. In direct negotiations with the Duke of Saxony, Moritz turned down the request for passage—even though he had initially favored the creation of the force—because he feared that it would provide an excuse for the emperor's forces to invade Hessian territory.[21]

Moritz's efforts to maintain formal neutrality did not help him for long. In early 1623, General Tilly moved into the valley of the Werra from Hersfeld, on the pretext that Moritz was disobeying the emperor. Tilly skillfully exploited the tensions between the noble Estates of Hesse and the landgrave to make his occupation easier. The nobility mode no pretense of resisting Tilly's army and yielded immediately to superior force. They had no reason to sacrifice their own lands on the Werra, so they agreed to a *salva guardia*, an agreement between troops and local lords that gave tacit approval to Tilly's occupation of the villages along the Werra in exchange for "protection" of those villages against abuses by the troops. Moritz's militia was no match for the veterans in Tilly's army. It was quickly swept aside, and much of the Hessian countryside was occupied.

Moritz was incensed by the failure of the territorial Estates to offer any assistance to his militia. He complained that "last winter, shortly before the holidays, the knights in general and especially those in the district (*Bezirk*) on the Werra River, showed themselves to be so shameful and irresponsible in the face of obvious danger, that all chronicles should be filled with their deeds.[22] Moritz's adversarial relationship with the nobility prior to the invasion only increased the finger pointing, since the easy victory by Tilly's forces could be attributed either to the failure to organize an effective militia or to the recklessness of pursuing a policy in opposition to the legitimate interests of the emperor. Moritz's appointed investigator of the debacle, Dr. Wolfgang Gunther, naturally concurred with Moritz's assessment of the nobility's behavior, which sharpened the divisions between Moritz and the Estates.[23] In practice, Moritz could do little but rail against his nobles. He was in no position either to defend them against Tilly or to oblige them to take arms against Tilly. So while Moritz and the nobility argued over who was responsible for the debacle, the villages of the Werra suffered under military occupation.

The approach of Tilly's troops in 1623 established the basic patterns of interaction between the occupying force and the territory it occupied for the early part of the war. This is true of all levels of interaction, from the commanders of the armies to the common soldiers. Tilly negotiated a provisions ordinance for his troops that provided for a straightforward system of distributing the burdens on the occupied territory.[24] Each officer and soldier was allotted a fixed sum of money per week, from 49 Reichsthaler for an *Obrist* to 1 Rthlr for a common soldier. The rules of acceptable behavior for officers and men were quite similar to those for civil officials of a territorial ruler. No one was allowed to take more than his allotted share, or he would be punished severely. The ordinance expressly forbade soldiers or officers to demand "spices, confections, or other delicacies"; it allowed for no more than the necessary provision of wood and light. All forms of extortion of the peasantry were condemned. Indeed, Tilly encouraged his officers "to approach the poor people with commiseration and mercy, and not to demand more from them than they can supply."[25] Another section of the ordinance ordered that commanders cooperate with territorial administrators in keeping a weekly record of which soldiers were quartered with which households. Unfortunately, no copies of these lists survived, nor is there any evidence that they were kept. It is telling, however, that Tilly tried to use local officials as part of the apparatus for securing provisions for his troops; for war to nourish itself, it was useful to employ the overseer of the harvest. The terms of the provisions ordinance were burdensome for the villagers, but they were as clear and fairly apportioned as many of the burdens imposed by the landgrave's own administration.

As villagers were aware, the problems with Tilly's provisions ordinance lay not in the written terms but in their execution. One problem was the relative inflexibility of the local economy in responding to any increased demands on its resources. Even before the coming of troops, there were many villagers who were on the margins of subsistence. These people were pushed beyond the margin when asked to support a soldier, or perhaps even two or more soldiers with their entourage of wives, children, and hangers-on.[26] The fact that the *Amtmann* agreed that troops could take a given amount from a village was no guarantee that the village could provide that amount. The other problem was the inability of the commanders to maintain troop discipline and to ensure that the terms were followed. Even if the soldiers adhered to the provisions ordinance and did not plunder or extort, the exactions for the troops were a severe burden on the villagers. When soldiers resorted to plunder, the costs to the villagers were compounded. Heinrich Rodingus, the *Rentmeister* in Sontra, captured some of the frustration of those who suffered from plundering soldiers when he described the fate of the landgrave's own supply of forage in 1623:

> The Bavarian cavalry and several servants of the *Obrist Leutnant* Herbersdorf forced me with violence and great threats to open the grain supply to them and they took the available wheat, spelt, and oats from me to feed the animals; but they did not stop there, but also broke open the lock on the stalls and took away your entire supply of hay, and used all the stocks of coal except for one *Fuder* in the kitchen of the *Obrist*.[27]

Of course, if soldiers took such liberties with the property of the landgrave in the presence of one of his officials, they would have had few qualms about doing the same to the property of villagers. The plundering of the landgrave's property was not mere wanton destruction, however. The soldiers apparently did not take any objects of value from the building besides food for the animals and themselves, since the *Rentmeister* would have mentioned other losses if they had occurred. The primary objective of the soldiers was to find provisions, not to destroy property in the occupied territory. Indeed, what is most striking about the early years of the war is how unusual complaints about the behavior of soldiers were. There were virtually no letters from the villages of the Werra to the landgrave complaining of ill treatment by soldiers in the early part of the war.

Villagers had no say at the level of negotiations that determined the burdens placed on each *Amt* and village. They were left with three basic responses to those burden: passive acceptance, with supplications to reduce the worst effects; flight; or active resistance. It is easy enough to identify the advantages and disadvantages of each response, and the decision to adopt one or another must have been based on calculations of their feasibility. Some inhabitants of the village chose one option and others chose a different option, though the impetus to conform probably produced fairly uniform behavior.

Of the responses, active resistance was the hardest to justify. If it took the form of attacks on occupying troops, the villagers were certain to face reprisals. But if resistance did not include armed action, it could not drive the troops away. The balance of forces was so unequal that such attacks were suicidal. The motif of peasants attacking soldiers is common in engravings of the period, but these invariably show attacks on small detachments of soldiers that appear to be outside the protection of a larger force such as Tilly's.[28] Villagers were dissuaded from attacking troops not only because such attacks were risky but also because they were illegitimate within the structure of *Herrschaft*. As soon as an agreement was worked out between the landgrave or the Estates and the occupying forces, villagers who attacked soldiers might face reprisals from the territorial administration as well as from the troops. The issuance of a *salva guardia* meant that the agents of *Herrschaft* formally approved the presence of troops within the territory. To resist the *salva guardia* was thus to undercut legitimate rule. Armed peasants were viewed as a threat by the landgrave's officials as well as by regular troops.[29] When an official in Eschwege reported in 1626 that the peasants "have come together in great numbers and especially in *Amt* Sontra and Rotenburg have begun to beat the old drum," and that they have "resolved to fend off the occupation with force,"[30] he did not write with approval. He was terrified of the possibility of a peasant insurrection. Even this report seems to have been unfounded. There is no evidence that the villagers of the Werra ever tried to fend off occupation by force.

Flight was a more realistic response to the troops than resistance, but it was possible only if the village was prepared in advance. Villagers remained alert while troops were in the field, especially if they were in the vicinity. Most villages of the Werra relied on information from neighboring towns to learn about the disposition of the troops. Sontra sent messengers as far afield as the Wetterau when it was suspected that Tilly's troops might be headed toward the Werra. It was comparatively easy to flee to a nearby town with walls, and it was often prudent to do so for a brief period until the details of a provisions ordinance were worked out. Eschwege and Sontra could both be defended in a brief siege, though neither had modern defense works. If villagers were forewarned when troops were coming, they took precautions to protect valuables such as silver coins by either hiding them or bringing them to town with them. Grain was also stored in towns in large magazines, though villagers were suspicious of the administrators of the magazines and complained of any losses.[31] The presence of the magazines and of the *Amtmann* and other officials created an obligation for the town to house villagers when troops approached. All this might draw a villager to town when the troops drew near, but an unattended house in the village was susceptible to pillage and burning. It made sense to flee only when the danger to one's life and personal property outweighed the disadvantages of leaving one's household and fields unattended.

In the first years of the war, most villagers adopted the option of passive acceptance. They stayed in the village and tried to cope with the presence of the occupying troops as best they could. The villagers provided their share of provisions for the troops quartered in their houses, as specified in the provisions ordinance. They also gathered money and produce to fulfill the village's obligations for the maintenance of the troops. Fulfilling the burdens placed on the village was the least disruptive response, and it was much the same as fulfilling obligations to other forms of Herrschaft. It was a familiar way of responding to the uncertainty of forces outside the village's control. Villagers were resigned to the depredations of the soldiers if they remained within "acceptable" limits and responded to them as they would to any unwelcome incursion of an outside authority—by hiding as much as they could and arguing for a reduction of their burden.

How frequently were the villagers of the Werra forced to draw on this repertory of responses after their first contact with the troops in 1622 and 1623? In the absence of the local registers that were supposed to be produced as part of the provisions ordinance, it is difficult to know precisely. Once interaction became routine, there was little need for local officials to correspond with the central administration. One illustration of how occupation affected the life of the village in the first years of the war is an account of payments to various troops from the village of Heldra in Amt Wanfried.[32] The account does not tell us precisely how often troops were quartered in the village, but it does indicate how often the village was drawn into negotiated payments to troops through salva guardia and contributions, which were always backed with the threat of occupation.

Heldra made payments to twenty different forces over the ten-year period from 1623 to 1633. The register began with three weeks of payment to the regiments of Collalto in 1623. Immediately following its payments to Collalto, the village began a seventy-eight-week span of payments to Colonel Wurzburg until June 1625. In the summer of 1625, a company of cavalry under Galleas received payments for an unspecified but short period of time, as did a regiment under Don Balthasar later that year. For three weeks in the first half of 1626, Heldra made payments to cavalry under von Merode. On 11 July it began payments to Herberstdorff's regiment (the force that had behaved so badly in Sontra three years earlier), which lasted until 21 May 1627. In December 1627, the village began its single longest period of payment: to Ferdinand Oppen of the Wurzburg regiment for nearly two years, until September 1629. In December 1629, it began making payments to Tilly's artillery that went on for more than a year, until April 1631. In 1631, as Gustavus Adolphus made his advance and Tilly completed his siege of Magdeburg, the burdens on Heldra became more varied. The village supplied Gleim's company for eight weeks and Lucan's for an unspecified length of time. Bongartz's cavalry of Tilly's army spent three days in the area, presumably after the defeat at Breitenfeld, and was followed for one month by two companies of infantry under Rodenburg. At the very end of 1631, Swedish cavalry spent fourteen days near Treffurt, supported by funds from Heldra. In 1632, Heldra made payments to Gleim's troops for two months, Lucan's for one month, and Stange's for twenty weeks, as well as a nonspecified payment to Oberproviantschreiber Zacharias Hufselen, presumably a Hessian official. Finally, in 1633, Heldra made payments to two forces: for one month to troops under Count Eberstein and for three months to the Hessian cavalry at Kassel.

The register breaks off at this point, just before the region's most desperate years of the war were about to begin. The account shows that Heldra was burdened with extraordinary payments because of the close proximity of troops more than two-thirds of the time between 1623 and 1633. In the crucial years 1626–1627 and 1631–1632, the demands on the village were unrelenting. The payments went to both Hessian troops and invading forces, with the latter receiving the majority. The comparatively regular schedule of payments suggests that the inhabitants of Heldra remained in the village to fulfill the obligations to the troops. Payments were either long and drawn out or very brief, but they were a constant feature of village life after 1623.

Fulfilling village obligations to the occupying troops did not mean that villagers did nothing to fend off the burdens. The primary tools at their disposal were the traditional relations embodied in the principle of *Herrschaft*, which they used as best they could to defend themselves from inordinate burdens. The same conditions that made armed resistance to occupying forces illegitimate made arguments for a reduction of burdens all the more legitimate. If the agents of *Herrschaft* accepted a *salva guardia* from invading troops, they were responsible for ensuring that the terms were adhered to. When the demands of the troops exceeded the village's ability to supply them without undermining the livelihood of village inhabitants, the principle of *Schutz und Schirm* required the authorities to grant relief either by convincing the troops to take less or by reducing seigneurial and tax burdens in proportion to the size of the troops' demands. The result was a flood of supplications to the landgrave and his officials, and a smaller flood to the commanders of the occupying troops, that combined legalistic appeals with emotional statements of how heavily the burden weighed on the local community.

Historians often discount the institutional and psychological impact of the war, viewing the ways in which that impact was expressed as an obstacle to understanding what damage the war "really" inflicted. S. H. Steinberg, for example, argued that most of the descriptions of death and destruction were from educated chroniclers who were predisposed to exaggerate the extent of destruction because their property was particularly vulnerable and money for "culture" was less available.[33] He used this "fact" to argue that the war did not have any notable effect on German society. He adduced no evidence to support his claims, but Gerhard Benecke, in a careful analysis of urban debts and claims of damage in the town of Lemgo, supported Steinberg's argument, concluding that "a war damage claim was an unscrupulous attempt to get tax-reduction from the territorial authorities irrespective of neighbours' problems. It was not a credible account of actual war damage."[34] According to Benecke, the main obstacle to overcoming the exaggeration of local chroniclers is the excessive gullibility of modern historians. He argued:

No straight-forward picture emerges from the Lippe records of the war and occupation years, unless the naive view is taken, and every time a general plea for exhaustion and dearth is made in order to avoid further taxes, it is accepted at face value and ascribed to war horrors—a poetic license more applicable to post war literature as shown by Grimmelshausen's best-seller "Simplicius Simplicissimus."[35]

Although there is every reason to agree with Steinberg and Benecke that not all descriptions of war horrors should be accepted without question, they are inclined to overcompensate for the potential bias of the sources by assuming that if damage cannot be proved, the claim must be false. Benecke provides no means of deciding which general pleas for exhaustion and dearth were made to avoid further taxes and which were made because the region was experiencing exhaustion and dearth—except for his assumption of bias, which seems no more useful as a general principle than the assumption of truth. Descriptions of exhaustion and dearth are one of the most common sources from the war era, and rather than dismissing them as biased and thus useless as historical evidence, one should view them as one of the ways in which villagers coped with the war.[36]

Many supplications invoked *Herrschaft* and appealed to *Schutz und Schirm* in order to link protection of the village with the defense of Hesse and legitimate social order. Most focused on the inequity of burdens. Supplicants lost no opportunity to describe themselves as "poor overburdened villages" from which one could scarce expect to raise another *Heller* of supplies. At the same time, villagers complained profusely whenever it appeared that one individual or one village was not carrying its share of the burden. Villagers were undoubtedly selfish in protecting their own interests. A supplication is, by definition, an act of special pleading. Villagers tried to shift burdens to some other village or region, with no consideration of how that would affect the other region. But the audience for the supplications was far from naive about the good intentions of supplicants. The landgrave and his officials had a strong interest in extracting resources from their subjects and were disinclined to grant releases from seigneurial obligations without a compelling reason. Both sides were aware of the conflicting interests between village and administration. Local officials, such as the *Amtmann*, served as a conduit of "objective" information about local conditions, tempering any wild exaggeration of local circumstances. Therefore, the presence of local officials shaped how villagers could make their claims of damage. The central administration was receptive to claims of damage when all the normal channels for checking into those claims pointed to their veracity. Even in the last years of the war, the central administration made some effort to verify claims, providing perhaps the best evidence that such claims were taken seriously. The council of the landgrave noted with regret in 1648 that "when we write to our officials for information as has always been the case, we see from the letters that they send that they completely agree with the complaints of the subjects and confirm and strengthen the claims of the damage."[37]

All features of supplications were routine for seventeenth-century German states. At first, the only distinctive feature of wartime supplications was that they invoked the war as the cause of distress rather than fires or bad harvests. The constant recurrence of the burdens of war quickly created a distinctive rhythm of supplication, however, that transformed disputes over equitable distribution from the prewar era. For example, the town and villages of *Amt* Sontra carried on a running feud over their shares of the contribution that harked back to disputes over the Treysa Assessment.[38] The town of Sontra insisted that the villages of the *Amt* pay twice as much as the town in contributions because there were so many more people in the villages; the villages countered that the burden should be split evenly because the town had more wealth. Feuds of this sort were bound to escalate as each town and village tried to use every technique available to reduce its own burdens.

Although the town of Sontra and the villages of the *Amt* were disputing the distribution between them, in 1625 they both challenged the noble village of Herleshausen's exemption from the payment of wood. The noble lord Herman von Wersabe responded with a seventeen-page letter defending the exemption of his village.[39] Wersabe based his defense on both the specifics of the various ordinances that fixed the burdens of his village and an emotional appeal on behalf of the village, which was already overburdened. He pointed out that the written terms of occupation, negotiated with a Rittmeister von Rineck, made no mention of wood deliveries from noble villages: "All and every Contribution was specified therein, but wood was not considered."[40] He added wryly that the cavalry, which was so quick to come to collect late payments of cash, never bothered Herleshausen about its failure to provide wood. Wersabe went on to describe how Herleshausen was contributing so many other things to the troops that supplying wood as well would make the burden intolerable. Counting contributions in money and in hay, oats, and straw, his village was providing 105 taler to the troops. By comparison, Sontra was providing only 40 taler for wood and 34 taler for oil.[41] Wersabe believed that Sontra was contributing far below its ability, while Herleshausen was being pushed beyond its capacity to pay. He described Sontra's complaint as "completely contrary to Christian love and all fairness"[42] and insinuated that once Herleshausen began delivering wood to the troops in Sontra, the town would start to demand oil and light as well. He capped his argument by stating that since Herleshausen had no wood to begin with, the villagers would have to buy their wood from merchants in Sontra or elsewhere to send to Sontra.

Wersabe's defense of Herleshausen's exemption from wood deliveries introduces many of the conflicts that resulted from trying to lessen the burdens on individual villages. Supplications sometimes tried to play off the central administration's suspicions about the motives of its subjects. Wersabe's response to Sontra raises the issue of material motives by suggesting that Sontra's merchants wanted to force Herleshausen to buy wood from them. Such an imputation no doubt conformed to the expectations of the landgrave and his officials about peasants and burghers, who, in the view of the educated elite, were notoriously self-interested.

The landgrave's response to the dispute between Amt Sontra and Herleshausen did not survive. In general, however, the central administration was skeptical about complaints, so even the most compelling arguments were unlikely to prompt a change in policy. The Ämter Treffurt and Wanfried wrote copious complaints to Kassel when Tilly's troops arrived in late 1623.[43] Wilhelm Bernhard von Hagen reported from Wanfried that the regiments of Collalto and Truchseß had taken contributions of over 400 fl from the Amt and had kidnapped the Bürgermeister and Stadtschreiber in order to extort another 1,000 fl. These problems were only the prelude to a larger problem: Treffurt and Wanfried were each housing a company of troops—the same as Amt Eschwege/Bilstein—though it had more than fifteen villages and Wanfried and Treffurt had only four villages each. Hagen's initial complaint met with little success in Kassel, even though the council knew as well as Hagen the inequity of Wanfried's four villages being asked to support as many troops as Eschwege's fifteen. The council responded that there was nothing it could do for Wanfried and Treffurt because the situation was bad everywhere. Finally, Treffurt managed to remove some of the burden by appealing directly to Tilly. Tilly agreed to billet some troops in nearby Amt Melsungen in order to relieve some of the strain, but a further reduction in burdens was blocked by Moritz's unwillingness to allow troops to occupy the area around Kaufungen.[44]

Supplications from localities became part of a wider range of correspondence concerning the disposition of troops. There was constant communication between occupiers and occupied on multiple levels throughout the war. The rulers of a territory had a strong interest in keeping foreign troops from occupying the territory. They searched for evidence that their villages were suffering from the strains of military occupation in order to convince commanders that there were no resources to support winter quarters. The strains of the war legitimated strong language about the degree of suffering in the countryside. In 1624, the nobility of Hesse had already adopted an apocalyptic tone in assessing the extent of damage. The Estates of Hesse wrote to Landgrave Moritz:

> What God the omnipotent and Lord of all Lords threatened his disobedient people through the prophets, such, alas God have mercy, your principality has experienced for some time now, with great, even extreme, melancholic pain, misery and sighs, yes with the loss of everything that belongs to it. . . . Yes, one can see, it is as if God wished to overturn our land and people and remove us from his sight, because the sword reaches to the soul and there is no one who can save us from the hand of calamity.[45]

Moritz, who was otherwise in constant conflict with his territorial nobility, adopted similar arguments in his correspondence with the nobility and with his own officials when he wrote about the "barbaric and tyrannical" actions of enemy troops.[46] As a result, the territorial administration and even the occupying troops buttressed the descriptions in the supplications from the local level. By 1626, Tilly himself described the "distress and poverty of the currently completely exhausted and worn down lands."[47]

The supplications from villagers conformed to the presuppositions and political calculations of the landgrave and the nobility. While Moritz and the Estates debated the proper response to Tilly's invasion in 1623 and used the devastation caused by the invasion to buttress their arguments, the village of Rittmannshausen constructed its own description of what happened as a result of the debacle. Three years after the event, the villagers wrote to the landgrave describing the origins and consequences of the actions of the von Boyneburg's administrator Weitzel during the occupation of 1623.[48] The landgrave's official had offered to let the villagers store valuables in the town for the duration of the danger, but the von Boyneburg family produced a *salva guardia* with Tilly's troops. Weitzel guaranteed the security of all village property against plunder and forbade the villagers to move their valuables to town, presumably to keep the valuables from coming under the control of the landgrave's officials, who opposed the *salva guardia*. Unfortunately for Weitzel and the villagers of Rittmannshausen, the troops were not as disciplined as the *salva guardia* required, and they began to ransack houses for grain and forage. The loss of food supplies and forage was compounded by the fact that many villagers had hidden other valuables among the straw and hay. All the hay was carted off to the noble's house in nearby Netra and dispensed to the troops, and whatever valuables were hidden among the straw disappeared. The villagers demanded restitution of their losses not from the soldiers but from the official who had thwarted their efforts to protect their property. They emphasized their anger at the officials of the nobility by describing the *salva guardia* as "completely unnecessary and ruinous." Their criticism of the action of the nobility was part of a more general attempt to demand that the provisions of *Schutz und Schirm* be sustained in the Werra region despite the war.

The villages of the Werra adjusted to the conditions of the first few years of the Thirty Years' War with discomfort, but they did adjust. Between 1623 and 1626, the numbers of complaints and their vehemence generally increased, but the form and basic content did not change dramatically. Each year brought greater pressure on the already unstable economic base of the village. It was possible for the villagers to deal with adversity in the usual ways and to tolerate the impositions of the troops for a while, but eventually they were strained beyond their limits. Flight became more common as the conditions of occupation became worse.

The year 1626 marked a watershed between two phases of the Thirty
Years' War in Hesse. The pattern of interaction between the village and
soldiers created during Tilly's first invasion began to break down in Hesse,
and new patterns were established as Tilly and Wallenstein returned. A
striking sign of the change in interaction is that in 1626 the parish register
of Grandenborn mentions for the first time the burial of four parishioners
"killed by Tilly's troops."[49]

Among the casualties of the repeated occupations of the eastern regions
of Hesse during the first decade of the war were the ideological underpinnings of Schutz und Schirm, which were destroyed when neither the landgrave
nor the local nobles were able to protect anyone. Finally the nobles of the
Werra region abandoned all pretense of defending their lands and fled from
the region. Their precipitous departure lent credence to the apocalyptic
picture they had painted in 1624, while the rural population struggled to
make its way in the face of new relationships of power and dependence.
The villagers of Grandenborn reported to the landgrave in 1626 that the
von Boyneburg "fled our beloved fatherland by fog and night (for what
reason we do not know)" and left them "with neither advice nor support."
But even worse was the fact that "we poor subjects have not only been
wiped out by the various and sundry invasions, but also we have been overburdened by our noble overlords with unbearable money payments."[50] As a
result, the villagers renounced their noble lords and appealed to the landgrave
to become the immediate protector and overlord of the village. The villages of Netra, Röhrda, and Rittmannshausen followed Grandenborn's lead
and appealed to the landgrave two weeks later.[51] Conditions at the local
level had deteriorated to the point that villagers grasped desperately at any
source of protection.

The crisis at the local level reverberated in the central administration.
Moritz and the Estates were still at loggerheads over Moritz's war policy.
The nobility clamored for the dismissal of Dr. Gunther, who had attacked
their behavior in 1623, and they insisted that Moritz reach an accord with
the emperor's forces.[52] All this suggests that Grandenborn's plea would have
been received sympathetically by Moritz, who continued to rail at the territorial nobles for their ineffectual resistance to Tilly's troops, but he was in
no position to offer the villages any more protection than the von Boyneburg
had provided. The military campaigns of 1626 led to the final collapse of
Moritz's internal administration and the bankruptcy of his treasury. The
failure of Protestant arms and the mounting fiscal crisis weakened his position immensely. Tilly once again took advantage of the discord and convoked
an assembly of the Hessian Estates in 1626 to demand Moritz's abdication.
Hessian troops controlled only the fortresses of Kassel and Ziegenhain; the
rest of the territory was in Tilly's hands. In 1627, Moritz realized that he
was incapable of dislodging Tilly or gaining any further support within his
territory, so he abdicated in favor of his son, Wilhelm V.[53]

The events of 1626 and 1627 led to administrative confusion for the villages of the Werra. When Moritz abdicated, he separated a number of *Ämter*, including Sontra, Eschwege, and Wanfried, and gave seigneurial authority over them to his second son, Hermann, who thus became landgrave of Hesse-Rotenburg. This *Rotenburger Quart* remained integral with Hesse-Kassel for purposes of administration and taxation, but the regular revenues from the land as seigneurial jurisdiction went to Hermann.[54] Moritz thereby undercut the process of consolidation between seigneurial and state administration in exchange for doubtful dynastic advantages. The *Quart* was too small to be a power of any magnitude, and the loss of revenues was bound to weaken the already weak Hesse-Kassel further. The agreement complicated an already complex set of jurisdictions. The landgraves of Hesse-Rotenburg proved to be weak and were dominated by Hesse-Kassel and its more dynamic ruler during the rest of the war.

For the villages on the Werra, the return of Tilly's troops in 1626 proved almost as disastrous as it was for Moritz's administration. This time, the troops brought plague and dysentery with them. The epidemic had catastrophic consequences in some villages, combining demographic disaster with the regular burdens of war. The demographic disaster led to a change in the tone of supplications and in the descriptions of death and destruction. The people of the Werra began to express their despair in ways that were never seen by those with the power to alleviate the burden. One of the most poignant commentaries was on the tombstone of the pastor of Ulfen. It mentioned that 349 people had died of the "red dysentery" that year and referred to a quote from Sirach to remind people of the enormity of the tragedy.

Troops returned to the Werra frequently in the years after 1626. Meanwhile, Wilhelm V pursued a cautious neutral policy in his first years as landgrave. He repaired some of the rift with the Estates, in part by bringing Moritz's investigator, Dr. Gunther, to trial.[55] Wilhelm's initial neutrality did not spare the countryside from the depredations of troops, and the respite from full-scale conflict was too short to allow the villages to recover. Eventually, Wilhelm renewed Hesse's commitment to the Protestant cause; the issue of the Marburg succession continued to guide Hessian policy, and the lands remained firmly in the hands of Hesse-Darmstadt. Gustavus Adolphus's entry into the war provided Wilhelm with the opportunity to renounce his neutrality and rejoin the conflict.[56]

The organized exaction of contributions continued to break down, and stoic resolve and grumbling acceptance were transformed into desperate avoidance. All villages claimed that they had nothing left to give, and most villagers began to resort to flight as their first response to news that troops were coming. Recourse to new kinds of descriptions was necessary because the traditional practice of supplication was exhausted. Villages continued to submit supplications to the new landgrave, but they came in such numbers that the administration was no longer capable of responding to them, much less rectifying the problems.[57] Landgrave Hermann of Hesse-Rotenburg admitted his inability to offer assistance to any part of his land in a letter to the superintendent in Eschwege in 1641. He expressed sympathy for the "miserable" conditions caused by military occupation but admitted that he could do nothing to alleviate them in Eschwege because the rest of his territory was suffering extraordinarily too.[58] It was now pointless for a village to try to foist a burden onto another village or district, since the language of despair had become so generalized that all villages were known to be suffering. Grievances became plaints, with no expectation of redress other than that God might grant the village peace so that it could go about its business without disruption. The breakdown of "legitimate authority" allowed, indeed nearly forced, language to become more and more piteous.

Constant flight exacerbated the breakdown of both administrative and social order. The account books for Sontra in 1634 reported that no fines were collected that year "because we had to flee and were not at home."[59] A fine recorded from Ulfen shows that some parents fled, leaving their children behind in the village with the few adults that remained.[60] Only a small core of villagers remained; a large number of villagers disappeared to Kassel or still farther away for long periods of time. Toward the end of the war, villagers from the Werra fled as far as Bremen and Holstein, while others went to Braunschweig and the Pfalz.[61]

The already desperate situation became worse in 1636 and 1637, when a second epidemic struck the Werra valley.[62] In addition, the villages were plundered by marauding troops, who no longer made any pretense of adhering to a provisions ordinance. In December 1636, the district administrator of Sontra, Peter Stückrodt, corresponded with the landgrave about the miserable conditions in his district.[63] Sontra was no longer concerned with minor squabbles over wood deliveries from Herleshausen but was instead desperately struggling to survive. A sign of that desperation is that the traditional conduit of information about local circumstances was now the author of a supplication. Stückrodt's letter was prompted by a new contribution of 139 *Reichstaler* imposed on the district on 15 December. He explained that the entire quarter of Sontra was "ruined to the ground" and could pay nothing. Unfortunately, the soldiers came anyway, and when the town could not pay, they took all the horses and cattle as ransom. To underscore the seriousness of the situation, Stückrodt explained that he could "vow with God and pure truth that there is no way that we can collect this contribution without the few horses and cattle" and requested that the landgrave do something to retrieve the animals. He went on to explain that hunger and misery were so great that people were buried without coffins in their torn clothing, and the rest would surely die of hunger or leave the region permanently. His depiction of misery culminated with the request that the landgrave send a deputy to visit the region to see for himself how feeble were the prospects of collecting arrears or even future revenues. Stückrodt's letter was an admission and an explanation of his inability to perform his duties as district administrator. Prior to the war, district administrators made little effort to protect their districts from exorbitant burdens.

Stückrodt was not the only commentator to adopt the strategy of inviting an investigation of his district to reinforce the veracity of damage claims. Unlike propagandistic pamphlets, which also claimed to be "nonpartisan" and "truthful," an invitation to come see for oneself could be accepted by the "audience." Therefore, such an invitation could be extended only if one was confident that the landgrave would agree with the assessment if he were to come. Landgrave Wilhelm did not, however, personally visit his devastated lands during the war. Indeed, for many of the crucial years of the war, he was in the Netherlands to escape the dangers that befell Hesse. Despite entreaties from his own council that he return to show direct leadership, Wilhelm refused because of the constant presence of enemy troops.[64] His refusal served in its own way to confirm and justify the rhetoric used at the local level.

The change in the rhetorical tone of descriptions of local suffering followed the escalation of local horrors. By the mid-1630s, the wantonness of the occupying troops made it imperative that villagers flee to safety as quickly as possible. Being caught by soldiers in the open was tantamount to a death sentence. Those villagers unfortunate enough to be caught out could disappear entirely. The pastor of Grandenborn noted the fate of one poor victim in the list of burials in the parish register: "Melchior the sowherd stayed outside during the plundering, he is said to be buried near Eschwege."[65] Other villagers were spared a similar fate by their quick response to warnings about approaching troops.

The brutality of the troops escalated in 1637.[66] Croatian soldiers under General Isolani arrived in the Werra that year and ransacked the entire region. The town of Eschwege was burned and the surrounding villages pillaged. Six people in Grandenborn were killed by the Croatians, including the village head, who was beaten to death.[67] Eventually, any group of unruly troops with a foreign accent came to be called Croatians. The brutality of the Thirty Years' War was now at its height, and the Croatians were a symbol of how brutal the war had become.

By 1638, much of the Hessian countryside was desolated. No one doubted that the situation in the villages was horrible. After Wilhelm V died in 1637, the new regent Amalie Elisabeth sent several of the supplications she had received to the council, with the observation that she received comparable descriptions of despair "almost daily."[68] The council was so powerless that its only recourse was to turn weakness into an asset. When a new occupation threatened, the council wrote to Amalie Elisabeth, "we had hoped that when the enemy troops recognized the obvious and notable lack of resources of the poor peasants of this land, they would quit and leave, but instead they have done the contrary," with the result that ruin and devastation would be worse than before.[69] In response to the universal tone of despair (and in an effort to maintain whatever vestiges of revenues and *Schutz und Schirm* she could), Amalie Elisabeth sent out a directive to assess the extent of damage in February 1639.[70] The survey asked for information on the number of married householders and widows left in each village, along with the number of cows, sheep, pigs, horses, oxen, and ploughs and the amount of land planted for the winter. The order was short and direct, and it demanded a response within three weeks. There was no demand for explanations or lengthy descriptions in the order, but many villages took the opportunity to provide them to the regent.

The villages of the Werra described their situations in great detail. Each individual inhabitant of the villages of Netra, Röhrda, Grandenborn, Thurnhosbach, Rechtebach, Wichmannshausen, Reichensachsen, Langenhain, Hoheneiche, and Oetmannshausen was carefully enumerated. The cumulative effect of dozens of entries that read like the first entry from Netra— "Hans Weitzel, married, has no animals and a miserable little hut"—was clear evidence of the desperate circumstances in all the villages. Each village also wrote a brief description of the contrast between its current situation and its situation before the war. Villages might have consulted with one another as they prepared their descriptions, but each description was particular to its source. Most notable for its idiosyncrasy is the report from Grandenborn. The villagers' descriptions were highlighted by strong flourishes that heightened their expression of despair. As they pointed out: "everything is in ashes and burned down, which is clear to see, alas, God have mercy, and we poor people must continue to pay the entire burden of the war for the whole village as if it was still all standing and in good shape." The fields of the village were "so overgrown that now there is nothing on the lands, but they are completely ruined by the mice in the grass and the cold frosts."[71] According to the report, the village was at the mercy of the marauding troops because it was so far from any secure fortress.[72] The result was unmitigated misery for everyone in the village. Grandenborn then concluded: "God the almighty change things for the better and give us his merciful grace and remove the great burden of war from us and grant us poor Hessian subjects dear peace, so help us God."[73]

A constant refrain in the reports from the villages along the Werra is that the few individuals left in the village had to carry the fiscal burden of the whole village as if it were still at peak productive capacity.[74] All villages hoped to use the inquiry from the regent to reduce the financial burden, and the plea from Grandenborn made sure that this issue came to her attention. It was a common practice to insist that one's own village was the most depressed and ruined of them all and therefore deserved special dispensation, but Grandenborn's argument could not be rejected by Amalie Elisabeth out of hand.

The question of whether it was proper to continue to exploit the resources of an already overexploited peasantry had become part of the wider discussions of the war.[75] The whole system of contributions was explicitly attacked as an unreasonable imposition on the countryside in a lengthy pamphlet by Andreas Ortelius, "Blood-, Fear-, Tears-Money, The extorted, intolerable extraordinary Contribution-, Ransom-, . . . Money, as it is Practiced in the Current, most Destructive War Policies, is nothing other than the Poor People's Sweat and Blood."[76] Grandenborn's report provided a local confirmation of Ortelius's argument, with the additional comment that the effects of the contributions were "clear to see"—a rhetorical flourish comparable to Stückrodt's invitation to the landgrave to send an agent to come see for himself. Those observers who were around corroborated the claims of the villages.

The force of the pleas from the countryside may have been blunted by the fact that they followed the format of traditional peasant grievances, but villagers had no other means of communicating their suffering to the wider world aside from appeals to the landgrave. At the very least, villagers were aware that the extent of damage was great enough to elicit a sympathetic hearing from the landgrave. It was the regent, after all, who had been concerned about the economic status of the land and had asked for the information from the villages. The regent could appoint a special commission to investigate the claims if she had serious doubts about their accuracy.

Grandenborn's claims might be weighed against those of other villages in the same district, but it was more difficult for the central administration to deny the veracity of such claims when other districts reported comparable levels of damage. The desolate state of the village suffused every part of the report of the village of Rambach in 1639, highlighting the general mood of despair with many of the same rhetorical techniques:

> Today . . . the Herr Oberschultheiss from Wanfried called together the entire *Gemeinde* of Rambach by ringing the bell . . . there he saw with a saddened heart how pitifully more than half of the village lays in ashes and found those married people and how with much difficulty (as alas, is clear) they run their households. Widows, who run their own households, but are in utter poverty—2, one of whom has a pile of poor little ill-bred children.
>
> Men, old and some of whom are infected and burdened with an evil raging disease, so that almost no one can be of any assistance to another—7
>
> Widows who stray about with their poor children and breed misery—6
>
> Table of animals and what the village saved over winter—cows 2, sheep 0, horses 0, oxen 1, pigs 0, plows 1
>
> A whole wagon with yoke could be put together in an emergency but we would not trust it to last one mile with just half a load.[77]

The report to the regent from Reichensachsen was less sensational and more direct in tying the plight of the village to the heavy fiscal burdens on the village. Reichensachsen reported that "we have been assessed such a heavy and unsupportable contribution" that it was impossible to purchase animals to replace those that were lost.[78] They returned to the subject of the contribution in a brief description of the continuous decline of the village during the war:

> NB We repeat that at the beginning of the invasion by Tilly in 1623 this village had 172 hearths, but after the terrible Croatian arson only 72, including the tiniest, remained and in the Götzian passage another 12 burned down and other houses and barns were set on fire. Even though another 13 tiny houses now have been built, it does not help at all, and it is truly pitiable that we poor people have not had our contribution reduced by a single *Heller* despite the great damage, and we once again beg for God's sake and in all submissiveness, that that might occur.[79]

Among the lists is scattered information suggesting that more than just excessive financial burdens troubled the village. Many men had been killed by the Croatians in 1637, leaving widows behind. The report from Reichensachsen emphasized the direct fiscal impact of the war on the village, but it also included descriptions of individual misery. Claus Tholle reportedly was killed and his body thrown into the fire. His widow and children were left with nothing but a "miserable hut" and had to beg for their food.[80] The experience of misery was shared by all members of the village, not just its immediate victims.

Pastor Lorenz Ludolph began to keep a parish register for Reichensachsen in 1639, the same year that the village sent its report to the regent. The marginal notations in that parish register are the most complete description of what occurred to the Werra region in the last years of the war. Aside from the observation that he had to abandon keeping records of burials "in such difficult times," he first began to describe the situation in the village in 1640.[81] He kept track of the destruction of the village and the disruption of the routines of work and worship as a result of frequent flights. His notations confirmed the impression of despair described by the village in 1639 and continued to document his experiences and those of his parishioners until the end of the war.

Ludolph's marginal notes in the parish register present the usual problems of interpretation. They were more concerned with how the disruptions affected his spiritual duties and the physical condition of his parishioners than with contributions, which he did not mention. Yet his descriptions closely followed those in the villages' reports to the regent. It is possible that Ludolph's account was read by his superiors at some point—most probably by the superintendent in Eschwege—but the register was primarily for use in the village alone. Ludolph was probably motivated to describe the situation in the village so as to capture the moment for posterity and to give vent to his frustration at being unable to protect his flock. His account was not designed to win freedom from fiscal burdens for the village, since there was little to be gained by writing copious complaints in a parish register, where they would not reach a wide audience. The superintendent never mentioned discussing the burdens of Reichensachsen with Ludolph,[82] but Ludolph had no need to remind the superintendent that the war was disruptive, since the superintendent was forced to flee in June 1640 and seek shelter in Kassel.[83] Ludolph's description of events began with just that general flight to Kassel on 17 May 1640:

> First of all, fled for 3 weeks as Weimar's army marched through all at once to Saalfeld to meet with the Swedes. Thereafter, shortly after Pentecost, fled again; this flight lasted 10 weeks at a stretch, since the Swedish, Weimar's, the Lüneburger, and Hessian armies all at once invaded the Werra region and occupied it. 17. VIII we came home and the Gospel Mark 4: <Omnia bene fecit> etc. was preached for the first time again. During this flight many animals and horses died of hunger. The people also suffered from great hunger, so that, after we returned and ate enough bread, the people all became sick, so that almost no one healthy was left in the village.[84]

The presentation of information is very straightforward. There is a small element of self-justification, as Ludolph explained how much work the situation forced on him, but he is also concerned to show that his parishioners suffered greatly because of their flight. The flight was necessary, even though the troops were supposed allies of Hesse, because they represented a threat to the security of the villagers. Ludolph, like the scribe from Grandenborn, complained about the huge mice, "as big as cats," that overran the fields and consumed much of the crop before the villagers could harvest it. Everyone was on the verge of starvation, and even the richest had been reduced to begging. Ludolph complained that he had not seen meat for over a year. It is doubtful that anyone saw more than meager handfuls of grain. These horrible conditions prevailed even when it was possible for the villagers to reside in their homes and must have intensified when the village was in flight. As the duration of the flights increased, Ludolph made more of an effort to explain the villagers' situation in vivid terms. In discussing the devastation of the fields, he wrote, "the little that we could sow in the winter anno 40 and also the summer crop was all eaten by mice, so we did not harvest much. One went to the fields to cut and the grain was stripped away so bare that one could not tell what kind of, or even if, grain had been planted there."[85]

There was a self-consciousness in Ludolph's notations in the parish register that suggests a striving for literary effect. Perhaps the best illustration of this self-consciousness is his observation at the end of nearly eight pages of description that "I must stop describing the situation, not only because it is impossible to describe it, but also because I did not undertake to write a chronicle of Reichensachsen, but instead to keep a catalogum baptizatorum et copulatorum"[86] At another point, he introduced his description of the events of the year 1642 with the observation that "all the misery continued just as bad as in the previous year, so that the despair pressed all the harder. . . . Whoever has not himself seen and lived through such circumstances cannot believe what I note here."[87] Both these statements pose a conundrum for those historians who discount the degree of suffering caused by the war. Ludolph was not pleading for a reduction in the tax burden, though his descriptions were certainly similar to those of villagers who made such pleas; nor was he complaining about the lack of funds for culture, as Steinberg would have it. He was trying to make sense of what had happened around him on a very personal level. His drift toward histrionics in his descriptions is a sign of his own despair. He used all the rhetorical resources of an educated person to capture the full measure of his own experiences and make them accessible to posterity. The fact that he addressed posterity is, in its own way, a sign of the seriousness with which Ludolph created his message.

In June 1642, Ludolph was presented with an opportunity to distill his impressions of the war experience and present them to the village as a whole. Sabine von Boyneburg genannt von Hoinstein, the wife of one of the leading *Grundherrn* in the village, died, and a funeral was held with a "respectable collection of the nobles and several villages." Ludolph presented the funeral oration, which he then wrote into the parish register. The work is suffused with comparisons between the Old Testament and the afflictions of Reichensachsen. After a preliminary section primarily in Latin, in which Ludolph made frequent reference to passages from Psalms (especially Psalms 55, 56, 139, and 142),[88] there is a "Transition to Our Current State," which recounts in greater detail the points of comparison between Reichensachsen and the afflicted of the Old Testament. The format of this section of the funeral oration is itself indicative of how Ludolph understood his message. He underscored the themes that he wished to illustrate with his biblical passages and noted both the themes and the passages in the margins of the text in order to draw attention to them. Ludolph cited Zechariah 13:5 and Amos 7:14 ("Then answered Amos, and said to Amaziah, I was no prophet, neither was I a prophet's son; but I was a herdsman, and a gatherer of sycamore fruit") to underscore that the desperate circumstances gave both him and his listeners the ability to interpret suffering as a prophetic message. Central to the imagery of Ludolph's oration are passages from Hosea, Job, Jeremiah, and Lamentations (the same Old Testament prophets invoked by the Estates of Hesse in their report of 1624), which he linked with themes that were central to the experience of the villages in the region: protection, towns, *salva guardia*, friendship and neighborliness, men, wife and children, nobles, church, houses, fields, town hall, the dead. His exposition was punctuated by the exclamation, "O, that we have sinned so much!"

The funeral oration for Sabine von Boyneburg was long, and the constant refrain of sin and suffering must have struck Ludolph's audience. The oration undoubtedly was calculated to appeal to his local audience, but there was no need for Ludolph to persuade the villagers of Reichensachsen that they were suffering. His rhetoric of death and destruction had to serve a different purpose—to offer hope and give the suffering a meaning that could be cathartic. After highlighting the biblical passages and themes in the margins for the majority of the text, Ludolph wrote the last two pages in one stretch, with no indication of the sources, though the images there are also primarily from the Bible. Following his final exclamation, "O, that we have sinned so much!" Ludolph tried to capture all the horrors of the war in a single statement of the wages of sin:

> Is there even one house, one alley, one corner, one street, one field, one road, one trail, one footpath, one hill, one hedge, one mountain, one valley that has not been sprinkled with our blood and marked by the blood of the killed! And those of us who still live and remain here . . . what else are we but a repast for fire and the sword, which await us. O Reichensachsen how your magnificence is thrown to the ground! They treat you like an unclean vessel! You have become like a common whore, whoever thinks of you wants to quarter by you! Whoever can go no-where, comes to you, whoever can find nothing to plunder comes to you! All your injuries cannot be counted! In addition, they open their mouths up wide against you—that is your reward—whistle at you, blacken your teeth and say "he ha" we have plundered and hunted you and we like it, we have treated you like discarded water and spurned you; You may say: I say to you all who pass by, Look for yourself and see if there is any pain that has passed us by, for the Lord has filled me with woe on the day of his anger, he has sent a fire from hell to my bones and let it boil, he has tied a net around my feet and knocked me down, he has made me desolate, so that I must mourn daily. I the pastor and all who pass by you may say: O Reichensachsen, with whom can I compare you and how shall I account for you? With whom can I compare you that I could console you? For your suffering is great as a sea, who can heal you? O Reichensachsen, never forget this condition![89]

The service ended with I Thessalonians 5:23: "And the very God of peace sanctify you wholly; and I pray God your whole spirit and soul and body be preserved blameless unto the coming of our Lord Jesus Christ."

The reference to "peace" in Thessalonians redirects our attention to how narratives of death and destruction shifted toward the end of the war. We have already seen that a plea for peace was part of Grandenborn's depiction of its suffering in 1639. The yearning for peace became an alternative way of talking about death and destruction that served to revive hope in a desolated community. Peace had, of course, figured in pamphlets and correspondence from the beginning of the war, but the failure of all other rhetorical strategies to find a way out of the war made the yearning for peace the most powerful image in the last years. According to the poets and pamphleteers in the 1640s, Germany "sighed" for peace, and when it finally came they "shouted with joy."[90] Ludolph elaborated on the benefits of peace in his funeral oration in a way that was certain to appeal to the hopes of his audience: "the lord grant that our sons grow up in their youth like plants and our daughters like the bay trees, and that our palaces and magazines be full, so that they can produce one supply after another, that our sheep bear a thousand and a hundred thousand in our villages."[91]

But the war lasted for another six years after Ludolph's oration. The final years of the war brought no respite from hunger and occupation, nor from the constant flight that was now the standard response to the approach of troops. The final years of the war involved a fierce struggle between Hesse-Kassel and Hesse-Darmstadt, which was waged in part in the Werra region. The Werra remained a battlefield until the final year of the war. Ludolph reported that the villagers fled for eighteen weeks in 1646 and yet again in 1647, only to return to the village at Candlemas 1648. This last threat to the Werra region was severe enough that the superintendent in Eschwege again fled to the security of Kassel for a brief period in 1647. All these disruptions elicited some comment from Ludolph, as if by chronicling the events he would be better able to judge the spiritual welfare of his flock and make the events intelligible to them.

The long, drawn-out negotiations in Westphalia heightened anticipation of the coming peace. When the peace treaty was completed, the circuit was closed and the experience of the war as a whole became fixed. The rhetoric of death and destruction contributed to the contemporary understanding of the chronological contours of the war, from the outbreak in Bohemia in 1618 to the end in Westphalia in 1648.[92] The coming of peace was a time of great rejoicing, in part because it provided a final cathartic moment for the locality. Even if it did not end all the suffering at the local level, it ended the process that gave that suffering such rhetorical force. When peace finally came, the sense of yearning for peace and catharsis was expressed in the Werra region by the von Boyneburg family, who greeted the news of the formal confirmation of the Treaties of Westphalia in Nuremberg on New Year's Day 1650 with a wish for "a blissful peaceful (friedensreiche) and peaceable (fridsamen) new year."[93]

Of course, the end of the war did not mean the end of all troubles. There were still difficult times ahead, as the villagers slowly trickled home and the troops demobilized; but the peace made it possible for the village to regroup and to try to reestablish the former order that had been so disrupted by the last years of the war. The cycle of misery was finally broken, and a new basis for interaction between the locality and the outside world could now be established.

Notes

1. Hessian State Archives, Marburg (StAM) 4h 187, Moritz to Räte.
2. The two standard accounts of Hessian participation in the Thirty Years' War are Christoph Rommel, *Geschichte von Hessen*, vol. 6 (Marburg, 1836), and Franz v. Geyso, "Beiträge zur Politik und Kriegführung Hessens im Zeitalter des Dreißigjährigen Krieges," *Zeitschrift für Hessische Geschichte* 53 (1921): 14–30. Any analysis of Moritz's role in the war must begin with these works. Geyso judges Moritz's capabilities much more harshly than does Rommel. Our primary concern is with how Moritz's policies affected the Werra region, however, for which Rommel and Geyso give only scant information.
3. Standard and recent works on the Thirty Years' War are Moriz Ritter, *Deutsche Geschichte im Zeitalter der Gegenreformation und des Dreissigjährigen Krieges (1555–1648)*, vol. 3 (Stuttgart, 1908); C. V. Wedgwood, *The Thirty Years' War* (London, 1938); Geoffrey Parker, ed., *The Thirty Years' War* (Boston, 1984); J. V. Polisensky, *The Thirty Years' War*, trans. R. J. W. Evans (Berkeley, 1971); Günter Barudio, *Der Teutsche Krieg 1618–1648* (Frankfurt, 1985); Gerhard Schormann, *Der Dreißigjährige Krieg* (Göttingen, 1985).
4. See, for example, Collalto's request to march through Hesse in StAM 4h 502, which Moritz referred to his Räte on 23/7/1623.
5. StAM 5 14964.
6. On Ludwig of Hesse-Marburg's testament and its place in the tensions between Hesse-Marburg and Hesse-Kassel see Manfred Rudersdorf, *Ludwig IV Landgraf von Hessen-Marburg 1537–1604: Landesteilung und Luthertum in Hessen* (Mainz, 1991). On the general problem of the decision of the *Reichshofrat* against Moritz see Ritter, *Deutsche Geschichte*, 190–91.
7. Gunter Thies, *Territorialstaat und Landesverteidigung: Das Landesdefensionswerk in Hessen-Kassel unter Landgraf Moritz (1592–1627)* (Darmstadt and Marburg, 1973).
8. StAM 4h 208. Oddly, Thies, *Territorialstaat*, says nothing about the performance of the militia in battle. Although his formal endpoint is the end of Moritz's reign in 1627, he effectively ends his analysis in 1622, just before the invasion of Tilly's troops.
9. StAM 4h 95.
10. StAM 17d von Boyneburg, packet 17, 29/4/1622, Peter Betzer to Räte.
11. StAM Kop. 121, passim. .
12. Compare Chapter 1.
13. StAM Kop 121. Compare also F. L. Carsten, *Princes and Parliaments in Germany* (Oxford, 1959).
14. Carsten, *Princes and Parliaments*, 172–80, discusses Moritz's actions in terms of this struggle. He relies primarily on Rommel for his interpretation.
15. See Fritz Redlich, "Contributions in the Thirty Years' War," *Economic History Review* 12–13 (1959/60): 147–54, and Moriz Ritter, "Das Kontributionsystem Wallensteins," *Historische Zeitschrift* 90 (1903): 193–249. Although evidence from the Werra region is not conclusive, it seems that the mechanisms of collection and the actual term *contribution* were both employed before Wallenstein made them notorious.
16. StAM 4h 187, May 1619, Räte to Obrist Leutnant v. Ködderitz.
17. Hans Wertheim, *Der Tolle Halberstädter: Herzog Christian von Braunschweig im Pfälzischen Krieg 1621–1622*, vol. 1 (Berlin, 1929), 340–63.
18. StAM 4h 353.
19. See Wertheim, *Der Tolle Halberstädter*, 2: 131–33.
20. StAM 4h 451.

21. Wertheim, *Der Tolle Halberstädter*, 2: 363.
22. StAM 5 17061, Moritz to Räte, undated.
23. W. Grotefend, "Der Prozeß des landgräflichen Raths Dr. Wolfgang Gunther," *Hessenland* 12 (1898): 270.
24. See StAM 4h 405, Verpflegungs Ordinantz, 8/1/1624, for the following.
25. Ibid.
26. StAM 4h 531.
27. StAM 40d Sontra, 28/6/1623.
28. See Jane Susannah Fishman, *Boerenverdriet: Violence Between Peasants and Soldiers in Early Modern Netherlands Art* (Ann Arbor, 1982) and Herbert Langer, *The Thirty Years' War* (Poole, 1981).
29. This is an interesting lingering consequence of the Peasants' War of 1525. The English observer Fynes Moryson noted, "In generall, the Gentlemen feare the conspiracy of the common people, lest after the example of the Sweitzers, they should roote out the Gentry, or at least yeeld either none or voluntary obedience, at their owne pleasure." *An Itinerary Containing His Ten Yeeres Travell Through the Twelve Dominions of Germany, Bohmerland, Sweitzerland, Netherland, Denmarke, Poland, Italy, Turkey, France, England, Scotland, and Ireland*, vol. 3 (Glasgow, 1907), 192.
30. StAM 4c Hesse-Darmstadt 1873, 10/9/1626.
31. StAM 17e Eschwege 127.
32. StAM 17e Heldra 2.
33. S. H. Steinberg, *The "Thirty Years War" and the Conflict for European Hegemony 1600–1660* (New York, 1966).
34. Gerhard Benecke, "The Problem of Death and Destruction in the Thirty Years War: New Evidence from the Middle Weser Front," *European Studies Review* 2 (1972): 250. I do not believe that Benecke's evidence proves his point conclusively, even in the specific case of Lemgo. At the very least, Benecke needed to establish a more direct relationship between *public* debts and *private* damage on a large scale.
35. Ibid., 245–46. In his book based on the same material, Benecke expressed himself rather differently. He calls Grimmelshausen's work the "simpleton's best-seller," as if to suggest that only a simpleton could believe that Grimmelshausen's fiction could contain elements of truth. G. Benecke, *Society and Politics in Germany 1500–1700* (London, 1974), 233.
36. I treat this problem in greater depth in John Theibault, "The Rhetoric of Death and Destruction in the Thirty Years War," *Journal of Social History* 27 (1993): 271–90.
37. StAM 5 12201, 1/3/1648, Kammerräte to Amalie Elisabeth.
38. StAM 4h 569, 29/9/1624, for instance.
39. StAM 17/I 1002, 5/1/1625, Wersabe to Räte.
40. Ibid.
41. Ibid. Wersabe does not mention contributions in money from Sontra, nor does he explain how often the 105 taler and 74 taler were collected.
42. Ibid.
43. StAM 4h 531.
44. Ibid. Landgrave Moritz thwarted an effort to extend the quarter into *Amt* Kaufungen on the grounds that he did not want all his districts to be ruined. An interesting sidelight of the conflict is that neither *Amtschultheiss* wished to serve on a commission to investigate claims of damage. Melchior Philipp Trott excused himself from serving as a commissioner by explaining that he was weighed down by negotiations with Collalto and could use some "guete leute" ("good people") who could provide "gueten raht und taht" ("good ad-

vice and support"), instead of his having to go off to advise others.

45. StAM 73 32, 31/8/1624, Stände to Landgraf Moritz.
46. StAM 4h 502, 23/7/1623, and StAM 340 von Baumbach-Nentershausen II, 149, Landtagsabschied of 8/1626.
47. StAM 4h 753, Tilly to Moritz, 4/11/1626.
48. StAM 23a Landvogt an der Werra, 15/4/1626, Gemeinde zu Rittmannshausen to Moritz.
49. Pfarrarchiv Renda, Ki Grandenborn 1587–1669.
50. StAM 17d v. Boyneburg, Unv. Paket 19, 12/4/1626.
51. StAM 23a Landvogt an der Werra, 28/4/26, Netra, Röhrda, and Rittmannshausen to Landgrave Moritz.
52. Grotefend, "Der Prozeß," 271.
53. See Geyso, "Beiträge zur Politik," 29–30.
54. Uta Krüger-Lowenstein, *Die Rotenburger Quart* (Marburg, 1979). For the distinction between regular revenues and taxes, see Chapter 1.
55. Grotefend, "Der Prozeß," 298–301.
56. Geyso, "Beiträge zur Politik," 41ff. The period after 1633 in Wilhelm's administration is covered in Ruth Altmann, *Landgraf Wilhelm V von Hessen-Kassel im Kampf gegen Kaiser und Katholizismus 1633–1637* (Marburg, 1938).
57. Perhaps the best sign of this is in StAM 4h 718, which included more than a hundred letters of supplication received from different parts of Hesse in only six months in 1625 and 1626.
58. StAM 4c Hessen-Rheinfels-Rotenburg 836.
59. Ilse Gromes, ed., *Bußen aus den Amtsrechnungen des Amtes Sontra 1590–1648* (Sontra, 1977), 74.
60. Ibid., 69.
61. W. Kürschner, "Aus dem Kirchenbuch von Reichensachsen (und Langenhain) von 1639–1653," *Archiv für Hessiche Geschichte und Altertumskunde* NF 9 (1913): 56.
62. Ki Grandenborn.
63. StAM 4h 799, Peter Stückrodt to Landgrave Hermann of Hesse-Rotenburg, 21/12/1636.
64. StAM 4d 39, 4–14/10/1637, Räte to Landgraf Wilhelm, partially in code.
65. Ki Grandenborn.
66. A good recent description of the burning of Eschwege in 1637 and the process of rebuilding is Herbert Fritsche and Thomas Wiegand, *Eschwege 1637 Die Zerstörung der Stadt im Dreißigjährigen Krieg* (Eschwege, 1987).
67. Ki Grandenborn.
68. StAM 5 12201.
69. StAM 4d 39.
70. Hilmar Milbradt, *Das Hessische Mannschaftsregister von 1639* (Frankfurt, 1959), vi.
71. Ibid., 98.
72. Ibid.
73. Ibid., 97–98.
74. Ibid., 98.
75. See the title of the pamphlet by Johann Christoph Assum, "Telum necessitatis, paupertatis et impossibilitatis . . . nemlich die gegenwärtige nun viel Jährige: und zuvor unerhörte, auch noch unaufhörliche Kriegs-onera, und dannenhero Ihr und ihrer noch übrigen armen Unterthanen, biß auff den grund und boden außgeschöpfftes Vermögen kräfftiglich dagegen zu allegiren vorzuwenden . . ." ("Weapon of need, poverty, and powerlessness . . . namely the current war burdens that have lasted several years, have never before been known, and have yet to cease, and the resulting efforts to protect the wealth of the few remaining poor subjects and their exhausted resources") mentioned in Paul Hohenemser, ed.,

Flugschriften Sammlung Gustav Freytag (reprint) (Hildesheim, 1966), 377. An anonymous work addressed itself directly to the problem that Grandenborn raised about deserted farmsteads. "Wohlmeinender Christlicher und Politischer Discurs, Von Wüsten Güthern, Darinnen nachgezetate drey Fragen von denen fast in allen Landen befindlichen wüst- und öde liegenden Güthern tractiret und erörtert wird. I. Wohero die Verödung so unzehlich viel Gütter und die dahero dem gantzen Lande zuwachsene verödung entstehe. II. Wer Ursacher daß solche nicht wieder gebawet, sondern wie man täglich und kläglich erfähret, gemehret werden. III. Wie solchem Verwüstungen abzuhelffen, dero vor Augenscheinende total desolation vorgebawet und alles successive in vorigen Flor und Wohlstand gesetzet werden möchte." ("Well-meant Christian and political discourse of deserted lands, wherein the following three questions concerning the deserted and desolate lands that can be found in almost all territories are treated and explained: (1) From whence does the desertion of countless lands and the consequent growing desolation of the entire territory arise? (2) Who is responsible for the fact that these lands are not planted again, but instead, as one sees clearly and sadly, the desolation increases? (3) How can such desolation be averted, the evident complete desolation prevented, and everything consequently brought back to its earlier flourishing and healthy condition?") Ibid., 378.

76. Ibid., 378.
77. Milbradt, *Das hessiche Mannschaftsregister*, 115.
78. Ibid., 107.
79. Ibid.
80. Ibid., 106.
81. Kürschner, "Aus dem Kirchenbuch," 54.
82. Wilm Sippel, ed., *Forschungsberichte der Stiftung Sippel* (Göttingen, 1981), passim.
83. Ibid., 119.
84. StAM Ki Reichensachsen 1639–1653.
85. Ibid.
86. Kürschner, "Aus dem Kirchenbuch," 53.
87. Ibid.
88. Characteristic is Psalm 142. "I cried unto the LORD with my voice; with my voice did I make my supplication. / I poured out my complaint before him; I shewed him my trouble. / When my spirit was overwhelmed within me, then, I knewest my path. In the way wherein I walked they have privily laid a snare for me. / I looked on my right hand, and beheld, but *there was* no man that would know me: refuge failed me; no man cared for my soul. / I cried unto thee O LORD: I said, Thou *art* my refuge *and* my portion in the land of the living. / Attend unto my cry; for I am brought very low: deliver me from my persecutors; for they are stronger than I. / Bring my soul out of prison that I may praise thy name: the righteous shall compass me about; for thou shalt deal bountifully with me."
89. Ki Reichensachsen.
90. I. Weithase, *Die Darstellung von Krieg und Frieden in der Deutschen Barockdichtung* (Weimar, 1953), 43–52. "Friedeseufzende Teutschland" ("Germany Sighing for Peace") is used by Philipp Michael Moscherosch; "Friedewünschende" and "Friedejauchzende Teutschland" ("Germany wishing for" and "Jubilating for peace") are both used in dramas by Johann Rist.
91. StAM Ki Reichensachsen.
92. See K. Repgen, "Noch Einmal zum Begriff Dreißigjähriger Krieg," *Zeitschrift für Historische Forschung* 9 (1982): 347–52.
93. StAM 17e Bischhausen 4.

6

The Material Impact
of the War

The war undermined the ability of the village to reproduce itself. It placed unprecedented burdens on a relatively inflexible agricultural economy, which led to massive disruptions of the village's internal order. Property, labor, and capital were all vulnerable to the war. Most of the strategies used by the villagers to protect village resources failed. As a result, the measurable indices of destruction moved in tandem with the breakdown of local authority and the increasing intensity of descriptions of suffering. We must, therefore, consider the material impact of the war as part of the way that the village was defined during the war.

The prewar economy of the Werra region has already been discussed in some detail. That prewar situation provides a framework for understanding the economy of the region during the war. The economic structure can be separated into two broad categories, demography and productivity, though they are closely linked in many respects. The prewar demographic and economic indicators for the Werra do not point toward an imminent collapse; nor do they point toward robust growth. Population was increasing in conformity with the demographic pattern of the old regime. The productivity of the *Amt* was increasing, though much of that increase could be attributed to the larger number of people in the *Amt* and the inflation of grain prices rather than economic expansion on its own. Although it cannot be demonstrated that the Werra had not reached its Malthusian limits by the outset of the war, one cannot argue that the war struck a population or an economy in obvious crisis. The war precipitated the collapse of the village economy.

Different regions of Germany were affected quite differently by the war, and different sectors of the economy responded at different rates, but it is not clear how to judge the relationship of those facts. The work of Günther Franz gives a preliminary impression of the extent of depopulation caused by the war.[1] Based on an exhaustive study of the secondary literature, Franz presents a mosaic-like picture of the demographic impact. There were regions with no losses, such as Schleswig-Holstein and Austria; regions with losses of less than 10 percent, such as much of Lower Saxony; and regions that lost more than 50 percent of their population, such as Mecklenburg and the Palatinate. The average for Germany as a whole was a loss of 40 percent in the countryside and 33 percent in the towns.[2] The Werra region was one of the earliest and most frequent victims of the depredations of the troops. It is, therefore, representative of those regions hit hardest by the war. Franz's figures put the territory of Hesse-Kassel among the regions that suffered the greatest population losses. Hesse lost 40 to 50 percent of its population because of the war; in Thuringia, which bordered the Werra valley, the population loss was over 50 percent.

There is little analytical subtlety to Franz's presentation of figures. His estimate of a 40 to 50 percent population loss is imprecise because it is an average for the territory as a whole based on a very small body of evidence. Population levels were fluid, as villagers fled and returned, so there was no one point in time when losses could be measured adequately. It is, therefore, difficult to assess whether Franz measured the totals of 1648 against those of 1618 or compared the nadir of population during the war against a generalized prewar figure. He resorted to one or the other method, depending on the nature of his secondary sources. Nevertheless, the figures confirm what the expressions of misery described in the last chapter indicated: The population of the Werra was hit hard by the war. The war was not a simple Malthusian check but a disaster that had wide ramifications for the demographic system.

If we move away from Franz's general figures to the population trends of individual villages, the impact of depopulation on the organization of the village becomes more apparent. One of the few works to assess the demographic impact of war in relation to famine and disease—the other props of the Malthusian system—is Myron Gutmann's analysis of the Basse-Meuse from 1620 to 1750.[3] He demonstrated that the effects of war were almost always compounded by the effects of disease and famine fostered by military occupation. Very few deaths were caused by the soldiers themselves, but many deaths resulted from the problems of coping with the presence of troops. That same pattern characterized the Werra region, though the extent of disruption was much greater in the Werra than it was in the Basse-Meuse. The experience of Grandenborn—the only village for which we have extensive information about its response to demographic crisis under normal Malthusian conditions before the war—provides one concrete example of how the war affected the standard practices of the village. Two demographic crises took place in Grandenborn during the war. Neither crisis can be attributed entirely to the war, but both were exacerbated by the presence of troops. The immediate cause of the first of these crises was an outbreak of plague and dysentery, which was brought in by soldiers in 1626.

The 187 deaths recorded in that year stand out immediately as an extraordinary catastrophe for the village (Table 6.1).

The demographic response to the large numbers of deaths differed greatly from the response to crises of the old type. The village did not recuperate from the exceptional mortality of 1626 with the same vigor as it had in 1598. In the ten years before the 1626 crisis, there were an average of 14.6 baptisms a year. This was somewhat less than the 18.8 average for the spurt after 1598, but it was well in excess of the number of deaths in the same period. In the ten years after 1626, Grandenborn averaged only 8.6 baptisms a year. Instead of responding to depopulation with an increase in the number of births, as it had done in 1598, the village showed a decrease. The number of baptisms from 1627 to 1635 exceeded the number of burials by thirty-two, because the decrease in the mortality rate was even greater than the decrease in the birth rate, but the 187 people lost could not be replaced rapidly at that pace. The change in the demographic pattern can be attributed partly to the disruptions that accompanied the presence of the troops and partly to the severity of the population loss itself.

The crisis of 1626 in Grandenborn fits Alain Croix's definition of a *mortalité de crise*, in contrast to a standard Malthusian check.[4] The pattern of recovery associated with a smaller mortality crisis was temporarily suspended, and the ability of the demographic system to respond by immediately increasing the number of marriages and births was interrupted. The magnitude of the disaster that befell Grandenborn is even more evident when compared with the experience of the Basse-Meuse described by Gutmann. Gutmann analyzed the severity of demographic crises on the basis of an "index of extreme behavior," which measured how far the statistics for a given year deviated from what would have been expected had the year experienced "normal" mortality.[5] The highest index value for the parishes of the Basse-Meuse in the 120 years between 1628 and 1748 was 2.40 in 1676, which means that in 1676 the region suffered a mortality crisis nearly two-and-a-half times as severe as the death rate in a normal year.[6] In no other year was there an index value over 2.00. If we take an index value of 1.75 as indicative of a major crisis, the Basse-Meuse suffered five crises in that 120-year period.[7] The shortest time span between major crises was eighteen years. Index values for Grandenborn calculated in a manner similar to that for the Basse-Meuse offer a striking contrast. The highest index value for Grandenborn was 13.69 in 1626. Even accounting for the wider range of index values created by the smaller total population, Grandenborn's mortality crisis was of a different order. The rhythms of crisis and renewal were disrupted by the magnitude of the crisis. The tribulations of 1626 not only marked a change in the way the village interacted with the troops and the central administration but also altered the process by which the village reproduced itself.

If the events of 1626 plunged Grandenborn into crisis, then the events

TABLE 6.1
Number of Burials in Grandenborn, 1587–1647

YEAR	DEATHS	IEB	YEAR	DEATHS	IEB
1587	7	0.52	1618	2	0.15
1588	8	0.59	1619	7	0.51
1589	19	1.14	1620	7	0.51
1590	0	0	1621	9	0.66
1591	11	0.82	1622	15	1.10
1592	6	0.45	1623	8	0.57
1593	9	0.67	1624	12	0.88
1594	9	0.67	1625	5	0.37
1595	6	0.45	1626	187	13.69
1596	7	0.52	1627	11	0. 80
1597	19	1.41	1628	6	0.44
1598	89	6.59	1629	6	0.44
1599	6	0.44	1630	4	0.29
1600	7	0.52	1631	4	0.29
1601	8	0.81	1632	5	0.36
1602	6	0.44	1633	3	0.22
1603	7	0.52	1634	3	0.22
1604	11	0.81	1635	10	0.73
1605	8	0.59	1636	97	7.07
1606	5	0.37	1637	21	1.53
1607	23	1.70	1638	36	2.62
1608	8	0.56	1639	0	0
1609	9	0.66	1640	0	0
1610	5	0.37	1641	4	0.29
1611	7	0.52	1642	0	0
1612	7	0.52	1643	0	0
1613	4	0.29	1644	1	0.07
1614	13	0.96	1645	0	0
1615	10	0.74	1646	1	0.07
1616	14	1.03	1647	3	0.22
1617	8	0.59			

Source: Pfarrarchiv Renda, Ki Grandenborn.

Slope = .00572; Y-intercept = 13.44, with year 1587 = year 1.

IEB = index of extreme behavior, devised by Gutmann and explained in text.

of 1636 turned the crisis into catastrophe. Although the rhythm of renewal had been changed because of the magnitude of the mortality crisis of 1626, the village still struggled to reproduce itself. For nine years, the number of births exceeded the number of deaths. Such a rate of recovery would ordinarily lead to a rapid return to traditional demographic patterns. In 1636, however, Grandenborn was hit by another mortality crisis. Although it was not as severe as that of 1626, it equaled the worst crises identified for other regions of Europe. Ninety-seven people died in 1636, producing an index of extreme behavior of 7.07. If we recall that the Basse-Meuse suffered indices of 1.85 at twenty-year intervals, and that the highest mortality for a village in the Nantais was 733 percent of normal, we can see that the effects in Grandenborn must have been compounded by how soon the second crisis followed the first. The combination of two such immense catastrophes in such a short time span dramatically altered the demographic response of the village. The rhythms of birth and death that had echoed feebly in the time between the two crises came to a halt. At first, a new rhythm was established. The death rate remained high for another two years; a total of fifty-seven people died in 1637 and 1638. After that point, however, both the death and birth rates dwindled to almost nothing. Only ten more burials were recorded before 1648. Only thirty-three baptisms were recorded in the ten years after 1636. The difference in burials and baptisms produced a net increase of twenty-three inhabitants but was not enough to recover the losses from 1638, much less those from 1636 or 1626. The vital signs of population growth were almost nonexistent. The last ten years of the war took place in a different demographic environment from that of the beginning of the war.

It is difficult to gain a clear picture of how Grandenborn's experience compares with that of other villages in the Werra region. The mortality of 1626 was high in many other villages, but information is hard to find. For example, the parish register of Rockensüß, which commenced in 1623, had no record of burials before the end of the war, and the record of baptisms was riddled with gaps between 1623 and 1650.[8] The minister explained the gaps in the register by noting when he and the rest of the village were forced to flee. Between 1626 and the end of the war, there were eleven years with incomplete records of baptisms.

Many ministers faced with the prospect of recording such a large number of burials abandoned the project altogether. Pastor Ludolph of Reichensachsen reported that he could not maintain a list of burials "in such difficult times" and devoted his energies to recording baptisms and marriages instead.[9] His list of baptisms did not show the same devastating impact of the mortality crisis as did Grandenborn's, but this may be explained in part because it began in 1639. Reichensachsen averaged 16.7 births a year until the end of the war. It probably had many more births a year before the war, since it had more than twice as many householders as Grandenborn in 1623, but the fact that Reichensachsen had a stable birth rate suggests that the village was already in a position to recover in the 1640s.

The parish register of Abterode, Vockerode, and Wellingerode begins between the two great demographic crises of the war. The data from that register indicate few wrenching changes.[10] Abterode suffered a significant population loss in 1635 from the same plague that affected Grandenborn, registering 135 burials. The number of deaths remained higher than normal through 1638. The demographic consequences of the mortality crisis of 1635 in Abterode were less severe than those in Grandenborn, even though the numbers of burials were comparable. In Abterode, the number of burials after 1638 declined in comparison to the 1630–1634 period, but they did not come to a standstill. Abterode seemed to recover from the demographic crisis in the accustomed manner of the old-type crisis. It is likely that the village was able to recover so quickly because it had not suffered such a dramatic population loss in 1626.

It was, however, possible for a village to escape the more severe consequences of a crisis afflicting a neighboring village. The village of Vockerode, just over a kilometer away from Abterode, did not suffer a dramatic population loss in 1635. Only eighteen burials took place there that year. There is no apparent reason why Vockerode should have escaped the plague that afflicted its neighbors. It was located in a separate narrow valley, but Grandenborn was similarly isolated and suffered more severely. Whatever the reason, Vockerode remained fortunate for the rest of the 1630s. The average number of burials for the four years 1635–1638 was 21.5. This was higher than normal but did not constitute a crisis of mortality. The situation in Vockerode seemed closer in character to the crises of the Basse-Meuse than to that of Abterode. As a result, the surplus of baptisms over burials after 1638 quickly put Vockerode on the road to recovery.

In all villages of the Werra, demographic crisis accompanied the most destructive phases of the war. This fact helps make sense of the laments encountered in the preceding chapter. The worst descriptions of death and destruction almost always came in conjunction with manifest demographic catastrophes. Villagers may have had ulterior motives for stressing their misery, as some historians have claimed, but demographic data confirm that they were truly miserable.

The demographic impact of the war on the entire Werra region cannot be interpreted through parish registers alone. If we move from the close examination of the demographic experiences of individual villages to a more general assessment of the population of the region during the worst years of the war, we can see how much local variation there was. The 1639 survey instigated by Amalie Elisabeth, described in the preceding chapter, offers the broadest perspective on the demographic effects of the war in the Werra region. There are, however, three limitations to the information supplied by that survey. The first is that it does not cover all the *Ämter* of the

Werra region. The villages of *Amt* Eschwege/Bilstein were not included in the survey, which excludes the villages of Abterode, Vockerode, and Wellingerode from closer consideration of the concrete results of the demographic events already described.[11] The second limitation is that the account gives only the number of male heads of households and widows in each village, not the total number of inhabitants. Without information on household composition, it is impossible to tell how severe the decrease in the number of children was in comparison to the decrease in the number of household heads. It is also impossible to tell how much of the decrease in the number of households was caused by remarriage of widows, with its concomitant fusion of her household with her husband's, and how much was caused by the disappearance of entire households because all of its members had either died or fled. The third limitation is the year that the survey was made: The lists were created at a time when village life was most disrupted by the effects of the war. There were some villagers known to be living elsewhere, who would return when stability arrived. There were others who disappeared without a trace, but returned at the end of the war. But there were also nine additional years of warfare that were to take its toll on the people who remained. These limitations mean that we cannot derive precise figures for the impact of the war throughout the region, but we can get a sense of the scale of that impact.

The village-by-village surveys ordered by Amalie Elisabeth establish that the Werra had lost more than 50 percent of its population by 1639. The pattern for all three *Ämter* was similar (Table 6.2). The number of households in *Amt* Sontra had declined by 68.8 percent in comparison with 1583.[12] *Amt* Wanfried reported losses of 63.5 percent, and the villages of *Gericht* Boyneburg lost 54.4 percent of the number of households in 1583 and 59.4 percent of the households claimed in 1623. This loss of population affected different villages in varying degrees. In general, the largest villages suffered most (Tables 6.3 and 6.4). The *Höfe*, which consisted of only three or four

TABLE 6.2

Demographic Impact of the War in Villages of *Amt* Sontra, *Amt* Wanfried, and *Gericht* Boyneburg

SIZE	NUMBER	AVERAGE POPULATION	% REMAINING IN 1639	% REMAINING IN 1656
Small villages	13	19.8	55.1	74.6
Medium villages	12	58.8	35.2	60.5
Towns and large villages	4	168.0	34.7	60.0

Sources: StAM S 98; Hilmar Milbradt, *Das Hessische Mannschaftsregister von 1639* (Frankfurt: 1959); and Herbert Lamprecht, *Die Huldigung von 1656 in der Rotenburger Quart* (Frankfurt: 1985).

TABLE 6.3

Number of Householders in Selected Villages in Ämter Sontra and
Wanfried, 1583, 1639, 1656

	1583	1639	1656
Small villages			
Rauttenhausen	17	3	9
Berneburg	24	8	19
Dens	27	13	14
Munchhosbach	24	16	19
Medium villages			
Altenburschla	49	7	29
Breittau	57	11	36
Königswald	58	14	23
Rockensüß	63	18	45
Towns and large villages			
Ulfen	114	34	64
Wanfried	177	71	115
Sontra	231	58	134

Sources: StAM S 98; Hilmar Milbradt, Das Hessische Mannschaftsregister von 1639 (Frankfurt: 1959); and Herbert Lamprecht, Die Huldigung von 1659 in der Rotenburger Quart (Frankfurt: 1985).

TABLE 6.4

Growth and Collapse of Villages in Gericht Boyneburg,
1583, 1623, 1639

VILLAGE	1583	1623	1639
Thurnhosbach	12	15	6
Rechtebach	12	16	13
Oberdünzebach	17	24	11
Niederdünzebach	35	32	6
Grandenborn	60	82	15
Wichmannshausen	64	72	21
Röhrda	70	89	56
Netra	86	76	37
Reichensachsen	150	172	70

Sources: StAM S 98; Hilmar Milbradt, Das Hessische Mannschaftsregister von 1639 (Frankfurt: 1959); and Herbert Lamprecht, Die Huldigung von 1656 in der Rotenburger Quart (Frankfurt: 1985).

households, were able to maintain a stable population of householders. Some small villages also remained relatively stable. The small village of Rechtebach in *Gericht* Boyneburg even reported one more household in 1639 than had been present in 1583; it was the only village in the region to grow during the war. In *Amt* Sontra, the number of householders in Krauthausen and Weissenborn, which was fewer than twenty before the war, declined by only 27.8 percent and 25 percent, respectively. Those villages that began the war with more than fifty households all suffered losses greater than the average for the *Amt*. The town of Sontra and the villages of Rockensüß and Ulfen all lost between 70 and 75 percent of their households. The village of Breittau was especially hard hit, losing over 80 percent of its households. Great losses were not confined to the larger villages, however. The single greatest change came in the small village of Rauttenhausen, where seventeen households resided in 1583. In 1639, only three remained. In *Gericht* Boyneburg, large villages also suffered more substantial losses than small villages, though the contrast between large and small was not as striking. Grandenborn lost 75 percent of its households, a figure comparable to most of the larger villages of *Amt* Sontra, but Reichensachsen lost "only" 53.3 percent and had more households than the town of Sontra.

The figures for the percentage of households lost in Grandenborn and Reichensachsen are consistent with the rates of baptism in the two villages after 1639. Reichensachsen averaged 16.7 baptisms a year, and Grandenborn had almost none. Reichensachsen started out with more people in the village before the war but also had a less precipitous decline in population. A loss of 50 percent of households did not create the same demographic response as a loss of 75 percent of households. Neither village could be described as fortunate in its war experiences, but Reichensachsen was more fortunate than Grandenborn. The scale of population loss was a matter of luck as much as anything else, but the consequences of that luck were immediately apparent in the reports of 1639 and in the parish registers. The different experiences of Abterode and Vockerode in 1636, described above, were another example of the differences in fortune. The situation in Röhrda shows a similar pattern. Although it was just on the other side of the hill from Grandenborn, it lost only 20 percent of its households. The impact of the war, therefore, varied greatly even within very narrow geographical boundaries.

The survey of 1639 shows other evidence of severe demographic dislocation besides the small percentage of households remaining in the villages. The number of remaining households headed by widows was also extraordinarily high. In *Amt* Wanfried, more than half the remaining households were headed by widows.[13] It is possible that men were more liable to be killed by marauding troops than women or children, either because they had more information of the whereabouts of their valuables or because they were more likely to put up resistance. It was relatively rare, however, for villagers to die directly at the hands of soldiers. The reports of 1639 were

careful to note the gruesome deaths of a few villagers—such as Claus Tholle
of Reichensachsen, who was thrown into his burning house by soldiers—
but the number of such cases was small.[14] A far more common cause of
population decline during warfare was famine and disease, which struck a
weakened population. The adult male population ordinarily did not make
up an exceptional proportion of the victims of famine or disease; indeed,
children were more likely to suffer than adults. The high percentage of
households headed by widows is, therefore, a striking confirmation of how
far from a typical mortality crisis the crises of the war were. The decline in
the number of marriageable men forced a change in the perception of the
household as requiring a male head; widows had to be counted as heads of
households to preserve the stability of households within each village.

Charting the economic impact of the war presents some of the same problems as charting the demographic impact. Economic burdens were distributed somewhat more evenly across the region because they were easier to
control, but there were still tremendous fluctuations and local variations.
Two aspects of the direct economic impact of the war on the village fed on
each other and intensified the overall burden. First, the war extracted extraordinary payments such as contributions, which removed both capital
and produce. Then, as the war continued, it directly affected the region
through the destruction of buildings, equipment, food stocks, animals, and
ultimately people. These direct intrusions into the economy deflected the
regular forms of economic interaction and thus adversely affected the economy
even when troops were no longer present. Any assessment of the impact of
the war on the community must determine what local products the war
took from the village, what measurable damage it inflicted, and what the
damage did to local economic practice.

The first of these factors is the most straightforward, but even it is hard
to determine because of the obscure record-keeping methods of the era.
There are few extant account books that give a sense of the amount of
revenues extracted by contributions, and even these rarely include the costs
of fuel and salt, which were accepted as a normal part of the price of occupation. Provisions ordinances and *salva guardia* allowed for the continuation
of some local control over the process of collecting revenues, which meant
that some revenues that were "extracted" remained in the village in some form.

In principle, the money from the contribution was to be used for pur-
chasing provisions, so that the money returned to circulation. Gerhard Benecke
used this characteristic of the contribution to argue that its adverse impact
on ordinary taxpayers was exaggerated by those who had to pay it.[15] No
purchase records survive from the Werra region to indicate whether anyone
there profited from the armies' demand for provisions. Wealthier merchants
in Eschwege and Hannoversch Münden were probably the primary beneficiaries of grain sales to the troops. It is unlikely that much of the money

TABLE 6.5
Capital Value and Damages Claimed in the Werra Region, 1623–1625

DISTRICT	TREYSA VALUE (IN RTHLR)	DAMAGE CLAIMED (IN RTHLR)
Town and *Amt* Eschwege/Bilstein	315,300	281,570
Town and *Amt* Sontra	111,400	108,238
Town and *Amt* Wanfried	113,990	22,075
Kloster Cornberg	5,600	4,447
Vogtei Germerode	nd[a]	39,689
All Hesse	6,151,400	3,318,326

Source: StAM K 57 and StAM 4h 579.
[a]nd = no data.

collected by the troops returned to the village through the sale of grain. Wealthy villagers might have profited if they were able to market their grain at an opportune moment, but if they were caught with their grain at home when the troops arrived, they would have to accept what the troops offered instead of market price.

The entire system of local circulation of goods and money worked only as long as the troops remained in one place. When they moved on, they were likely to take local products with them. The central administration was sensitive to losses of revenue from the *Amt* and sought information to assess the extent of the damage. As early as 1625, the central administration asked local officials to report on the value of all goods supplied to invading troops as well as the extent of damage suffered by each *Amt*.[16] The reported losses for just two years, August 1623 to June 1625, were far in excess of the burdens placed on the *Amt* in ordinary years (Table 6.5). According to the Treysa Assessment, the town and *Amt* of Sontra had a taxable capital of 111,400 Reichsthaler (Rthlr) and paid 34 Rthlr in a standard tax period,[17] yet they reported losses of 108,238 Rthlr in 1625.[18] The neighboring town and *Amt* of Eschwege/Bilstein reported 281,570 Rthlr in losses. In both cases, the losses claimed were nearly equal to the total value of the prewar capital. At first glance, these claims are absurd. Although the figures are "precise," there is no connection to the exact values of specific objects that were claimed to have been lost. There were few accounts from the individual villages from which to derive the grand total for the *Amt*. But both villagers and administrators were aware that it was possible to extract more "value" out of peasants than was accessible through the traditional mechanisms of *Herrschaft*. The administration had asked for an account of all "money, victuals, and other expenditures, including the damages suffered in the process."[19] This meant that the report measured something more than just the fixed property of the *Amt*. Although the administration's inquiry enabled the local officials to exaggerate the extent of damage—since the value of property could not be determined precisely and the "other expenditures" could be construed very broadly—the total figure had to tally with what the administration knew that armies were capable of extracting.

Other, more detailed, accounts from the same period produced less imposing, though by no means negligible, totals. The account of payments over a ten-year period from Heldra to various troops came to a total of 1,660 Rthlr. The villages of Amt Eschwege kept a similar account of their payments of contributions from 11 October 1623 to 21 February 1624.[20] In those four months, they collected 8,556 Rthlr, all but 62 Rthlr of which was given to troops; 1,200 Rthlr went to the troops under the command of Collalto in October and November alone. The village of Abterode paid 564 Rthlr, which comes out to more than 6 Rthlr per household. Projected out over a twenty-two-month span, the total for the Amt reached over 45,000 Rthlr. That does not include data from the town of Eschwege, which must have spent more than the villages of the Amt combined, if the Treysa Assessment served as the basis of the tax. None of these figures included any sums for damage caused by the troops or for food and fuel given to troops while they were quartered in houses in the village. They lend at least a little more credence to the huge sums claimed in total damage, since they were certified accounts that were confirmed by the provisions officers of the troops themselves.

It is unlikely that any village or town escaped with no losses to plunder or ransom. Local officials were aware of the assessed value of their land according to the Treysa Assessment. They could push the limits of credulity somewhat, but they could not claim an implausible amount of damage for fear of an investigation by the central administration. The reports had, after all, been produced in response to a direct inquiry from the central administration and must have been signed by the Amtmann or Rentmeister, who would have to attest to their veracity. The central administration maintained faith in the accuracy of the reports of local administrators throughout the war. Even in 1648, the Räte in Kassel still relied on local administrators to confirm the damage claims made by villagers.[21] The Räte reacted to the reports with some dismay, as the local officials "confirmed and strengthened" the claims of the villagers; they did not reject the reports as biased, however, but concluded that "our most gracious prince and lord will not be able to collect even the smallest amount this year."[22]

It was, of course, still possible to collect the smallest quantities from the villages, even in their times of greatest need. But the war interrupted the normal channels through which the activities of government were financed and prevented the administration from collecting the quantities it had in the past. Much of the money that the villages produced was funneled into contributions, which imposed a tremendous cash burden on the village. The 8,500

Rthlr collected by the emperor's troops in 1624 was more than twice what the landgrave collected from the Amt in a year from his rights as Grundherr. Not all this money was lost to the community permanently. Contributions paid to foreign troops gave the villagers few opportunities to recover their losses, but contributions paid to the landgrave's own troops gave villagers more leeway in their financial maneuvers. One of the few village accounts of contributions that survived to the present shows how the process of collecting and disbursing contributions was manipulated in the village of Abterode to minimize its impact in the village.[23] Between February and August 1634, the village collected a total of 13 taler 28 albus per week, nearly the value of a small house. In September, the weekly total fell to 7 taler, but for short periods the sums grew markedly; in January 1634, the village collected 85 taler, and in December of that year another 70 taler. These were substantial sums for a single village. The money was picked up by soldiers quartering in the area, who received a gratuity out of the total collected. This procedure for collecting the contribution was not regulated. Villagers paid gratuities to up to sixteen soldiers, and at one point to "2 females, who extorted the Contribution."[24]

Money returned to, or remained in, the village in the form of collection costs and exemptions for services rendered that were deducted from the total ostensibly collected. The gratuities paid to the soldiers who picked up the money were just a small proportion of the total deductions. Of the 85 taler collected in January 1634 in Abterode, only 48 taler were delivered to the paymasters of Colonel Ungefug in Eschwege.[25] Fourteen taler were paid in wages to the village tax collector, who was a villager, and to the toll official in Allendorf. The rest of the money was disbursed to villagers for various reasons. The deductions ranged from 8 taler that Hans Gercke Schöpff retained "because of the debt that the Gemeine owes him," to $3\frac{1}{2}$ albus given to Lorenz Junge's son, "who carried a note from the Rentmeister to Eschwege."[26] Between wages and deductions, Abterode kept just under half of what it had collected. In many cases, the deductions were probably not collected at all but merely recorded as collected and disbursed in order to fulfill the tax quota. The power of the local tax collector was enhanced by this accounting procedure. He was well paid for his efforts, and he was in a position to reduce the burden on other villagers by giving them paid chores, such as delivering messages, that could be deducted from their contributions. Not surprisingly, village officials benefited most from the deductions, since they were most closely involved in the negotiations that went along with each new imposition. The ability to recoup some of the money collected in contributions may have provided some solace to the village, but it could not disguise the fact that the contribution drained the resources of the village. As it became harder for villagers to raise the sums for the contribution, many forms of economic activity that contributed to the landgrave's other revenues ceased.

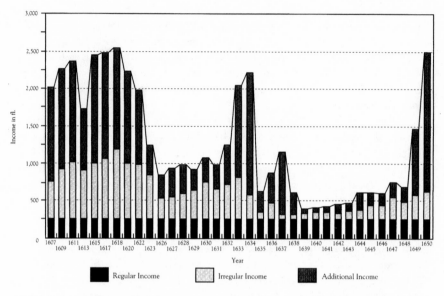

GRAPH 6.1   TOTAL INCOME IN *AMT* SONTRA BY TYPE OF INCOME,
1607–1650

Between contributions and the money collected by the landgrave as
Grundherr, the Werra was producing far more revenue than it had before
the war. But if the central administration needed any evidence that the
war affected the local economy severely, it had to look no further than the
Amt account books.[27] Seigneurial income began to drop steadily as the war
took its toll. Some of the income was inflexible and was collected no matter how prosperous the local economy was, but some of the income depended on the prosperity of the villages. As the war worsened, this source
of the landgrave's income collapsed.

The development of irregular income in *Amt* Sontra shows that the pattern of economic activity collapsed in tandem with demographic upheaval
(Graph 6.1). The years 1626 and 1635–1637 mark the two most notable
downswings in revenue, from which the *Amt* recovered slowly.[28] These are
also the years of greatest demographic crisis. Prior to the war, *Amt* Sontra
regularly collected more than 700 fl in irregular income, peaking at 923 fl
in 1618. Neither 1620 nor 1622 showed any appreciable slacking off in
economic activity in comparison with the prewar period, as irregular income still exceeded 700 fl. In the first year of direct contact with the
troops, 1623, decline set in. Irregular income fell below 600 fl for the first
time since 1607, to 585 fl. The next two years of accounts are missing, but
in 1626, the amount collected fell by more than 50 percent, to 271 fl.

Irregular income remained low in 1627. It started to grow again in 1628 but would not reach the 1623 level for the next several years. In 1635, the second phase of economic collapse rocked the *Amt*. The account registered a negative balance of income and expenditures for the first time. Only 100 fl were collected in irregular income, a drop of more than 50 percent below the previous low set in 1626. The result was that the *Amt* fell 346 fl short of balancing its accounts.

The negative balance indicated that the *Amt* was in severe economic difficulties. More and more sources of irregular income were drying up because they were destroyed or diverted to supporting the troops. The population decline contributed to the collapse of income because there were fewer people to meet the financial demands of the *Amt*. The costs of running the *Amt* did not decline, however. This meant that money that had ordinarily been sent to Kassel as surplus was no longer available. Irregular income hit bottom in 1638, at a mere 49 fl, just 5 percent of the 1618 level. From 1637 to 1642, *Amt* Sontra could collect no more than 100 fl in irregular income per year. Before the war, regular income had never exceeded irregular income; in 1639, 67 percent of the income collected in *Amt* Sontra was regular income and just 18 percent was irregular. We have already seen that regular income was collected by accounting fiat rather than through any recognizable collection mechanism. It is likely, therefore, that the actual amount of money in the hands of the *Rentmeister* from all sources in 1639 was far less than the reported 387 fl.[29] This was less than what a single village in *Amt* Eschwege/Bilstein had paid out in contributions over a four-month period in 1623–1624. It was a serious decline from the 2,542 fl in total income reported in 1618.[30]

Just as with the population crises, the intensity of economic collapse made it more difficult for the *Amt* to recover quickly. After 1642, the worst was over for the local economy, and the amount of irregular income increased gradually. In 1648, it reached a level comparable to that of 1626. But this meant that revenues were still only 25 percent of the prewar high set in 1618. Once resources were diverted from the economy of the *Amt*, it was hard to redirect them into that economy.

For the most part, the measures in the account books chart the economic activity of the villagers themselves only indirectly. The amount of revenue that the landgrave could extract on an irregular basis was affected by how prosperous the villagers were, but it was also dependent on how stable the local administration was. One sign that economic disruption contributed more than administrative troubles to the decline in revenues is the increasing numbers of arrears that turn up in the account books and eventually become separate accounts of their own. Administrative attention was diverted from enforcing ordinary dues to charting an extraordinary situation. In 1628, *Vogtei* Germerode already had arrears reported for 464 distinct pieces of property.[31] Arrears are a sign that the rural economy was no longer able to produce for seigneurial revenues as it had in the past, but they do not tell us what form the rural economy took in its efforts to serve both *Herrschaft* and the war.

One source for the Werra region enables us to trace the process of indebtedness and the efforts to keep up regular payments through a difficult period of the war. The Treusch von Buttlar managed to keep careful records of their income as *Grundherrn* in a *Salbuch* for the village of Lüderbach from 1627 to 1634.[32] The notable feature of this *Salbuch* is that it kept track of both how much the householder was supposed to pay and how much he or she actually paid each year. The difference was carried over to the next year's account, so a running total of debt was accumulated. This accounting procedure was quite different from that in the *Amt* accounts, where it was unclear whether previous years' debt had been paid off or not. Another interesting feature of the *Salbuch* for Lüderbach is that the Treusch noted every instance in which they permitted a villager to substitute one form of payment for another. The *Salbuch* shows that a makeshift local economy emerged as villagers scrambled to meet all their various obligations with the resources of overburdened property.

The *Salbuch* divided the population of Lüderbach into two groups: nineteen *Bauern* and forty one *Hintersiedler*. It gave the name of each property holder and a list of the yearly dues associated with that property, but there was no indication of how much land each villager owned. The *Salbuch* began with information on how far behind the payments were in 1626. This provides insight into the impact of the war up to 1626, which had been disruptive but not insuperable. Eight of the nineteen *Bauern* properties had no arrears in 1626, but only nine of the *Hintersiedler* had managed to keep up their payments. Those villagers who were securely over the margins of subsistence were able to respond effectively to the demands of the troops, but those at the margins were already beginning to fall behind. The difference between established and marginal landholders is even more evident if we look at the debts of those *Bauern* who were behind in their payments. Only one, Kleinhans Seiffhardt, was falling behind in cash payments and in rye, which suggested that the productivity of his estate was in jeopardy. Eight of the eleven who were behind in payments were behind in only oats or wood, both of which were in temporary short supply because of the troops. Bastian Morgenthal was short one *Schock* of eggs in addition to oats, but he was not behind in rye or cash; Georg Morgenthal was short two geese, two chickens, and four roosters, but he was not behind in rye, cash, or oats. The fact that all but one of the *Bauern* were able to keep up payments in the primary grain crop of the region and still had cash on hand indicates that their households continued to work their land productively, despite the disruptions of the plague and troops. In contrast, thirty of the *Hintersiedler* already had cash arrears. Although the villagers with greater resources were able to weather the storms of the first part of the war, the poorer members of the community were already being pushed over the edge of subsistence.

The resilience of the wealthier households began to break down in 1627, when the results of the occupation of 1626 began to affect the region more severely. No one in the village managed to make all payments that year, and twenty-five *Hintersiedler* and two *Bauern* made no payments at all. The inability to pay anything was a temporary condition for most, as the number of villagers paying nothing was reduced to twenty-four in 1628, twenty in 1629, and eleven in 1630, where it stabilized for the next two years. What is striking about the debts that grew in 1627 is that it became difficult to pay in rye and cash. Although it is not explicitly stated anywhere, it is likely that the shortage of cash was caused by the presence of troops, who made their fiscal demands before the Treusch could make theirs. As a result, the economy of Lüderbach turned to barter as the primary means of paying off debts. There were delays in making a full transition to a noncash economy between lord and peasant, but by 1630, ordinary payments were routinely bartered into different forms. Although the Treusch would have found cash a much more useful product, they compromised in order to achieve something resembling regular payment of the expected dues.

The patterns of barter established in Lüderbach are complex and do not allow for a straightforward synopsis. In general, villagers paid off their debts to the Treusch in two ways: either by substituting one product in kind for another or by substituting their own labor for money or a product in kind. For example, the *Hintersiedler* Lorentz Wetzstein paid off a debt of half a *Schock* of wood by delivering sixty eggs instead. Elsa Seiffhard paid off a 1-fl debt by tending the animals of the Treusch for "a few weeks" while the maid was sick. There are also a few arbitrary exemptions, such as the case of Claus Buel, who was released from one year's payments "for certain reasons." One of the most common labors was to make deliveries to various locations in Hesse, most often to Kassel. These deliveries were assigned a cash value and could be used to pay off debts in cash and in kind.

The barter economy that emerged in Lüderbach continued to affect large and marginal landholders in the village differently. In the period 1627 to 1633, there were 110 instances in which one payment in kind was substituted for another, eighty-eight of which were by *Bauern*. The Treusch began to accept slightly larger quantities of inferior grains from the larger farmers in order to ensure that the farms remained productive. Deliveries became the tasks of *Hintersiedler*, except when a team of horses or oxen was required. Of the ninety-six instances in which villagers were reported to have made deliveries to Kassel, only six were by *Bauern*. Both *Bauern* and *Hintersiedler* tried to fulfill their standard roles within the village economy, but the war made it impossible for them to succeed in traditional terms. The barter of services and different products was one way of continuing their traditional contributions in a different form.

The overall impression from the Lüderbach *Salbuch* is of an agricultural economy that was unable to produce for several years, overseen by a lord who wished to ensure that none of his prerogatives was jeopardized by the disruption. Similar compromises seem to have taken place in the contribution register for Abterode, which bartered tax payments for delivery services as a way of inflating the total amount collected. It is possible that similar barters took place in the *Amt* economy as well, but if they did, they were masked by the accounting procedures. The barter economy was a compromise that made the villagers indebted to their lords. By 1631, the situation in Lüderbach had become so unstable that villagers had to borrow from the Treusch in order to plant their next year's crop. In 1632, the rate of borrowing increased dramatically. For example, Bastian Morgenthal, who had had no debts in 1626 and had managed to pay off at least some of his debts every year, borrowed three *Malter* of rye, one *Malter* of barley, and two and a half *Malter* of oats in 1632. In 1635, Christoffel Sebach borrowed 10 Rthlr from the Treusch family's agent in the village to buy a new horse. Again, the *Bauern* were favored by the Treusch when it came to lending seed corn or money. It was in the Treusch's interest to see the village economy stabilized so that it could reproduce itself.

The *Salbuch* of Lüderbach stops recording the attempts of the Treusch family and the inhabitants of the village to cope with the extraordinary burdens of the war just before it took its second brutal turn. Presumably, the increased demands of 1636 and 1637 would have produced a total collapse of any effort to work out an agreement between lords and villagers. The evidence for the Werra region after the years 1636 and 1637 indicates that the region as a whole suffered terribly. The local economy suffered an absolute decline because of the war—not just a decline relative to the rest of Europe—and the decline was apportioned among the villages unevenly. Both demographic and economic trends were variable, but the magnitude of decline suggests that all villages suffered somewhat, and the problems of production were shared by all.

Villages depended on their livestock and crops for much of their wealth. They could secure mobile property by hiding it, but anything that was not hidden was easily removed by the soldiers. There are no complete or partial lists of household tools and livestock taken from individual villagers, but officials did record the landgrave's loss of personal property in the secularized monastery of Cornberg. Soldiers plundered the estate frequently and removed a variety of pans, pots, tools, and bedding.[33] Villagers may have been better able to hide their valuables but the losses at Cornberg show that soldiers caused significant material loss. In addition, soldiers took most of the villagers' animals, which further depleted the resources of the village. The number of sheep owned by the villagers of Rockensüß plunged from 763 in 1623 to zero in 1626.[34] No one in the village owned any sheep in 1627 either, but five villagers had a total of 548 sheep in 1628. It is not clear where the sheep came from or how they were acquired, but presumably some wealthier villagers had been able to hide enough money or valuables to purchase them from sellers outside the Amt once the troops were gone. That flock continued to grow until 1634, but a second wave of troops removed all the sheep in 1635. This time, no one attempted to restore them. By 1639, there were still no sheep to be found in Amt Sontra or in any of the neighboring Ämter.[35] No one in Rockensüß had any sheep until 1647. Pigs and poultry were also very scarce. The troops must have taken cattle and horses from the villagers as well, but since those animals were critical to the production of grain, the villagers replaced them as quickly as they could, even at the cost of building up debt on their property.[36] Indeed, the ransoming of cattle and horses was one of the most common means of extorting hidden valuables from wealthier villagers during the war.

The survey instigated by Amalie Elisabeth in 1639 once again provides a good overview of the extent to which the numbers of animals in the villages decreased as a result of the war. Reichensachsen claimed that there had been as many as 400 head of cattle in the village in 1625, but in 1639 there were just ten horses, four cows, one goat, and two pigs. Reichensachsen's claim of 400 cattle seems exaggerated, but there is no source to check it against, and it is not dramatically out of proportion to later estimates of the number of cows per person in many villages. Reports from neighboring Ämter show a similarly small number of animals remaining in 1639. There were only nine horses, eight oxen, and fourteen cows in all of Amt Wanfried. Amt Sontra did not suffer as significant losses of animals, with sixty-nine horses and seventy cows for a town and fourteen villages. The number of animals decreased in even greater proportion than the number of householders. For the soldiers, the animals of the village were a source of meat, but for the villagers, they were a necessary part of the agricultural cycle. Their absence disrupted the most essential part of the rural economy—the production of grain—so their absence was keenly felt.

Agriculture continued to be the mainstay of the rural economy, so the decline of grain production was the single most important consequence of the war. Not all problems of agricultural production were caused by the war—the "Little Ice Age" of the seventeenth century was at its worst during the war[37]—but the war disrupted production in several different ways. On the most obvious level, the continuing presence of troops meant that grain that could have been used to produce income for the peasantry was consumed by the army. In one year, more than half the rye produced on the landgrave's estate of Cornberg was taken by the troops before it could be threshed.[38] The lands of the villagers most likely experienced the same fate. But the presence of troops also had a direct impact on the rhythm of planting. When villagers fled, they were unable to plant or harvest at the optimum time. That could significantly reduce the amount of grain produced.

Production of barley on the lands of the estates of Cornberg dropped by over 50 percent in 1625 because "the lands could not be sown at the right time, because of the war, also because there was not enough fertilizer because the animals had to spend so much time in their stalls."[39]

The combination of lack of fertilizer, disrupted labor, and bad weather made it increasingly difficult to produce as much grain as had been produced before the war. Given the intensity of the war, it was certain that even one of those factors would have had an effect. In some years, all three worked together to produce disastrous harvests. During the 1620s, the *Rentmeister* reported frequent meteorological events that adversely affected the crops in Cornberg.[40] Freezing temperatures damaged the rye in 1621 and again in 1626. Blight struck the wheat and hail damaged the oats in 1627. Between 1626 and 1634, no year passed without some frost, drought, hail, or blight to affect one of the crops in Cornberg.

By 1634, however, the *Rentmeister's* observations about poor weather conditions were overshadowed by his assessment of the effects of marauding troops. Between 1634 and 1641, there was only one year, 1639, in which the war did not have a direct impact on the harvest in Cornberg. In 1638, the rye crop suffered a threefold plague of disrupted planting schedule, bad weather, and pests. The *Rentmeister* reported, "the reason why so little corn was produced this year is because of the constant flight, which meant that the crops could not be planted at the right time, nor as well as they ought to be, also the continual heat . . . burnt most everything, and the abundance of mice . . . caused immense damage."[41] The mice, which afflicted the entire region, were a sign that the villagers could no longer perform ordinary maintenance of the fields, which would have reduced the numbers of pests. The presence of soldiers caused a long-term decline in agricultural production, which exacerbated the decline caused by the weather. Even in the best years, land that had previously produced six times the amount of rye sown began to produce less than four times the amount sown. The years 1632 to 1643 were especially bad (Graph 6.2). Twice, the fields of Cornberg produced only as much seed as had been sown, which was almost worse than if no grain had been sown at all. On three other occasions, disruptions during the harvest made it impossible to calculate how much had been produced.[42]

The effects of the war are not seen in a single poor harvest but in the cumulative effects of a series of poor harvests, many of which were caused directly by the war. Nevertheless, the year 1639 provides the best indication of how deeply the decline in grain production hurt individual villages, because we can relate the yield ratios for the year with the figures for the number of *Acker* planted according to the survey for Amalie Elisabeth. The experiences of Rockensüß and Grandenborn illustrate the situation with particular clarity. Rockensüß reported eighteen married couples in residence. They had planted thirty *Acker* of land over the winter.[43] The total number

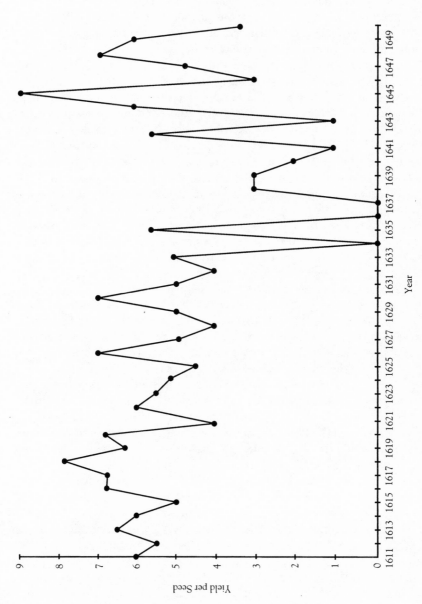

GRAPH 6.2 YIELD RATIOS OF RYE IN CORNBERG, 1611–1650

of *Acker* under cultivation in *Amt* Sontra was $432\frac{1}{2}$. Grandenborn had fifteen householders who had planted thirty-one *Acker* of land during the winter.[44] How much grain would that land produce? The harvest of 1639 was a poor one, primarily because the weather was uncooperative rather than because the war was especially severe that year. Cornberg returned only three times the amount of seed sown, while Germerode, which was usually far more productive than Cornberg, returned only $3\frac{5}{8}$ times the seed sown.[45] The *Rentmeister* reported in the margins of the account book that "the corn froze this year, which is why it did not produce the usual amount."[46] Villagers may have been able to make their own land more productive than that of the landgrave through more intensive work, but hard work could not compensate for all the obstacles to production. The decline in the productivity of the land of the villagers was probably comparable to the decline on the estates of the landgrave. The land in the villages of Rockensüß and Grandenborn was comparable in quality to that of Cornberg, so villagers there were likely to receive three times the amount of seed sown. It was standard practice in the Werra region to sow each *Acker* with four *Metzen* of seed. At that yield, the villages of Rockensüß and Grandenborn would have produced thirty and thirty-one *Viertel* of rye, respectively.[47] All of *Amt* Sontra would have produced about 430 *Viertel*.

The inadequacy of that yield is clear when it is expressed in terms of the money that it would yield. Rye sold for 3 fl 10 albus per *Viertel* in *Amt* Sontra in 1639, so the total value of grain produced by the two villages was a paltry 108 and 112 fl respectively.[48] The value for *Amt* Sontra as a whole was less than 1,500 fl. If the villagers wished to reserve enough seed to plant the same amount of land next winter, they had to hold on to one-third of the crop. The small yields may have compelled the villagers to consume some of next year's seed. A constant refrain in the list from Grandenborn in 1639 is that the amount of land sown was limited "because of the lack of seed."[49] This was, in part, a result of the marauding soldiers of the year before. It was risky for villagers to store seed when there was the constant danger of being plundered and losing it all.

The poor harvest must have continued that vicious circle. Much of the grain that was not saved for seed was consumed by the villagers rather than marketed. If we assume that one-quarter of the crop was put away for seed and that there were no children left in the village, there would have been ten *Metzen* (around three bushels) of grain available for each person in the village of Rockensüß that year. The problems caused by poor yields were compounded by the small amounts of land under cultivation because of the frequent incursions and the poverty and uncertainty that accompanied them.

The year 1639 was not uniquely desperate, however. In many respects, it was a good year. It was the only year between 1634 and 1641 in which soldiers did not remove some of the harvest either in the fields or from storage. Its yield ratio was also above the median for those eight years.

Nevertheless, the villages of the Werra could not produce enough to feed even their reduced populations.

Consecutive years of such small harvests made it difficult to keep up with the traditional demands of the *Amt*. The collapse of rye yields in Cornberg contributed to the collapse of income in rye for the *Amt* (Graph 6.3). The result was that a system of debts developed that permeated every level of society, from the household to the state. Except in cases such as Lüderbach, however, it is difficult to follow how the system of debt affected the region. The villages of *Amt* Sontra and *Gericht* Boyneburg made no mention of debts. Indeed, the documents of the region are remarkably silent about personal debts and the debts of the village as a whole throughout the seventeenth century. It seems unavoidable, however, that villagers were forced to borrow to meet the demands of the contribution and to buy new livestock. The villages of *Amt* Lichtenau, on the other side of the Meißner from *Gericht* Boyneburg, all reported more than 1,000 taler in debts owed by the villagers, "not including what they owe our gracious prince and lord in *Guldefrucht* and other things."[50] Other areas of Hesse reported comparable levels of debt. Households had debts of more than 100 taler, which was often more than the value of the land they had sown in 1639. If Rockensüß was at all similar to the villages of the neighboring *Amt*, however, it was likely to slide still further into debt at its 1639 level of productivity. Just over 100 fl worth of rye was not going to bring Rockensüß a speedy economic recovery.

The consequences of this diminished productive capacity were underscored by the proliferation of separate registers for arrears.[51] The combination of declining population and decreasing agricultural productivity produced a double bind for the village. Financial burdens increased, while the economic base shrank. One result of the complaints from the villages of the Werra was that the tax obligation of all the *Ämter* of the *Rotenburger Quart* was officially reduced by half by the end of the war.[52] But a tax reduction could not begin to restore the economic activity of the village to its prewar level. Only after the disruptions of the war ceased could the village recuperate and begin the process of rebuilding.

The economic and demographic data of the villages of the Werra confirm the picture drawn by the written supplications of villagers and the observations of witnesses: The war imposed unprecedented burdens on the village. The demographic indicators and measures of production followed similar trajectories. The factors that reduced productivity, such as poor harvests, also reduced the population through famine-induced population crises. Conversely, a reduced population meant a decrease in total production, even if productivity per person could be maintained. More striking is how closely the rhythm of demographic and economic contraction mirrored the villagers' subjective expression of their plight. Until 1626, the village adhered to the

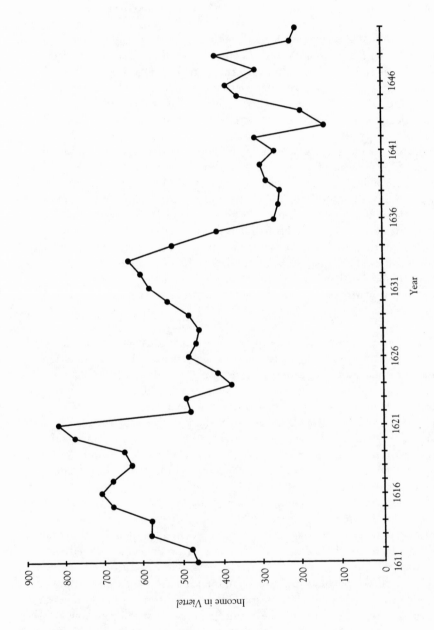

GRAPH 6.3   TOTAL RYE INCOME IN CORNBERG, 1611–1650

standard practice of complaint that was characteristic of the prewar period. During that same period, the economy and population responded to the strains of the war in the manner of the old demographic regime. After 1626, the village became less able to cope with the extraordinary burdens of the war. The economy and population were rocked by deep crises, and the village could no longer muster the resources to respond to crises in the standard way; nor would an ordinary response have been sufficient to overcome the extraordinary levels of damage. The demographic and economic indicators began to sputter, just as the language of complaint became more forlorn. The halting attempts of villagers to come to grips with the new situation were finally ruined by a second wave of crises after 1635. In the Werra region, at least, the vivid descriptions of devastation were a fair appraisal of an extraordinarily severe crisis.

After ten years of disruption, the villages of the Werra began to achieve a new equilibrium in the last years of the war. Although life was not back to normal, it was at least no longer desperate. Peace brought the village the opportunity to recover. It did not bring all the necessary tools for recovery, however. It would take time for the village to achieve its prewar condition, and there was no guarantee that it would be able to. The basic institutions had been tested by the war. Now they had to be applied to the unprecedented task of rebuilding a whole region of villages from the material and moral devastation of the war.

Notes

1. Günther Franz, *Der Dreißigjährige Krieg und das Deutsche Volk*, 4th ed (Stuttgart, 1978).
2. Ibid., 59.
3. Myron Gutmann, *War and Rural Life in the Early Modern Low Countries* (Princeton, 1980).
4. See Alain Croix, *Nantes et le pays Nantais* (Paris, 1974), 139. Croix devotes part of his study to a closer analysis of the rhythms of crises and arrives at a modification of Goubert's model. In particular, he notes that not all crises are followed by a period of recuperation: "We have passed from the *crise de mortalité*, a brief phenomenon, always followed by recovery, to the *mortalité de crise*, which is characterized precisely by the absence of recovery." See also Jean Jacquart, "La Fronde des Princes dans la Region Parisienne et ses Consequences Materielles," *Révue d'Histoire Modern et Contemporain* 7 (1960): 257–90, and Jean Jacquart, *La Crise Rurale en Ile-de-France 1550–1670* (Paris, 1974).
5. Gutmann, *War and Rural Life*, 231–32. There are some limitations on how directly Gutmann's evidence can be compared with the evidence from Grandenborn. Gutmann is able to draw on a much larger number of parishes to build his index. His numbers flatten out the moments of extreme crisis in two ways. First, the effects of crisis in one parish may be offset by the slightly different timing of a crisis, or the absence of a crisis altogether, in another parish. Second, a larger number of "events" reduces the magnitude of variation

that is likely. The parish registers also varied in their propensity to include stillborn, unbaptized, and other babies who died in earliest infancy. Nevertheless, the comparison is fruitful precisely because Gutmann is interested in the interrelationship between war, disease, and famine in a war-ravaged region.

6. Ibid., 154. Gutmann uses a linear regression to arrive at the expected value for each year, from which he calculates his index value. I followed his formula in generating the index values for the village of Grandenborn so that a direct comparison is possible. Gutmann discusses his reasons for choosing linear regression in an appendix. Although his explanation is compelling for the data he possessed, it cannot be applied unproblematically to Grandenborn's data. Note, for example, that using Gutmann's method, only seven of sixty values are within .20 of normal, and fifty years experience "below normal" mortality; more than half have index values below 0.67.

7. The years are 1634, 1671, 1694, 1729, and 1747. The data for 1635 and 1636 are incomplete and may be a sign of a more severe crisis. Gutmann makes no effort to decide how high an index value constitutes a severe crisis, nor does he attempt to compare the crises of the Basse-Meuse with those of France or elsewhere. The assumptions about severity based on his evidence are mine.

8. Pfarrarchiv Rockensüß, Ki Rockensüß 1623–1754.

9. W. Kürschner, "Aus dem Kirchenbuch von Reichensachsen (und Langenhain) von 1639–1653," *Archiv für Hessische Geschichte und Altertumskunde* NF 9 (1913): 54.

10. Pfarrarchiv Abterode, Ki Abterode 1630–1688.

11. Hilmar Milbradt, *Das Hessische Mannschaftsregister von 1639* (Frankfurt, 1959). Günther Franz explains the absence by the fact that the villages of the *Rotenburger Quart* were exempt, which is corroborated by the absence of Witzenhausen and Landeck but refuted by the presence of Sontra, Boyneburg, Wanfried, and Treffurt.

12. Compare Milbradt, *Das Hessische Mannschaftsregister*, with StAM S 98. For further evidence of the demographic impact of the war on other parts of Hesse-Kassel based on the same document, see Manfred Lasch, *Untersuchungen über Bevölkerung und Wirtschaft der Landgrafschaft Hesse-Kassel und der Stadt Kassel vom Dreißigjährigen Krieg bis zum Tode Landgraf Karls 1730* (Kassel, 1969).

13. Milbradt, *Das Hessische Mannschaftsregister*, 115. In this regard, Amt Sontra was not as hard hit. Only forty of 214 remaining households were headed by widows. This was only slightly higher than the number of widows in the cadastre of the late eighteenth century.

14. Ibid.

15. Gerhard Benecke, "The Problem of Death and Destruction in the Thirty Years' War: New Evidence from the Middle Weser Front," *European Studies Review* 2 (1972): 250.

16. Hessian State Archives, Marburg (STAM) 4h 579.

17. Compare StAM K57. For the Treysa Assessment, see Chapter 1.

18. StAM 4h 579.

19. Ibid.

20. StAM 5 14367.

21. StAM 5 12201, 1/3/1648, Kammerräte to Amalie Elisabeth.

22. Ibid.

23. StAM Rech II Abterode 1.

24. Ibid.

25. Ibid.

26. Ibid.

27. StAM Rech II Sontra 3.

28. Ibid. I did not attempt to construct an index of extreme behavior for the *Amt* accounts or for yields and productivity. Gutmann's data suggest that short-term collapses of productivity on a scale comparable to what I describe here took place in the Basse-Meuse. In particular, the crisis of 1671–1673 produced indices below 0.25, which seem to be comparable to what occurred in Sontra. The long stretch of well-below-average productivity in Sontra did not characterize the Basse-Meuse, however.

29. The bookkeeping assumption that all regular income must have been collected and disbursed is most clearly illustrated in the reports of income in kind in poultry. Until 1635, *Amt* Sontra kept a near perfect balance of income and expenditures in chickens; there was no carryover to the next year's account. In 1635, all the chickens were reported as collected, but only 118 were spent, leaving $525\frac{1}{2}$ chickens "in storage." Each year the number of chickens in storage mounted until there were $3,796\frac{3}{4}$ of them. Some had ostensibly been sitting there for eight years.

30. StAM 5 14973. Abterode paid 564 Rthlr between 11 October 1623 and 21 February 1624; compare with StAM Rech II Sontra 3.

31. StAM 40d Germerode Lf Nr. 151.

32. StAM S 590.

33. StAM Rech II Cornberg 3.

34. StAM Rech II Sontra 3.

35. Milbradt, *Das Hessische Mannschaftsregister*, 116–17.

36. StAM 5 12201. The village of Laudenbach in *Amt* Lichthenau claimed to have lost 900 Rthlr worth of horses and cattle in 1642. This is almost certainly an inflated figure. It is indicative of the vulnerability of livestock and the importance of draft animals to the village, however. It is noteworthy that *Amt* Sontra was stripped of sheep, pigs, and goats but still had a fair number of horses and cows in 1639.

37. H. H. Lamb, *Climate History of the Modern World* (London, 1982). In another work, Lamb popularized the term "Little Ice Age" to describe the period 1550–1700. Some climatologists argue that the late seventeenth century was more severe than the early part of the century, however. See, for example, Emmanuel Le Roy Ladurie, *Times of Feast, Times of Famine: A History of Climate since the Year 1000*, trans. Barbara Bray (New York, 1971).

38. StAM Rech II Cornberg 3.

39. Ibid., 1625.

40. StAM Rech II Cornberg 3.

41. Ibid. On the flight of 1640 and 1641 and the mice, compare Ludolph's parish register in Chapter 5.

42. Ibid. The years are 1634, 1636, and 1637. Compare these years with the demographic trends described above.

43. Milbradt, *Das Hessische Mannschaftsregister*, 117.

44. Ibid., 97.

45. StAM Rech II Cornberg 3 and Rech II Germerode 4.

46. StAM Rech II Cornberg 3.

47. Ibid. The 3:1 ratio produced almost exactly one *Viertel* per *Acker*.

48. StAM Rech II Sontra 3.

49. Milbradt, *Das Hessische Mannschaftsregister*, 97. This phrase follows all fifteen entries for the householders. Six of the fifteen entries also specify a lack of harness and plow as contributing to the small amount of land sown. Presumably this means that the other nine householders had some access to harnesses and plows. Unlike Rockensüß, Grandenborn did not indicate how many plows were in the village.

50. Milbradt, *Das Hessische Mannschaftsregister*, 89.
51. StAM Rech II Eschwege 15. Spezifikation was an allerhand Gattung frucht in diesem Jahr in den Interimbs-Abgange gesetzt wird [Specification of which of the varieties of grain have been placed in the Interim-arrears this year] 1642–44, 1646–48, etc. See also Rech II Germerode 9 and Rech II Sontra 4. The format of the arrears accounts was similar to that of the ordinary account books. They were an additional tool for keeping track of all the property that was no longer productive for the *Amt*. The fact that the local and central administrations needed such a tool indicates how severely the war affected the *Amt* as a whole.
52. StAM Kop 57.

7

Recovery and Reorganization

1637—Through vengeance and fire, Eschwege was turned to
ashes; 1660—In dear peacetime this city hall was rebuilt.
  —Carved on the facade of Eschwege's *Rathaus*[1]

The war was over in 1648, and the conclusion of peace created a sense of
closure about the events of the war, which was a first step toward psychological recovery. But the village did not "start over" in 1648, nor did it
return to the situation of 1618. We must treat the terms "recovery" and
"rebuilding" carefully; it cannot be assumed that all activities of the villagers
were dedicated to recapturing what had existed before the war. Neither the
administration nor the villagers were so constrained by tradition that they
did not see an opportunity to change the village to better suit their changing needs.[2] Change in outward form and interaction is only to be expected,
given the fact that the prewar village was a product of continual give-and-
take between its inhabitants and outside authority. At the same time, we
must be careful not to attribute all postwar changes to the immediate impact of the war. The war had an unavoidable influence on almost everything that took place in the village, but it did not cause everything that
took place. Recovery was affected not only by the death and destruction
but also by the response of the villages even as the war raged.

The most obvious and consequential characteristic of the postwar situation in the Werra region is that the village survived. No villages disappeared entirely—neither as human communities nor as ensembles of land
and buildings—from the Werra region as a result of the war. In contrast to
the crises of the late Middle Ages, the war did not produce a large number
of deserted villages.[3] The continued existence of all the prewar villages
nevertheless seems somewhat surprising given the extent to which the war
disrupted the ordinary activities of the villagers. Their survival is testimony
to the extent to which the village had become the place where the interests of individuals, households, and lineages intersected and sometimes
conflicted with those of the administrative hierarchy and the upper levels
of Hessian society. The need for such a location still existed at the end of

the war, and the war had created no alternative institutions to fill the need. The layout, boundaries, and offices of the village continued in their prewar forms. In that sense, one might argue that the village survived the war in a recognizable form.

Although the announcement of the Treaties of Westphalia was widely recognized as the end of the long war, the process of recovery did not begin in 1648. Instead, the villages recuperated at their own pace, beginning during the war. The recovery from the war can be traced in two phases. The first phase was dedicated to making the villages fit for human habitation again after the devastation during the war. That was the immediate task that had to be carried out with the available resources, one of which was the sense of the village that the people involved in rebuilding it preserved. The second phase allowed the unfolding of tendencies that remained below the surface so long as the population, physical layout, and economic capacity of the village were so far below their prewar levels. With time, the experience of the war became more remote and the experience of rebuilding more central. The change created new attitudes and interests that had to be accommodated within the compass of the village.

This chapter reintroduces the different perspectives on the village presented in the first four chapters in order to show how the same issues were at stake even in the fluid situation of recovery. What did the village now mean to the central administration and its conception of an ordered state? How did the inhabitants of the village construct their village as a corporate body and social unity? How were the different groups within the village guided in their interactions by their positions in households, kin networks, social strata, occupational groups, and informal social groups?

The continued presence of the state and other forms of *Herrschaft* in the villages after the Thirty Years' War has been noted by other scholars. Ingomar Bog, for example, argued that the efforts of territorial rulers to protect agricultural production during the war created the basis for "mercantilist" policies in the later seventeenth century.[4] But the role of the state in supporting the village was not limited to its actions during the war. Administrative systematization achieved before the war provided the framework for restoring the village on the same principles after the war. The central administration of the seventeenth century possessed a complete catalogue of all the villages in Hesse, whereas in the fourteenth century it had possessed only rudimentary information. The fiscal features of the village codified in the *Amt* account books were the main conduits of information. Thus, the amount of administrative attention paid to the place of the village in the territorial state had a direct bearing on the process of recovery. The *Amt* account books provided detailed information on individual bits of property in the villages and, by extension, on the existence of the village as a whole. Bureaucratic zeal ensured that that information was used to maintain the village as a unit of administration. The central administration was so dedicated to the bureaucratic structure it had created before the war that it insisted that prewar levels of revenue be reestablished immediately. The separate registers of arrears were kept to indicate not only what revenues the landgrave had lost but also where revenues were still to be collected and thus by what right they were justified. The purpose of the registers of arrears was to ensure that the landgrave's perquisites did not lapse. The systematic presentation of information in account books made it easier for the central administration to keep track of its legal jurisdiction but made it more difficult for villagers to change the contours of that jurisdiction.

The delicate negotiations over the legitimacy of *Herrschaft* had been torn apart by the insistent demands of the new military lords. A necessary step toward reestablishing negotiations was for the landgrave to gain control over the impositions of the military. This was not possible during the war, when troops were hard for the rulers to control and acted as a direct competitor to state authority. But the peace enabled territorial rulers to curb the local dominance of troops, allowing the landgrave to reassume his traditional role of protector. Although the landgrave's failure to protect his subjects during the war had corroded the traditional legitimacy of *Herrschaft*, the confusion and desperation underscored the necessity of some kind of protection and thus provided a basis for the revival of *Herrschaft* after the war. Much of the process that enabled the landgrave to gain control over the troops within his territory took place at a political level beyond the view of the villagers, but the suffering inflicted by the war could be used as a strategy for justifying renewed central authority over the main instrument of force—the military. The struggle to restore the legitimacy of *Herrschaft* became part of the older struggle between centralizing territorial ruler and recalcitrant Estates—now intensified by the stirrings of the idea of a standing army funded by regular tax revenues.[5]

Ironically, the new basis of taxation that emerged had been invented and elaborated during the war precisely because of the inadequacy of the traditional practice of *Schutz und Schirm*: the contribution. The contribution was grafted on to the traditional fiscal structure of the *Amt*.[6] Taxes had always been a separate legal category from the *Zins* and other dues that made up the revenues of the *Amt*. *Amt* revenues continued to be collected avidly after the war, but the transition to a "tax state" was taking firmer root. Occupying troops had imposed their own framework for collecting taxes, which they justified with reference to extraordinary necessity (*Notdurft*). Those taxes continued after the war, as the central administration adopted the mechanisms and terminology of the troops. The war had ruined the territorial nobility and enabled the landgrave to overcome their objections to an extraordinary tax. By 1651, the need for a regular contribution for the defense of the territory was established, despite the attempts of the nobility to regain their old powers over taxation as territorial Estates.[7]

Although it is clear that the state managed to impose the contribution on its own terms over the course of the war, it is not clear how that imposition was achieved. With the exception of the contribution account from Abterode, there are almost no records that indicate how much revenue the contribution produced during the war. The same administration that kept such thorough records for the seigneurial revenues of the *Amt* in even the worst years of the war seemed almost incapable of determining how money was collected for the contribution. This lack of precise information continued into the postwar period, so it is difficult to see the extent to which demands of the state came to supplant demands of the seigneurial jurisdiction of the landgrave.[8] The chance survival of collection receipts for one month's contributions in *Amt* Sontra in 1683 demonstrates that the principle of collecting taxes based on households rather than letting the village apportion the burden as it wished was firmly established.[9] The solidification of the contribution as the primary source of revenue for the Hessian state was capped in the eighteenth century by the creation of cadastres, which finally gave the central administration a statistical picture of the tax burden within the village.

The imposition of the contribution was an extension of the codification and fixing of location by official documents before the war, which was characteristic of the *Salbücher*, *Amt* accounts, and registers of arrears. But one result of the contribution was that the village became even more closely associated with the administrative hierarchy through the mechanisms of collection. The central administration continued to rely on the officers of the village as a link in the administrative chain. Village officers became more visible in official records after the war. The village head and *Vormunder* were instrumental in the *Amt*, and state taxation relied on the village as its basic organizing unit. The range of responsibilities of village officials thereby increased. In Abterode, a separate office of contribution collector developed. During the war, the position was makeshift, and the collector was paid out of the taxes collected. From 1634 to 1637, the village head, Lucas Zimmermann, collected the contribution.[10] Between December 1637 and November 1638, three different villagers had that duty. In the period after the war, the position of contribution collector became a more regular office of the village. Claus Wiegand acted as collector for six years, 1665–1671; Johannes Fischer was in office for seven years, 1676–1683.[11]

The increasing prominence of village officers in administrative duties may be seen either as a triumph of local autonomy or as the culmination of the bureaucratization of the communal will.[12] The two are not incompatible possibilities within the administrative hierarchy created by the landgrave. In either case, this increasing prominence did not stop villages from contesting the boundaries of *Herrschaft* whenever they thought it necessary or likely to be successful. One can see disputes becoming more juridical, as villages became more familiar with the terms of legal debate.[13] Supplications from villages began to use legal or pseudolegal Latin constructions to make their points. One village prefaced a traditional supplication for a reduction of its fiscal burden with a brief disquisition that argued that the conservation of a republic depended on maintaining the geometric and harmonic proportions of the territory; it then pointed out why the current burden upset those proportions. Another sign of the willingness of the villages to accept new juridical procedures to protect their positions is that many villages retained attorneys to present their cases before the landgrave's council.[14] Both the adoption of legalistic rhetoric and recourse to attorneys fostered a closer identification between order within the village and definitions of legitimacy created outside the village, as much by the strategies that villagers and their attorneys used to block further penetration into the village as by the ways in which legalistic thinking represented the landgrave's interests at the local level. Conflicts within the territorial state had been channeled in new ways but had not been circumvented.[15] The central administration and many of the villagers had a common interest in restoring the economic vitality of the village, which made it possible for them to cooperate on a wide range of jurisdictional issues, but they also recognized when their interests were opposed.

The secular administration was not the only route by which *Herrschaft* was linked to the revival of the village. The words of support and explanation by pastors such as Ludolph in Reichensachsen undoubtedly kept religion as one of the organizing principles of the village during the most desperate years of the war. The war helped tighten the bond between the church and the village. Six villagers in Rockensüß made charitable donations to the endowment of the parish in 1626;[16] in 1635, another two donations were made. This enthusiasm for good works in a time of crisis may indicate that Moritz's attempts to introduce Calvinist practices had not succeeded in overcoming Catholic remnants in local practices, but it also indicates that some villagers believed that the church was worthy of support, even (or especially) when the survival of the village was threatened. In any case, the strong spiritual conflicts unleashed by the *Verbesserungspunkte* had disappeared by the end of the war. The work diary of superintendent Hütterodt shows only minor residual conflicts over liturgical practice in the villages. What had been an object of controversy before the war had become a source of stability and continuity in the postwar era.

Maintaining the presence of the church in the village meant that the system of administration represented by the church was also reproduced. Pastors made a great effort to maintain their parish registers even after fleeing the village, to preserve some of the ties that made religion an integral part of the village. During the war, accounts and parish registers were often lost to the marauding troops. Shortly after the war, however, most parishes began keeping regular registers again.[17] Keeping track of souls in registers serves as a means of holding the village together in times of secular breakdown.

After the war, the keeping of religious records expanded at about the same rate as the keeping of secular records, so the association of church and moral police was strengthened.

The ties between church and village are illustrated concretely in the reconstruction of churches throughout the region. Many external signs of the church's presence in the village suffered during the war but were restored with the coming of peace. The parish buildings and schoolhouse in Breittau were destroyed in 1637, so the minister was forced to live with other villagers until the end of the war.[18] Altar cloths and goblets also disappeared during the war. Yet even those villages whose church buildings were devastated continued to be served by the church administration. The superintendent in Eschwege kept a careful account of all vacant positions for pastors in the area and acted as quickly as possible to fill them.[19] Rebuilding the church and, more particularly, the parish house was not always the top priority of the villagers, who had many construction projects to keep them occupied. But the churches were rebuilt, and the construction costs were often partially financed by villagers who bought pews in the church.[20] The rebuilt churches reaffirmed the individual identity of the village, and the rebuilt pews reaffirmed the villagers' commitment to their public faith.

Rebuilding churches was also part of a broader effort to reconstruct the interior dimension that contributed to village identity. Even in the worst years of the war, the few remaining villagers made an effort to reconstruct as much of their shattered surroundings as they could. We have already seen that Reichensachsen reported building thirteen new houses—albeit small and frail ones—by 1639, just two years after the town had been ransacked by Isolani's Croatians. There was, therefore, no firm dividing line between the disruptions of war and the recovery of peace for most villagers.

The initial problem of recovery was how to begin when so many aspects of the demographic and economic order had been disrupted or even eliminated for so long. Despite the interest of the central administration in accelerating the process, most of the recovery had to come from within. The tangible signs were the reconstruction of houses and community buildings, the resurgence of economic activity, and the return to prewar population levels. It is not clear how, or how quickly, villagers managed to rebuild the houses that had been destroyed during the war. Small houses could be built quickly but might not last long. There was a construction boom after the war, as both churches and houses were refurbished. Houses from the 1650s and 1660s survive in the Werra region today, a sign that the builders tried to make the buildings permanent. The reconstruction of houses with visible associations to a specific family—indicated by names and biblical passages inscribed above the door or along the roofline—reflected the new confidence in the locality in peacetime. The optimistic message on Balsser Kochrich's house cited at the beginning of Chapter 4 is a sign of a general confidence in the process of rebuilding. By the 1680s, the village head of Wichmannshausen made an even more ostentatious statement of confidence in the village by affixing a sundial with his name on it to his house.[21] It was no longer necessary to build just to have a roof over one's head. The interior space of the village was now restored with permanent structures.

As villagers reconstructed their physical environment, they also needed to reconstruct their social world. Villagers had to do the work of rebuilding, but who was now a villager? The return of people who had disappeared during the war and were unaccounted for became one test of the resiliency of internal ties. Migration was a common response to the war, but with the coming of a general peace, it was safe to return to where one's primary property was. Part of the experience of rebuilding was joining together the interests of those who returned after years of exile and those who had stayed behind during the most turbulent years. Pastor Ludolph, the minister of Reichensachsen, noted the process of repopulation in his account of souls.[22] In 1646, he listed eleven individuals as having returned *ab exilio*. In 1647, another sixteen returned. Some of these returning exiles were expected, but others had been presumed dead. Shortly after Sophia, Hans Möller's "widow," had been granted a dispensation to remarry in 1648, Möller returned, as the pastor noted with some irritation in his parish register.[23] These returning exiles contributed to the population recovery that was already under way by the end of the war. In 1646, Ludolph counted 451 souls in Reichensachsen. In 1647, the total had risen to 478, and by 1652 it reached 573.

Only a small part of the recovery of population can be attributed to new settlers coming into the village to work abandoned lands. Ludolph listed two households with a total of eight members who moved to Reichensachsen from elsewhere in 1646, in comparison to eight households who returned from flight.[24] In 1647, only one new resident was recorded. No one new took up residence in 1652. The account books of the *Amt* also show no great increase in the amount of *Inzogsgeld* collected from newcomers to the *Amt*, though the administration waived that requirement for demobilized soldiers in order to encourage new settlers.[25] Even though the villages were struggling to rebuild after the war, they were not receptive to newcomers. Villagers resented the special exemption the soldiers received, since soldiers had caused the devastation that made resettlement necessary. The administration found it necessary to issue edicts threatening to punish any villagers who tried to keep demobilized soldiers from settling in Hesse.[26] Aside from those edicts, the Hessian landgraves did not undertake an active policy of recruiting foreigners to repopulate the Werra valley immediately after the war.[27] The task of rebuilding the village and restoring its population fell primarily on those families that had resided in the area before or during the war.

The social network of the village was made up of intersecting interests of households and lineages and of different social and economic groups. Some lineages and households had more at stake in the village than others and contributed more to its reconstruction. This segment of the population may have been most responsible for hindering the resettlement of demobilized soldiers. There are few ways to identify those groups that played the greatest role in the survival of the village, except by their continued presence in the village at the time of crisis. Family names give only a rough sense of the centrality or marginality of individual households, since some names were shared by households that belonged to different groups; the long-term existence of a name within the village, however, is a good sign that the basic lineage was not marginal. Family names such as Ruppel, Homan, Landau, and Jacob were shared by many households in Rockensüß in the seventeenth century. Those names were held by a disproportionate share of the village heads and *Vormunder* of the village during that time.[28] They also indicated families with a disproportionate influence on how the village survived the war.

In 1612, Rockensüß had twenty-seven different family names among its sixty-seven households.[29] Although the village had only eighteen households in 1639, the core of traditional households returned to reconstruct the village after the war. Fifteen of the original twenty-seven family names were still in the village in 1665. Nine were still there in 1710. It was common for some family names to die out in a forty-year period in normal times, without any outside influences such as a war. The continued existence of fifteen family names through the tribulations of the Thirty Years' War reflects a strong attachment to the village by those families.

The long-term impact of the leading families of the village was modified by the demographic organization of the recovery. The village returned to a traditional demographic pattern after the war—one that took thirty years of peace to overcome the population loss of thirty years of war. After the war, the number of births exceeded the number of deaths by a substantial margin in every village of the Werra region. For a few years, the surplus of births led to a skewed age structure of the population, but the return of adult members of the village from migration may have blunted the effects of the imbalance. By 1676, the demographic system had returned to its old equilibrium. The proof came after a mortality crisis in Abterode that year: The birthrate rose to its highest level in the entire parish register immediately afterward in order to recoup the losses.[30] The normal pattern of crisis and renewal had been restored.

Although repopulation and reconstruction of the core of the village presented a major challenge to the inhabitants, it was equally important that they bring the surrounding fields back into full use and reestablish ownership. Historians have often assumed that villagers took advantage of the decreased population to work those bits of property that yielded the most grain for the lowest dues and rent, abandoning those that paid high dues or produced poor yields.[31] They did that to a small extent, but the central administration was aware of the possibility of subterfuge and tried to protect its interests. The officials of regent Amalie Elisabeth observed in 1642 that:

> Many people and villages appropriate the best bits and lands from the deserted *Hufen* land and similar lands with dues, whose rightful lords have died or left, and pull them to themselves, and divide them up under some pretext or other, but fail to pay the lord the dues that belong with the land, and use them freely, without any imposition, and at the same time, they sometimes leave their own *Hufen* land and similar property deserted and overgrown, to our disadvantage.[32]

This observation should caution us against assuming that the central administration did not recognize the villagers' strategies. To combat subterfuge, the central administration insisted that the old records be kept and adhered to, with the result that accounts of arrears proliferated as a means of locating the property that had to be brought back into cultivation.

In 1642, an account identified 192 rye payments in arrears for small pieces of land from villagers in Abterode.[33] This account was a year-to-year list of which properties were producing no revenue for the landgrave. Parallel with the recovery of population, the number of entries in the account dropped rapidly as the end of the war approached, indicating that the officials were able to reestablish the traditional mechanisms for payment and bring the land back under cultivation. Sixty-eight of the 192 payments were not mentioned in the account of arrears for 1643, presumably because they were now being collected. Another sixty entries disappeared in the 1644 account.[34] By 1650, there were only seven payments of the original 192 that continued to be listed in arrears. The last disappeared from the records in 1656.

The rapid decline in the number of properties in arrears in Abterode indicates that people did not manage to escape traditional burdens on a wide scale, as Amalie Elisabeth's officials feared. Conflicting jurisdictions complicated the process of bringing land back into cultivation, but the fiscal interests of all *Grundherrn* were the same: to eliminate arrears and return land to productive use. All local officials tried to keep track of who was making use of what bits of land within the village. If only part of a property could be brought back into circulation immediately, officials kept track of the part that was productive and encouraged people to pick up the rest of the land as well. Fritz Leinbach's land, for example, was 1 *Metzen* $2\frac{1}{2}$ *Becher* in arrears from 1642 to 1644; but in 1644, someone (the register does not indicate whether it was Leinbach or someone else) paid 1 *Becher* of the regular payment, which was noted in the account of arrears. Shortly thereafter, Leinbach's land disappeared from the account, which means that it was fully cultivated. The process of recovery of uncultivated land is best illustrated in the land of Hans König, the innkeeper of Abterode, which remained in arrears longer than most. In the original account of arrears in 1642, it was reported as 7 *Metzen* $1\frac{1}{4}$ *Becher* behind the payments.[35] König's land ordinarily paid 8 *Metzen* $\frac{1}{4}$ *Becher*, but someone else had planted part of the land and paid 3 *Becher* of that total. The small bit of land that produced 3 *Becher* worth of revenue was duly accounted for in the records. Villagers could not simply take over Hans König's abandoned land without paying the *Zins*, even in the immediate wake of some of the worst years of the war. In 1643, the amount of Hans König's land used by others rose, so the land was only 5 *Metzen* $2\frac{3}{4}$ *Becher* in arrears.[36] In 1650, the land was only 4 *Metzen* in arrears.

Almost all the land in arrears in Abterode was arable if people could be found to work it. Only 6 *Metzen* of grain were deemed uncollectible because they were due from land that was "laying deserted, and cannot be found."[37] Such land could have been bits of property that were worked secretly so as to avoid paying *Zins*, but it seems more likely that it was land that had been engulfed by the woods that bordered on the village and was, therefore, literally "not to be found." The fact that local officials could keep track of 1 *Becher* owed on Fritz Leinbach's land and 3 *Becher* owed by others for the innkeeper's property suggests that officials would not lose track of the other land unless it could no longer be worked. Although the administration may not have been able to identify who worked every bit of land, its insistence that the old forms of tenure be maintained in the traditional manner ensured that the village continued to be a part of seigneurial practice after the war.

The effort to resuscitate seigneurial revenues interfered with the villagers' own efforts to revive production. From the perspective of the villagers, the central administration demanded payment for land that was unfit for crops because it was overgrown. Accommodating the demands of the administration raised the question of how the burdens of reconstruction should be apportioned within the village. The disposition of land within the village could exacerbate tensions between outsiders, wealthier villagers, and the rest of the village and between exiles and those who had remained behind during the war. The Werra region was not near a major urban center, so there was little likelihood that villages were going to fall prey to massive investments that would displace peasants from their land, as happened in the Parisian basin after the Wars of Religion and the Fronde.[38] Regional officials did, however, try to establish themselves as major landholders in the regions where they were employed, by taking advantage of the decimated population.

A dispute between the village of Altenburschla and the heirs of the former *Amtschultheiss* of Wanfried, Johann Werner Geise, shows how the economic dislocations of the war changed the nature of the local land market in a way that had repercussions for the recovery process.[39] In 1639, Geise purchased part of the village's communal woods and meadows from the village. Geise was aware that this was a controversial act and took great care to ensure that it could not be disputed in the future. He had a bill of sale (*Kaufbrief*) drawn up, which was signed by the village head, the two village jurors, and the *Heimbürge* (the local name for *Vormunder*) as well as four other villagers, and had this notarized by the mayor of Wanfried. Despite this careful planning, the village disputed the right of Geise's heirs to keep the property in 1659. The fact that "the village" brought a complaint to the landgrave about an action taken by the village head and other members of the village elite is indicative of the tensions within the village during the process of recovery. There is some evidence that the complaint represented attempts by the exiles to restore village property that had been lost by the people who stayed behind, but it is conceivable that the complaint was initiated by the elite as a strategy for undoing something that had been done out of necessity during the war. Initially, the landgrave's administration was sympathetic to the claims of Geise's heirs, who argued that they had enjoyed uninterrupted use of the property for twenty years, but the village of Altenburschla argued that the land had been purchased improperly. Some of the villagers who had agreed to sell parts of the village commons to Geise had also bought parcels for themselves, which made their agreement suspicious. Altenburschla also argued that the village officers were not empowered to sell village land, especially when most village inhabitants were in flight. There had been no meeting of the village assembly, so the village had not agreed to make the sale. Eventually, the central administration found this claim convincing and ordered the Geise family to give the land back to the village in exchange for the price Geise had paid in 1639. Altenburschla's challenge to the sale of village property during the war demonstrates how the acceptance of juridical settlement of disputes could be connected to the return of the village population after the coming of peace. Administrative recovery and the recovery of land and population reinforced one another in establishing a new legitimate order in the countryside.

Geise's manipulation of the land market in Altenburschla was made possible by the economic crisis at the local level described in the previous chapter. The magnitude of economic collapse made it more difficult for the *Amt* to recover quickly. Revenues in 1648 were still only 25 percent of what they had been in 1618. Nor were there any clear prospects for the revenues to grow quickly. The *Amt* was no longer able to recreate the level of economic activity that had made the large prewar totals possible. The central administration noted that and struggled to revive the flagging income from the *Amt*, but the local economy was incapable of generating enough revenue to match prewar totals. As a result, revenues grew until the 1660s and then stabilized at a level well below that of 1618. The shift from "finance state" to "tax state" was accelerated by the breakdown of the profitability of traditional seigneurial sources of income.

One reason for the difficulty in reviving seigneurial revenues was the effect of peace on the regional markets. Although peace quickly boosted land productivity, more grain was being grown everywhere, which led to a sharp drop in prices. Grain from Thuringia flooded into the Werra region, forcing prices down further.[40] By the 1650s, rye was selling for $1\frac{1}{2}$ Rthlr per *Viertel* in the Werra region, down from 4 Rthlr in 1618, and there were numerous complaints about foreign grain ruining local producers. The landgrave tried to stem the tide by limiting imports, but that did little to bolster local prices. Many villagers of the Werra produced primarily for their own consumption, but the lower prices hampered their efforts to pay for new construction and to pay off debts left from the war.

Lower grain prices led to lower land prices. The first reaction of the fiscal administrators to the declining revenues caused by the breakdown of the land market was to blame local officials for not attending to their jobs as the landgrave's agents with sufficient zeal. One of the most precipitous declines in *Amt* income was in the amount collected in *Lehngeld* from the sale of peasant property in the village (Graph 7.1). The *Oberrentmeister* in Kassel appended a note to the accounts of *Amt* Sontra in 1665, claiming:

> Since it is apparent from old accounts, and primarily the completed assessments, that the *Lehngeld* produced an average of 159 fl per year, the *Rentmeister* should, therefore, energetically investigate all bits of land that are subject to *Lehngeld*, and put them in an accurate specification, which should be included with a future account.[41]

Amt Sontra had produced only 19 fl in *Lehngeld* in 1665, and the *Oberrentmeister* pushed the local officials to step up their collection. Income from *Lehngeld* did rise the next year to 50 fl, but this was as far as the pressure from the central administration could push the local economy. *Lehngeld* averaged just 52 fl for the next fourteen years. The 1618 total of 163 fl was no longer attainable in *Amt* Sontra despite admonitions from the central administration.

Lower *Lehngeld* revenues did not mean that villagers had abandoned the land market altogether. In fact, the number of properties subject to *Lehngeld* sold in *Amt* Sontra reached prewar levels in 1660. There were annual fluctuations in the number of pieces sold after that date, but the market was generally active. There were several factors that contributed to the small returns on *Lehngeld*. *Lehngeld* was a flat percentage fee on all property sold, so diminished revenues based on an equal number of sales meant that the property being sold was inexpensive. The most obvious explanation is that the combination of low population and plentiful land depressed prices. That is not the entire explanation, however. More valuable pieces of property did not come onto the market; large properties circulated in a different manner from small pieces. It did not make economic sense to put the best pieces of property on the market at a time when they would bring only a mediocre return. Even before the war, large properties contributed to *Lehngeld* revenues mainly because partible inheritance required one heir to buy out the others, not because a major property was being sold by a lineage. The postwar demographic situation made partible inheritance and the practice of buying out other heirs less a factor in the transfer of property in the

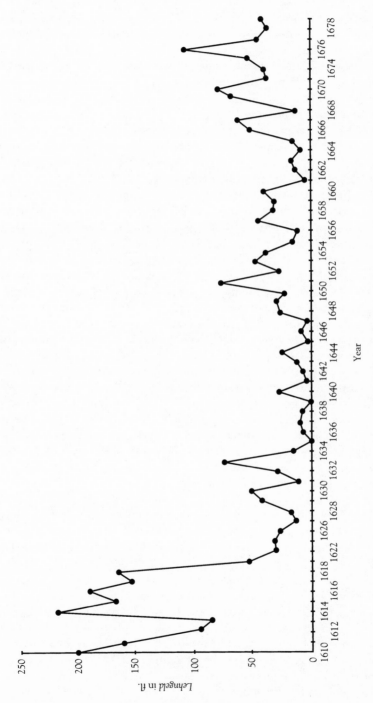

GRAPH 7.1 DECLINE AND RECOVERY OF LEHNGELD IN SONTRA, 1610–1680

village. This may have occurred because there were fewer heirs to buy out or because the heirs could divide money and property without resorting to formal sales. In either case, the decline in *Lehngeld* was caused by changes in the economic profile of the village itself.

The combination of economic forces made it difficult to maintain a profitable agricultural economy for the village elite, but most managed to hold on, perhaps by relying on subsistence production for the worst years of the agricultural depression. One actor in the rural economy did become the victim of the agricultural depression: the local nobles. The fiscal strains of the war had a compound effect on noble property. Debts had accumulated during the war, but the agricultural depression undercut the nobility's primary sources of potential income. Intensified production on seigneurial lands was unlikely to produce sufficient revenue, and the peasantry had no surplus cash to substitute for produce in kind. At first, the von Boyneburg family saw the coming of peace as an opportunity to restore the productivity of their estates.[42] There had been no account of the von Boyneburg properties in Bischhausen for twenty-two years by 1650, so they hoped that renewed vigilance would lead to quick profits. The family was heavily burdened with debts as a result of the war. The regent of the landgrave was already preparing to purchase the entire estate of Bischhausen from the von Boyneburg in 1650. Discord between different branches of the family and the vain hope that the lands could quickly be made profitable dragged out negotiations over the sale of the estate for several years. Finally, the von Boyneburg had to admit defeat in the attempt to pay off their debts. In the most dramatic administrative change in the Werra region after the war, they sold Bischhausen to the landgrave in 1654. The lands were then integrated into the landgrave's domain as *Gericht* Bischhausen.[43] The sale of *Gericht* Bischhausen, combined with the devastation of the castle Boyneburg during the war, emphasized how the presence of the nobility at the local level began to wane because of its inability to maintain even the outward trappings of authority during the war.

One of the sweeping generalizations sometimes made about the impact of the war is that it cleared away the inefficient old forms of economic organization and opened the rural world to more modern economic practices.[44] The war was therefore a progressive force despite its destructiveness. But Friedrich Lütge observed that the Malthusian check of the Thirty Years' War in fact gave a reprieve to the traditional agrarian economy of the late sixteenth century, which had been strained to near the breaking point.[45] Without the intervention of the war, population pressures would have forced a more rapid shift to market relations and wage labor. The war removed the incentive for modernizing the economy after 1650, and thus no mechanism to foster modernization came into existence.

The economic activity described so far was neither progressive nor regressive. It was a sign of instability and a groping for routes to short-term recovery that could move in either direction. Lütge's argument is important because the German economy of the late seventeenth and eighteenth centuries obviously did not lead to industrialization. If old forms were swept away, modern capitalist practices did not fill the vacuum. Market forces and rural industry had already penetrated the countryside to some extent before the war. It is impossible to know whether that trend would have continued or accelerated if the war had not intervened, but the presence of those market relations also makes it impossible to attribute postwar changes in labor and land to the war itself. The balance of rural artisanal activity and peasant agriculture varied before the war and continued to vary after the war, depending on the size and configuration of the village. But in the Werra region, one element of Lütge's argument holds true: The village elite, made up of large landholders, were most active in preserving the village and reformulating it in their image. When people ran away from the village for long periods of time during the war, the larger cultivators who adhered most consciously to the model of the "whole house" were the first to return and try to reestablish their economic base.

But if "progressive" tendencies did not define the village after the war, neither did "reactionary" tendencies. There was no effort to revert to pure agricultural production, so artisanal or unskilled labor became much more prominent in the village by the early eighteenth century than it had been in the early seventeenth. The way in which the village recovered from the war contributed to the increasing prominence of labor in the village. It is difficult to measure the degree of market integration of agricultural production, but market fluctuations had a social impact. Real wages remained high following the war, while prices of cereals collapsed.[46] Although the trends in Germany are parallel to those in other parts of Europe, the impact of the war made them much more dramatic in Germany. A sudden end to the disruption of agriculture led to overproduction. Meanwhile, the depopulation caused by the war reduced the demand for grain and decreased the labor supply. Economic historians have noted that opportunities for unskilled labor were so great that farmhands often worked without contracts because they could be so mobile. In Franconia, guilds proliferated in the countryside after the war, as trades tried to take advantage of favorable circumstances.[47] There was no incentive to shift from wage labor to subsistence farming, so there was no great influx of smallholders into the elite of large landholders. It is likely that access to the most productive properties in the village continued to be controlled by an elite anyway, so the smallholders of the village naturally turned to wage labor as their primary means of support. The result was that rural labor became a more prominent feature of the village economy after the war.

The connections between population growth and the structure of the village economy are complex. Prior to the war, some villages had developed a broad

TABLE 7.1

Number of Households in *Amt* Eschwege/Bilstein

VILLAGE	1583	1681
Eschwege	733	560
Abterode (with Freiheit)	100	121
Niederhona	69	60
Oberhona	60	50
Eltmannshausen	53	48
Weidenhausen	38	50
Wellingerode	25	31
Frankershausen	96	106
Vockerode	66	74
Frankenhain	53	51
Dudenrode	26	27
Hitzenrode	48	51

Sources: StAM S 98 and S 100.

spectrum of rural trades; others continued to be dominated by traditional rural cultivation. The relative importance of artisanal and unskilled labor varied, depending on village size and proximity to different markets. Large villages such as Abterode and Reichensachsen were the sites of some administrative activities, which may have encouraged small craft production to supply the needs of intensified seigneurial activity in the village economy before the war. Administrative centers were also more susceptible to penetration into the land market by local elites; *Amtmann* Johann Beerman gathered large landholdings in Abterode between 1630 and 1641. Small villages and villages that were far from towns maintained their traditional practices.

After the war, these same factors came into play, with the additional overlay of depopulation caused by war itself. Population began to rise generally throughout the region, but it did not do so in a uniform manner. In 1681, the landgrave had another Village Book of Hesse assembled.[48] A comparison with the Village Book of 1583 shows that some villages had recovered their prewar numbers of households and others languished (Tables 7.1, 7.2, and 7.3). The rate of growth in the villages of *Amt* Eschwege/Bilstein was much greater than that in *Gericht* Boyneburg or *Amt* Sontra. The uneven growth rate suggests both great difficulties in overcoming the depopulation and some peculiar procedures for counting the number of households. The figure for Rockensüß in 1681, for example, seems out of line with the evidence from the *Amt* accounts, where the number of householders paying "hearth chickens" increased steadily. In general, however, one can see that the villages closest to the towns of Eschwege and Allendorf recovered their

TABLE 7.2
Numbers of Households in *Gericht* Boyneburg

VILLAGE	1583	1623	1681
Netra	86	76	63
Hoheneiche	50	nd[a]	36
Oetmannshausen	20	nd	24
Reichensachsen	150	172	104
Röhrda	70	89	57
Bischhausen	80	nd	60
Rittmannshausen	20	nd	11
Kirchhosbach	36	nd	20
Thurnhosbach	12	15	15
Grandenborn	60	82	64
Rechtebach	12	16	15
Wichmannshausen	64	72	42

Sources: StAM S 98; Hilmar Milbradt, *Das Hessische Mannschaftsregister von 1639* (Frankfurt: 1959); StAM S 100.

[a]nd = no data.

populations more quickly than did villages that were far from an economic or administrative center. This is all the more striking because the towns themselves did not grow at the same rate; most had reached only two-thirds of their prewar population by the 1680s. The case of Abterode is the most dramatic illustration of the trend. The number of households there was already greater in 1681 than it had been before the war. Abterode was also one of the villages with the most rural artisanal activity prior to the war, so much of its postwar expansion may have been the result of the quick reintroduction of rural trades.

The transformation of the village up to 1681 set the stage for another wave of changes in the early eighteenth century, as the Werra region participated in the European population expansion that redefined and eventually obliterated the Malthusian limit of the old demographic regime. Although many villages lagged behind in 1681, all had exceeded their prewar population totals by the 1720s and 1730s. This expansion was not accomplished through dramatic expansion of the amount of land under cultivation or notable innovations in cultivating technique; it was based on rural trades that affected both the village elite and its marginal members. Trade may have been preferred despite the abundance of land because of the low prices for agricultural products. This discouraged a complete return to agricultural production and made the regular wages of a trade more attractive, even though artisans and tradesmen continued to practice subsistence agriculture.

TABLE 7.3

Number of Households in *Amt* Sontra

VILLAGE	1583	1656	1663	1681
Sontra	231	134	nd[a]	156
Weissenborn	16	11	10	8
Harnol	13	nd	6	8
Krauthausen	18	20	17	15
Ulfen	114	62	67	65
Wolferode	15	12	10	10
Breitau	57	36	36	31
Rockensüß	63	45	39	29
Dens	27	14	12	13
Berneburg	24	19	16	21
Königswald	58	23	24	31
Mönchhosbach	24	19	17	20
Rauttenhausen	17	9	7	8

Sources: StAM S 98; Herbert Lamprecht, *Die Huldigung von 1656 in der Rotenburger Quart* (Frankfurt: 1985); StAM 17/1 2389; and StAM S 100.
[a]nd = no data.

The result was that, although the village continued to produce agricultural products for its own consumption and for the fulfillment of dues to the landgrave, individual members of the village developed economic ties to the wider world that were not under the purview of the central administration or the traditional coercion of neighbors in the village.

The increasing visibility of trade meant that the imprecise social distinctions of the prewar period became more firmly entrenched.[49] The village economy was no longer strictly agricultural, and the social categories of the village came to reflect that change. One indication of the change is in the cadastre of Grandenborn, drawn up in 1745. It included a summary at the end that divided the inhabitants of the village into five groups according to their landholdings and occupations (Tables 7.4 and 7.5).[50] Unfortunately, the names that the scribe gave to the different groups have disappeared, so the characteristics of each group must be ascertained from the statistics of the group as a whole. Fortunately, the characteristics of each group are apparent from even a cursory glance at the table that the scribe produced.

Group one was evidently the non-householding poor, known as *Beisitzer*. One house for forty-two people meant that the people in this group resided in the houses of other villagers. The households of this group averaged between 2.9 and 7.7 *Acker* of land.[51] The holdings per household were among the smallest in the village—far below the average holdings per person in

TABLE 7.4

Social Strata in Grandenborn According to the Cadastre of 1745

GROUP	1	2	3	4	5	6	7	8
1	42	8	13	1	0	397	$62\frac{5}{8}$	212
2	92	20	20	22	2	8,121	$1,144\frac{3}{8}$	206
3	87	20	21	13	10	1,428	$166\frac{7}{8}$	308
4	65	15	14	12	0	3,329	$481\frac{1}{4}$	200
5	60	11	12	$13\frac{1}{2}$	0	6,295	$872\frac{7}{8}$	16
Totals	346	74	80	$61\frac{1}{2}$	12	19,570	2,728	942

Source: StAM Kat Grandenborn B6.

Key: 1 = Total Population, 2 = Men, 3 = Women, 4 = Houses with Outbuildings, 5 = Simple Houses, 6 = Total Capital Value (in fl, rounded down), 7 = Number of *Acker*, 8 = Value of Trade (in fl)

TABLE 7.5

Distribution of Property among Social Strata in Grandenborn

GROUP	1	2	3	4	5	6[B]	7
1[a]	4.8	1.4	2.3	30.5	16.3	37.8	2 albus 6 heller
2	47.6	12.4	41.9	338.4	8.6	248.3	16 albus 11 heller
3	7.2	1.9	6.1	62.1	13.4	68.2	4 albus 6 heller
4	40.0	7.4	17.6	277.4	16.7	242.7	16 albus 8 heller
5	64.6	14.5	32.0	466.3	1.2	355.8	24 albus 3 heller

Source: StAM Kat Grandenborn B6.

Key: 1 = *Acker*/House, 2 = *Acker*/Person, 3 = Percent of Village Land, 4 = Total Value of Property/House, 5 = Value of Trade/House, 6 = Total Taxable Value/House, 7 = Average Contribution/House

[a]The values per house for group 1 are calculated on the assumption that each adult woman represents one house. It would be pointless to present the data on the basis of the one house in the group.

[b]The total taxable value can be lower than the value of property because dues for the land are subtracted from the value of the land to calculate tax obligations; trades received no comparable reduction.

the most prosperous categories. It is perhaps surprising that the *Beisitzer* should possess even this much land. One possible explanation is that an old widow or widower might still hold a large plot of land while living as a lodger in someone else's house. This could account for most of the 62 *Acker* held by the group. The cadastre lists fifteen entries with no land at all.[52] Many of those were identified as *Beisitzer*, and the others probably were as well. With the exception of perhaps one or two landholders, members of this first group were the poorest in the village.

The only group that was as poor as the *Beisitzer* was the third group on the Grandenborn list, which can be described as the housed poor. They would most likely have identified themselves as *Kötner*. Their average of 7.2 *Acker* per household and 1.9 *Acker* per person was very close to the average for the *Beisitzer*. What distinguished this group from the first one was the possession of houses. Of the twenty-three houses in this group, only thirteen had any outbuildings for agricultural equipment; the rest were simple houses with an assessed value of perhaps 16 fl. This group shared in all the privileges of the village because they owned houses. Over 28 percent of the assessed value of the use of the *Gemeinde* property went to members of this group. This figure is not out of proportion to their numbers, but it was an appreciable amount in comparison to the amount of land they controlled in the village. It is likely that all these householders also had plots of land, but they were far too small to support the households. The differences in landholdings and village access made this group socially distinct from the *Beisitzer*, but both groups were poor. Almost all the day laborers in the village must have come from these two groups. These two groups had more in common with each other than with the other groups in the village. In all, these two groups of the poorest villagers accounted for 37.3 percent of the people in the village.

The magnitude of the difference between the section of the population that could survive only by working for others and those who tried to support themselves from their land can be seen in the fourth group in Grandenborn. This is the group of small-scale farmers who supplemented their income by some labor or handicraft and the craftsmen who supplemented their income by working small plots of land. They, too, might have called themselves *Kötner* rather than *Hufenbauer*, but most likely they identified themselves by their trade. The size of holdings in this group is much larger than in the two previous groups. All the houses in the group possessed outbuildings for agricultural implements or supplies. Each house averaged 40 *Acker* of land, and there were 7.4 *Acker* per person. The latter figure is close to the average for the village as a whole, but the former figure is greater than the village average. The average number of *Acker* per house may be inflated slightly because some households owned only half a house, so that one house counted for two households, but that would not have altered the figure dramatically. The difference between 40 *Acker* and 7.2

Acker was an enormous one, but this middling group was not comfortably situated. One striking thing about this group is its comparatively small size. What one might expect to be the "broad base" of the village actually constituted just 18.8 percent of its inhabitants. There was a distinct gap between the truly poor and the village elite that was only partially bridged by this middling group. This group was, nevertheless, the median group of villagers, as 17.6 percent of the land was in the hands of this 18.8 percent of the population. The success of this group was dependent on a judicious blend of craft labor and work in the fields.

Groups two and five in the Grandenborn cadastre represented the wealthy villagers. Both were groups of substantial landholders, though group five was somewhat wealthier than group two. The most likely reason for dividing the wealthiest villagers into two groups can be found in the column for income from trades (see Table 7.4). Group five was entirely dependent on agriculture for its wealth, and group two had substantial income from trade in addition to large landholdings. Group five can therefore be described as large-scale farmers and group two as tradesmen with large landholdings. These two groups dominated the economic life of the village. They owned nearly 75 percent of the land in the village. The average amount of land per house and per person far exceeded the village average. The overwhelming agricultural wealth of these groups is indicated by the fact that they owned forty-four of the fifty horses in the village. Although they were a minority, they were a substantial proportion of the population, constituting 43.9 percent of the inhabitants—significantly more than the percentage of distinctly poor. Large landholdings did not guarantee prosperity, of course. Even the largest landholders had to work hard and employ all the labor power of the household in order to prosper. They could, however, look forward to occasional surpluses instead of struggling from year to year just to survive.

Grandenborn's cadastre was distinctive because the scribe took the time to identify the characteristics of five social groups. But in other respects it lends itself to direct comparison with the cadastres of other villages produced at the same time. Grandenborn was one of villages of the Werra most dependent on agriculture before the war. That is why the large landholders continued to be such a large proportion of the population at the time of the cadastre. Grandenborn continued to have many more pure farmers than other large villages in the eighteenth century, but the penetration of artisanal or unskilled labor had progressed to the point that the majority of heads of households were identified by an occupation other than farmer. This pattern was all the more apparent in those villages that had been receptive to artisanal activity before the war. After the war, rapid growth combined with a diminished core of established families to open the village to economic change even as it preserved traditional forms of agricultural production and property holding. Some of the established families remained large-scale cultivators, and others expanded into profitable

TABLE 7.6

Occupational Structure of Selected Villages in the Eighteenth Century

	ROCKENSÜß 1724	ORFERODE 1724	VOCKERODE 1737	GRANDENBORN 1745
Miller, tavern	3	1	4	3
Farmer only	9	4	18	26
Day laborer	12	22	17	20
Weaver	17	6	8	22
Tailor	5	4	0	2
Butcher trade	0	1	3	0
Animal herder	7	1	4	6
Teamster	0	7	17	0
Salt carrier	0	29	0	0
Miner	1	0	7	0
Smith	5	3	2	2
Housing trade	4	3	2	3
Woodworker	5	3	2	2
Other	14	6	7	13
Totals	82	90	91	99

Sources: StAM 17e Sontra 1, StAM 17e Germerode 15, StAM Kat II Vockerode B1, StAM Kat II Grandenborn B6.

Note: People listed as "day laborer and . . ." are included as day laborers, except in the case of women in Grandenborn listed as "day laborer and spinner," because the other lists mentioned the occupations of only male heads of households. Housing trades include carpentry and masonry; woodworking trades include wagon making, barrel making, and cabinetry; others include the lame and old, soldiers, and a few trades that did not fit any of the above categories.

trades to supplement their landed wealth. The small landholders, who were receptive to taking up a trade before the war, had no immediate incentive to become pure cultivators after it. The changes affected even villages that still had land available to support agriculture. The burgeoning of artisanal activity in the villages of the Werra, especially in linen weaving and tailoring, indicates that rural cottage industry was taking root.

The specific pattern of rural industry in individual villages depended on the extent of rural industry in the village before the war and the options for diversification after the war. The different configurations of four villages with similar numbers of householders in the eighteenth century show that proximity to a production center had a profound influence on the trades practiced in the village (Table 7.6). The diversification of trades in Rockensüß, a village somewhat less isolated than Grandenborn but still primarily agricultural before the war, shows how far advanced the penetration of trades had become. Day laborers and pure farmers combined made up only 25.6 percent of the households. That percentage equaled the percentage of the population engaged in skilled trades other than weaving. And weaving was by far the most common trade in Rockensüß, just as it was the most common "skilled" trade in Grandenborn.

The structures of Grandenborn and Rockensüß in the eighteenth century are characteristic of the diversification of isolated agricultural villages. Vockerode and Orferode illustrate how that diversification was shaped by local opportunities in villages that were not isolated. There was comparatively little weaving in those villages because mining, salt production, and proximity to trade routes gave small landholders other employment options. The most striking opportunity was in Orferode, where nearly one-third of the households relied on salt carrying for income and only 4 percent of the households engaged exclusively in agriculture. Despite the importance of the salt trade for much of the village, the village elite continued to view agriculture as the primary economic activity of the village. They noted that they were not on the main road but were on the salt route from the works at Allendorf to Waldcappel, "from which the inhabitants here do not derive the slightest use, but on the contrary much damage to their property."[53] Vockerode was less exclusively dependent on the local mines, but the villagers had adapted to their proximity to Eschwege and the trade routes by acting as teamsters and participating in the animal trade, much as the neighboring villagers of Abterode did.

These changes in economic composition were obviously significant to the way in which the village was perceived from within, even though the compiler of Orferode's cadastre did not acknowledge their importance. The fact that information is available about the transformation is a sign that the central administration had also succeeded in redefining the village to some extent. The cadastres were part of a two-pronged attempt to give new meaning to the village in the context of state administration, which systematized local variation under the administrative regime of the seigneurial *Amt.* Cadastres were created on a village-by-village basis, with careful documentation of both the properties of all landholders within the boundaries and the physical characteristics of the village as a whole. The "preliminary descriptions" (*Vorbeschreibungen*) gave a brief overview of those formal characteristics, so local custom was no longer as impenetrable as it had been.[54]

The second aspect of the formal administrative role of the village to be codified in the early eighteenth century was internal police. That was accomplished by the promulgation of a communal ordinance (*Gemeinde Ordnung*) in 1739.[55] The regulations promulgated in the ordinance were not new; all of them had appeared in some previous ordinance over the centuries since Landgrave Philipp's reign. But the communal ordinance was an important step in the codification of administrative practice because it drew together these various ordinances under the designation *Gemeinde*. The near-simultaneous creation of these two instruments of administration shows that the distinct functions of fiscal and police authority were finally located in the village itself instead of being filtered through the remnants of the seigneurial and ecclesiastical structures attached to the village.

The ongoing interaction between central administration and villagers before and during the war continued afterwards. All the participants in the interaction continued to pursue their own goals. The result was that the central administration succeeded in establishing a more effective presence at the village level, and many of the villages of the Werra were transformed into centers of artisanal activity and labor rather than of self-sufficient agriculture. The cadastres and Gemeinde Ordnung were the culmination of the process of establishing the presence of the central administration that had begun with arrears accounts and officers for collecting the contribution. Even as villagers contested the administration's vision of how they were to be taxed and policed, they adopted more of the terms of debate that the administration provided and made it easier for codification to take place.

The transformation of the economic and social sphere was similarly shaped by a combination of intention and chance. The process whereby wage labor became a prominent feature of the rural world was shaped by the way in which depopulation became repopulation in the 1660s and 1670s. Instead of a generally stagnant population with periodic small mortality crises, the Werra region experienced sustained population growth throughout the second half of the seventeenth century. The Werra region was also spared the depredations of the wars of Louis XIV that undermined the attempts of towns like Nördlingen to revive after the Thirty Years' War.[56] Initially, this growth was sustained by high wages because of a shortage of labor. Wage prosperity made it unnecessary to challenge the elite households that controlled the market in desirable land. But population growth was so rapid that land again became a scarce commodity by the end of the seventeenth century, when the village elite had already retrenched. The forms that the villages of the Werra took in the early eighteenth century depended on a complex interaction of administration, internal perception, and social interaction that shaped the experience of the Thirty Years' War.

There were two responses in the Werra region to the transformation of the social life of the village by the early eighteenth century. One was the turn to cottage industry, which led to an incomplete form of "proto-industrialization" in the countryside. The other response can be seen in the bureaucratic zeal with which the state gained a closer view of the internal structure of the village. Administrators became more adept at using the instruments of the early modern "police state." They applied their attention to the burgeoning number of young men who were no longer essential for agricultural production, whom they identified by age, occupation, and marital status in order to supply yet another fiscal interest of the state. These men became the primary export of the Hessian state in the eighteenth century: mercenary soldiers.[57]

There is, then, an ironic epilogue to the long-term and much refracted consequences of the Thirty Years' War in the Werra region. It was a commonplace of the seventeenth century that war had to nourish itself. And the war did manage to nourish itself off the rural economy centered on the village for nearly thirty years. The war's efforts to nourish itself created strains that abetted changes that "rationalized" bureaucracy and opened the village to economic practices that had been nascent before the war. This transformation cultivated the new crop of soldiers, ready to nourish a different kind of warfare in a different social, economic, and political environment one hundred years later. Thus, despite the differences that emerged over the next century, the village remained and continued to shape the interests of both rulers and ruled by its mere presence and by how it was experienced.

Notes

1. "Des Brand 1637 Durch Rach und Rauch in Aschweg Eschweg ist Gebracht. Des Baw 1660 In Lieber Friedenszeit itzt Rathaus steht gemacht." Herbert Fritsche, *Eschwege 1637* (Eschwege, 1987), 103–4, argued that the *Rathaus* had already been restored in 1650 and that the date carved into the facade is incorrect.
2. Rudolf Schlögl, *Bauern, Krieg und Staat* (Göttingen, 1988), 15, also noted this.
3. Wilhelm Abel, *Die Wüstungen des Ausgehenden Mittelalters*, 2d ed. (Stuttgart, 1955). Guy Bois, *The Crisis of Feudalism: Economy and Society in Eastern Normandy* (Cambridge, 1984), 62, points out that in Normandy even the crises of the fourteenth and fifteenth centuries did not lead to many deserted villages.
4. Ingomar Bog, *Die bäuerliche Wirtschaft im Zeitalter des Dreissigjährigen Krieges* (Coburg, 1952), 154–66.
5. Francis L. Carsten, *Princes and Parliaments in Germany* (Oxford, 1959).
6. Compare Kersten Krüger, *Finanzstaat Hessen 1500–1567* (Marburg, 1980).
7. Hessian State Archives, Marburg (StAM) 4c Hessen-Rheinfels-Rotenburg 704.
8. The contrast between the completeness and bureaucratic thoroughness of "seigneurial" accounts and the haphazardness of "state" accounts is one of the most striking problems of my research. The absence of tax documents is coupled with an absence of information on individual and communal debts, which makes it extraordinarily difficult to see behind the accounting procedure to the actual economic impact of different financial burdens.
9. StAM 4h 4462. There is also an interesting testimonial note written by the village head and *Vorsteher* of Königswald to the effect that the commander of the force to whom they delivered the contribution "behaved honorably and upstandingly and that no one may say anything against his behavior."
10. StAM Rech II Abterode 1.
11. Ibid.
12. For a good elucidation of the difference between the exercise of *Herrschaft* with the active cooperation of the ruled and the transition to *Herrschaft* as rule over the ruled, see Heide Wunder, *Die Bäuerliche Gemeinde in Deutschland* (Göttingen, 1986).
13. The idea of "juridification" is from Winfried Schulze, "Die veränderte Bedeutung Sozialer Konflikte im 16. und 17. Jahrhundert," in Hans-Ulrich Wehler, ed., *Der Deutsche Bauernkrieg* (Göttingen, 1975), 277–302. See also Winfried Schulze, "Geben Aufruhr und Empörung Anlaß zu heilsamen Gesetzen?" in Winfried

Schulze, ed., *Aufstände Revolten und Prozesse* (Stuttgart, 1983), 261–82.

14. StAM 17e Abterode 7 includes a patent empowering Philipp Thomas Crollium to serve as attorney for the village in a case against the town of Eschwege.

15. Werner Troβbach, *Soziale Bewegung und Politische Erfahrung: Bäuerliche Widerstand im Hessischen Territorien, 1648–1806* (Weingarten, 1987).

16. Pfarrarchiv Sontra, Kopialbuch.

17. The vast majority of registers from the Werra region date from the 1650s because of the disruptions of the war. This is said explicitly in the preface to the parish register of Wichmannshausen. Ki Wichmannshausen.

18. Wilm Sippel, ed., *Forschungsberichte der Stiftung Sippel* vol. 5 (Göttingen, 1981), 31.

19. Ibid., 208.

20. Pfarrarchiv Wichmannshausen, Kirchenrechnungen 1657–1680.

21. This sundial and the inscriptions on houses can be seen today in the Werra region.

22. StAM Ki Reichensachsen 1638–1654.

23. Surprisingly, this case does not appear to have been brought to the attention of the superintendent, since he does not mention it in his diary. Sophia Möller's ability to get a dispensation to remarry, even without proof of her husband's death, may be compared with the unwillingness of Bertrande de Rols to get a dispensation in Natalie Davis, *The Return of Martin Guerre* (Cambridge, MA, 1979).

24. StAM Ki Reichensachsen. The term he uses for the new residents is *hierher gezogen* instead of *ab exilio wiederkommen*.

25. Compare StAM Rech II Sontra 3, passim. It is possible that *Amt* officials looked the other way as new settlers moved in in order to recover lost revenues. Bookkeeping at the level of the *Amt* fell into great disarray during the war. The names on the list of *Rauchhühner* in many villages of *Amt* Sontra remained unchanged from 1622 to 1665. Amalie Elisabeth officially exempted demobilized soldiers from *Inzogsgeld* in a patent of 3 March 1649, but I have been able to locate no other exemptions. StAM 5 16752.

26. StAM 5 16752. A second patent of 20 March 1649 ordered local officials to protect former soldiers "gegen aller unbillichen gewalt, zuenöchtigung und beschimpfung . . . und den Underthanen bey hoher straffe, daβ sie sich dergleichen allerdings endhalten" ("against any unfair force, importuning, and insults . . . and to keep our subjects from doing such things by means of heavy penalties").

27. See Günther Franz, *Der Dreiβigjährige Krieg und das Deutsche Volk*, 4th ed. (Stuttgart, 1979), 52–84. In the 1680s, Hesse-Kassel became a refuge for Huguenots. This had little impact on the postwar recovery in Hesse generally, nor was the Werra region a popular destination for the Huguenots who came to Hesse.

28. See StAM Rech II Sontra 3.

29. Ibid.

30. Ki Abterode.

31. Franz, *Der Dreiβigjährige Krieg*, 107–12.

32. StAM 5, 12201, 24/8/1642.

33. StAM Rech II Eschwege 15, 1642.

34. Ibid., 1643ff.

35. Ibid.

36. Note that the account did not identify accumulated debt but only the amount of land still not producing revenue.

37. StAM Rech II Eschwege 15, 1643.

38. It is hardly a surprising conclusion that Eschwege did not exert the same pull

on the Werra as Paris did on the Hurepoix in the Ile-de-France. See Jean
Jacquart, *La Crise Rurale en Ile-de-France* (Paris, 1974), for an example of increasing urban investment in the countryside in an age of economic dislocation.

39. StAM 17e Altenburschla 2.
40. StAM Rech II Sontra 3.
41. Ibid., 1665.
42. StAM 17e Bischhausen 4.
43. StAM Rech II Bischhausen 1, 1654.
44. See, for example, E. J. Hobsbawm, "The Crisis of the Seventeenth Century,"
in T. Aston, ed., *Crisis in Europe, 1560–1660* (London, 1965), 5–58.
45. Friedrich Lütge, "Die Wirtschaftliche Lage Deutschlands vor Ausbruch des
Dreißigjährigen Krieges," in Friedrich Lütge, *Studien zur Sozial- und
Wirtschaftsgeschichte* (Stuttgart, 1963) 336–95.
46. I have been unable to confirm that wages in the Werra region in fact remained high, though there is little reason to doubt that they did. The collapse
of cereal prices is easier to establish. My observations here are based on the
more general survey by Wilhelm Abel, *Agricultural Fluctuations in Europe from
the Thirteenth to the Twentieth Centuries* (New York, 1980), 158–61, 180–86.
47. Bog, *Die bäuerliche Wirtschaft*, 98–101.
48. StAM S 100.
49. Franz, *Der Dreißigjährige Krieg*, 109, argues the opposite—that there was a blurring
of distinctions between strata in the village. If this occurred, it could only
have taken place during the war itself. The postwar pattern of rebuilding did
not foster village equality.
50. StAM Kat Grandenborn B6. The table in the cadastre gives information for
the following categories: total number of persons; number of men, women,
sons, daughters; amount of contribution; taxable capital; total dues and fees
from tenure; value of fees in kind in money; value of animals; value of trade;
number of horses, cows, sheep; total regular capital value; value of communal
rights; value of house and land; amount of land held; number of houses with
outbuildings; number of simple houses. The figures for *Acker* per house, *Acker*
per person, and percentage of land in the village are all easily derived from
those categories.
51. If every adult female is assumed to be dependent on a male in the category of
Beisitzer—an unlikely prospect, since single women were more common in
marginal groups than they were in more ordinary households—then a household averaged 7.7 *Acker*. But if we assume that all the women were independent heads of households, the average holdings of the household are reduced
to 2.9 *Acker*. The actual average is probably closer to the lower figure.
52. StAM Kat Grandenborn B6.
53. StAM Kat Orferode 3.
54. On the richness of the cadastres as sources, see Klaus Greve and Kersten Krüger,
"Steuerstaat und Sozialstruktur—Finanzsoziologische Auswertung der Hessische
Katastervorbeschreibungen für Waldkappel 1744 und Herleshausen 1748,"
Geschichte und Gesellschaft 8 (1982): 295–332, and, more generally, Karl
Kroeschell, "Zur Rechtlichen Bedeutung der Amtsbücher vom 16. bis 18.
Jahrhundert," in Hans Schneider and Volkmar Gotz, eds., *Im Dienst an Recht
und Staat. Festschrift für Werner Weber zum 70. Geburtstag* (Berlin, 1974),
69–101.
55. A copy of the complete *Gemeinde Ordnung* is in the Stadtarchiv Eschwege.
56. See Christopher Friedrichs, *Urban Society in an Age of War: Nördlingen, 1580–
1720* (Princeton, 1979), 292–97, for his strongest statement on the importance
of the wars of the later seventeenth century for Nördlingen's retarded development.

57. A more thorough analysis of the connections between rural social organization and the mercenary armies of the eighteenth century, with many points of connection to the issues raised here, is Peter Keir Taylor, "The Household's Most Expendable People: The Draft and Peasant Society in Eighteenth Century Hessen-Kassel," dissertation University of Iowa, 1987. A more general treatment of the Hessian state in that era is Charles Ingrao, *The Hessian Mercenary State: Ideas, Institutions, and Reform under Frederick II, 1760–1785* (Cambridge, 1987). Neither work seeks to situate the eighteenth-century experience in the context of the legacy of the Thirty Years' War.

Conclusion

This book argues for the integration of the Thirty Years' War into a broader social and cultural history of early modern Germany. Essential to my presentation is the argument that that integration must take place through close attention to the local context in which the war was experienced. It is, therefore, also an argument against many of the presuppositions influencing other works that have investigated the development of the rural world in the early modern period. For example, there is Peter Kriedte's claim that "[d]isregarding primarily exogenous factors like the Thirty Years' War . . . the demographic movement of the 17th Century was a reaction to the excessive population growth of the 16th which ended in a deterioration of the overall economic situation. . . . In this sense, demographic decline was a reflection of both a 'Malthusian' and a social crisis."[1] The problem with such a formulation is not how it characterizes the demographic regime of the sixteenth century but how it brackets out precisely the problems that need to be addressed for the seventeenth. One cannot "disregard" the war in the Werra region and arrive at some picture of how society would have developed in its absence. Nor can one isolate the war as an "exogenous" factor that comes unexpectedly and then disappears. The war and the village were bound together from the outset, because both were products of the same social and cultural system.

The point of my approach is to see how structures and events influenced each other, instead of trying to reduce one to a function of the other. For this reason, this book has followed three principles. The first is that the direction of events at the local level was not inevitable but depended on how a series of interests and events intersected to produce change. The second is that the only way to understand how they intersected is to identify as many of the strands that were expressed at the local level as possible. And the third is that the village was the place at which competing conceptions of social order were focused. We observed these principles from different angles of vision, which gave us several perspectives on what the village meant. First, we observed the village as a unit, an object in its own right. Next, we saw that the unity of the village consisted of how its parts came together in various combinations. And finally, we saw the village as it was caught up in processes of transformation. The experience of the war in the village is not a different story but another side of the same story.

The problem with presenting both a prewar and a wartime view of the village is that such an approach suggests that the village was static before

221

the war and began to change because of the war. But central to our understanding of the village is that it was never static. The contours of the village were constantly being tested and reformulated. Each of the broad
perspectives mentioned above offered evidence of the contest that was at
the heart of village identity. The unity of the village was created by the
efforts of administrators to see a unity there, in order to consolidate their
control over local processes. Villagers themselves also defined the village
as a unit, because a sense of place was their means of pursuing day-to-day
interactions with their neighbors. The two views of unity—that of the villagers and that of administrators—were not identical. They posed alternative models that influenced each other reciprocally. The effectiveness of
all instruments of dominance was limited by the problem of acquiring the
local knowledge necessary to force obedience. And all efforts to enforce the
ideas of the central administration on the populace created opportunities
for the villagers to impose their own sense of obligation on the administration. Villagers were simultaneously implicated in their own subjection and
able to change the behavior of their dominators by the nature of the contest over village identity.

Reciprocal influence and contested definitions extended through all the
layers of village perception. *Herrschaft* and community took the forms they
did not only because of the way they interacted but also because of the way
each was contested from within. *Herrschaft* embodied both police and seigneurial conceptions of administrative order. Often the two conceptions
worked together, but sometimes they worked at cross-purposes, and the resolution of the conflict between the two visions redefined how *Herrschaft*
functioned in the village. At the same time, *Herrschaft* represented the interests of competing groups—the landed nobility and the state—who had
their own distinct agendas for administration. Both were interested in extracting resources and commanding obedience to secular and spiritual demands. The attempt to accommodate one group's view of administration
often undermined the interests of the other group. The creation of the Village
Book, the issuance of territorial ordinances, and the institution of the
Verbesserungspunkte were all part of the contest not only between villagers
and state but between the state and the nobility as well.

A similar conflict of competing visions can be seen when we look at
how community defined the unity of the village. Neighborliness involved
coercion in order to achieve a single voice. Those who were silenced by
the expression of unity had to find other ways of making their voices heard.
Sharing the space of the village enabled all who lived there to have some
influence on how the internal contours were defined, but some had more
influence than others. Participation in the contest over the internal definition of the village was shaped by the way in which individuals were located in other social groupings that made up the village.

We identified several different social roles that located individuals within the village: household, kinship, age, gender, wealth, occupation, and formal and informal association. One cannot take one social perspective and claim that it is the master perspective around which all others were constructed. Depending on circumstances, one or another of the perspectives would prove most important for situating an individual. Because of how *Herrschaft* and community functioned in the village, however, the social location of the household appeared to be most prominent. Patrimonial authority worked in tandem with administrative authority to construct a principle of social order. But only a minority of villagers could fill the role of patriarch. Hermann Rebel's idea that an individual simultaneously embodies several different social roles or expectations, so that the role rather than the individual is the "atom" of society, provides some guidance in seeing how these internal social perspectives worked.[2] Social roles generated expectations that had to be accommodated within the structure of the village, or the challenge to the internal definition would break down internal order.

Discussing the various social groups that made up the village also introduced a more abstract way of dividing the village into its constituent parts. Households, wealth, and informal association revolved around the fact that the village fulfilled both political and economic roles in the broader society. The structure of agricultural production and the European market shaped the internal contours of the village just as much as the expectations of the village's inhabitants did. Each village had a distinct connection to the market, and its internal composition reflected that connection. It is notable, however, that the economic and demographic expansion of the sixteenth century prompted some kind of response within almost every village. The seeds of nonagricultural production were sown in even the most agricultural villages. There is no way of knowing how those tendencies would have played out if the war had not intervened.

The Malthusian system clearly influenced, but did not determine, what happened to the villages of the Werra. The rhythm of economic and demographic expansion and contraction varied not only from country to country within Europe but even within regions. There was no simple ratio of people to productive land that determined the timing of crisis in a given location. Although local particularism was the norm in early modern Europe, no place was so isolated that it offered a pure Malthusianism, untouched by what was happening in adjacent regions. The expansion of the sixteenth century created constraints but did not determine the degree of social dislocation. Within the limits of those constraints lay a wide range of social responses, which formed the initial condition when crisis struck. At the same time, the specific form that the Malthusian crisis took had tremendous implications for the later trajectory of development. It made a difference that some villages in Germany, like the villages of the Werra region, experienced their Malthusian crises in the form of tremendous depopulation and disruption of production at a moment when it was far from clear that production and the organization of society faced irreversible problems, followed by a period of sustained growth. Other regions, like the Beauvaisis, experienced crisis in the form of dwindling resources throughout the seventeenth century, with a gently increasing spiral of epidemic disease and local production crises. To address that problem, one cannot ask merely what the war did to the village, but rather what the village did during the war.

A consideration of the war helps us understand the village in two distinct ways. First, the demands that the war placed on the resources of the village were such that it exposed underlying processes that remained hidden during "normal" interactions. War is, therefore, a powerful lens through which one may view the village as it tried to cope with extraordinary circumstances. It magnified the issues of *Herrschaft* and community, household and economy, described in the first four chapters. But as it exposed the underlying processes, it also provoked changes in them. The early modern village was not created to support war, nor was it designed to cope with the depredations of war. But the ability to conduct successful campaigns was based on the effective exploitation of the products of the village, so some kind of accommodation between the role of the village and the interests of the military was necessary whenever war broke out. The way in which the village responded to extraordinary circumstances produced changes in the village's internal order. Many features of the rural world were perpetuated after the war—some despite the war, and some because they provided one of the few ways of surviving the war. Other features changed rapidly after the war, primarily because the war had broken down local resistance. Actions taken at one point constrained later actions. The war affected the trajectory of development even when it was not the initial cause of that development. It compounded a traditional Malthusian check and gave the Werra region a distinctive rhythm of development.

"Ordinary" wars provoked strains in the balance of interests within the village—strains that could serve to change the internal dynamic. But the Thirty Years' War in the Werra region was no ordinary war; it was the worst that the village experienced. It disrupted the village in a manner that escalated as the war continued. The cumulative effect of these disruptions was to break down the cohesiveness of the village and to plunge it into misery. Initially, villagers reacted to the arrival of troops within a familiar framework of petitions and evasion of burdens. As the situation became more severe, the evasions and petitions became more desperate. The desperation was a response to the breakdown of the whole network of associations that had located the village in the broader social organization of early modern Germany. But the presence of troops not only caused psychological and organizational disruption of village life, it also had a direct material impact on the social order and physical layout of the village. Damage directly or indirectly attributable to the war disrupted the economy of the household and the village as a whole. The atmosphere of despair also contributed to further material damage by prompting villagers to leave. Damage threatened the ability of the village to reproduce itself. It struck at the core of village identity and put the resilience of the institutions of the village to a test.

The meaning of the war for the villages of the Werra region had two seemingly contradictory aspects. First, the war was every bit as destructive as the traditional historiography portrayed it. There is no way to avoid the conclusion that it was a catastrophe and that the apocalyptic language adopted by those who lived through it was consonant with their experiences. At the same time, however, the war was neither the beginning nor the end of anything. The village did not start from scratch in 1648, and its postwar situation must be understood in terms of the tendencies in the village before the war, not just in terms of the degree of destruction during the war. The point, however, is that the contradictory aspects must be treated together. The terrible destruction during the war became one with the social character of the village and accentuated the perpetual change of the village to a larger extent than was usual.

Even at the moment of greatest threat to the ability of the village to reproduce itself, the way in which the different interests were focused by the presence of the village helped the village survive. Historians have overemphasized the role of one of those interests, the state, in contributing to that survival. To some extent, all forms of *Herrschaft* tried to help villages overcome the threats to production stability, the activities of the Treusch von Buttlar in Lüderbach show how seigneurial authority could be used to protect the elite of agricultural producers. But the presence of the state in the village after the war came primarily from the state pursuing its own interests, in opposition to the continued efforts of the locality to preserve its insularity. For most of the war, *Herrschaft* failed to perform the most essential feature of *Schutz und Schirm*, and it was only because there was nowhere else to turn that villagers continued to make use of it at all. Most of the expressions of despair in the later years of the war show that villagers had turned to other sources of solace, such as the yearning for peace and pleas to God. The route that the state took to penetrate the community was not that of closer cooperation with elite villagers in order to foster greater productivity: instead, it grafted itself onto the institutions created by occupying armies to support themselves and held on to them tightly once the war was over.

The Thirty Years' War hit the Werra region harder and longer than almost any other part of Germany. The experience of the war lingered in the historical memory of the villagers and so came to define interaction in the postwar era. But once the war was over, it was over. A new phase of contesting and redefining began in which the village once again changed itself and was changed by the forces operating at the time. Unlike some parts of Germany, the Werra region was granted a long period of peace and stability.

With the exception of an epidemic in 1676, the "uncontrollable" aspects of the world seemed to be under control. The combination of the severe impact of the Thirty Years' War and the negligible impact of the wars of Louis XIV meant that the experience of the Werra region from 1580 to 1720 remained distinctive rather than being a model for other parts of Germany to follow. An older view of social history might, therefore, have dismissed what happened to the Werra region as unimportant. But the extremes that the Werra region experienced illustrate something very important about rural society of early modern Europe. They uncover the range of possible directions of development located within rural society and the resiliency of the village in the face of the most terrifying tragedies.

Notes

1. Peter Kriedte, *Peasants, Landlords and Merchant Capitalists: Europe and the World Economy* (Cambridge, 1983), 63.
2. Hermann Rebel, *Peasant Classes: The Bureaucratization of Property and Family Relations under Early Hapsburg Absolutism, 1511–1636* (Princeton, 1983), 220–29.

Index